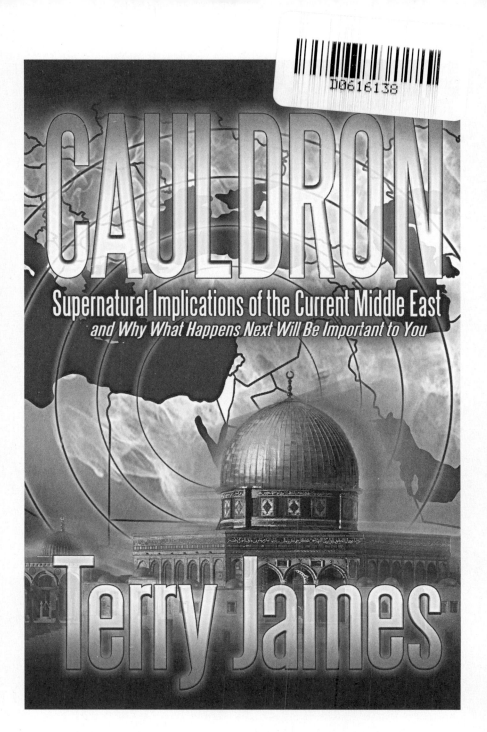

CAULDRON

Supernatural Implications of the Current Middle East
and Why What Happens Next Will Be Important to You

Terry James

DEFENDER

CRANE, MO

Defender
Crane, Missouri 65633
©2014 by Terry James

All rights reserved. Published 2014.
Printed in the United States of America.
ISBN: 978-0-9856045-5-451995

A CIP catalog record of this book is available from the Library of Congress.

Cover illustration and design by Daniel Wright: www.createdwright.com

Unless otherwise indicated, all Scripture quoted is from the King James Version (KJV) of the Bible.

DEDICATION

Dedicated to the memory of Zola Levitt, whose love for his Lord and passion for Israel continue to burn brightly through the ministry legacy he left to us.

Contents

FOREWORD

By Thomas R. Horn

THEY SAY THAT timing is everything, and in this newest nonfiction book by best-selling author Terry James, you are about to discover why I consider it to be one of the most important works—if not *the* most prescient document—of 2014. *Cauldron* uncovers with vivid description how prophecies from the Bible proclaimed far in advance appear now to be cascading around the world in phenomenally accurate fulfillment. Research and analysis within *Cauldron* will convince even the hardiest skeptic that something frightening yet marvelous is unfolding as the author takes you deep into the Middle East and around the world to chronicle, with pivotal skill, not only shocking events that seem torn from the pages of apocalyptic literature, but also the words and actions of global leaders who are now openly proclaiming the end times are here.

Critical prophetic events as covered by James include a gamut missed by most recent works of prophecy—an astonishing call by Muslims and Jews to build the Third Temple in Jerusalem; political and religious leaders advocating for a single global, financial, and political authority; and even what appears to be intentional movement by the international community that could initiate the battle of Armageddon.

As a judicious example of the findings in this investigative book, James points to the book of Ezekiel, where one of the most important prophets of the Old Testament provides very specific information regarding the final global battle—called in Ezekiel 38 "the battle of Gog and Magog." Ezekiel says this supernatural contest will occur in the latter times, after Israel is "gathered out of many people and nations" and is recognized as a nation once again. During that generation in which Israel is so reunified—which was accomplished on May 14, 1948, when David Ben-Gurion, the head of the Jewish Agency, proclaimed the establishment of the state of Israel and "U.S. President Harry S. Truman recognized the new nation on the same day"[1]—the Battle of Gog and Magog occurs. If a biblical generation is seventy years (see Psalms 90:10, Daniel 9, and related texts), counting forward from 1948 would seem to indicate that this decisive conflict, which leads to the final confrontation referred to in John's Apocalypse as the "battle of Armageddon," could happen very soon. In Ezekiel's vision, Iran (Persia) becomes the number-one confederate with Russia (Gog) in this invasion of Israel:

> And the word of the LORD came unto me, saying, Son of man, set thy face against Gog, the land of Magog [the Russian Federation]…and prophesy against him, And say, Thus saith the Lord GOD; Behold, I am against thee, O Gog, the chief prince of Meshech and Tubal: And I will…bring thee forth, and all thine army…. Persia [ancient kingdom of Iran], Ethiopia, and Libya with them." (Ezekiel 38:1–5)

Although Ezekiel explains how the invasion of Israel described above somehow goes wrong for Iran, Russia, and their confederates (actually leading them to turn on each other, according to chapter 38:21), one cannot read this prophetic foresight and fail to ponder the unprecedented events in recent days involving Iran and its leaders, Russia and its leaders, and the current push by the president of the United States to force Israel into a so-called peace deal with the Palestinians (whose lead-

ers openly call for the destruction of Israel and the slaughter of Jews[2])
while secretly negotiating a nuclear agreement with Iran, a fact made
public in November 2013.

"The Obama administration, with Secretary of State John Kerry in
the lead, joined with the international community in making an agreement with the Iranian regime that many view as a betrayal of Israel,"
notes James in a chapter of this book. "Just as the sanctions against Iran
for their pursuing development of a nuclear program to produce atomic
weaponry was beginning to make an impact, the U.S., in concert with
the world powers that constitute the international community, agreed to
lift part of those economic sanctions on Iran."

Of course, James sees through this façade of diplomacy and recog-
nizes the important, even staggeringly prophetic, implications of these
Machiavellian maneuverings. Israeli Prime Minister Benjamin Netanyahu saw through them as well and harshly condemned the nuclear deal
with Iran as a massive failure of foreign policy. "What was reached last
night in Geneva is not a historic agreement, it is a historic mistake," he
said, before concluding: "Today the world became a much more dangerous place because the most dangerous regime in the world made a
significant step in obtaining the most dangerous weapons in the world."

Netanyahu's economics minister, Naftali Bennett, then alleged, "If a
nuclear suitcase blows up five years from now in New York or Madrid it
will be because of the deal signed this morning."[3] Ironically, Saudi Arabia also viewed the U.S.-led and secretly bartered agreement with Iran as
a treachery due to its (the Saudis') historic affiliation with Washington,
which in modern history was demonstratively committed to protecting
the kingdom from Iran. This new agreement weakens the relationship
with Saudi Arabia, a fact that, all by itself, could have destabilizing and
prophetic effects throughout the Middle East.

Given Iran's consistency with not honoring such "deals" and the
hearty evidence that it is in fact developing nuclear bomb technology
as well as likely purchasing WMDs (weapons of mass destruction) on
the black market with stated ambitions of annihilating Israel, James

says what people not living in the Middle East should understand is the resolve that Jews like Netanyahu have for protecting themselves and the security of their nation, not to mention God's promise of the same. Because of this resolve, Obama's *fait accompli* regarding peace deals with Israel's enemies could result literally overnight in the battle described by Ezekiel and in the book of Revelation. The modern people of Israel—from civilians to government and military leaders—have powerful memories of those who have promised to exterminate them, including Nazi Germany in the past and modern Iran today, and survival *by any means necessary* thus pervades their hearts at this stage in history. This was reflected most recently by Netanyahu himself during the 2013 General Debate of the 68th Session of the United Nations, when the prime minister, before the nations of the world, admitted that Israel *is at the center of Bible prophecy,* saying:

> [O]ne cold day in the late 19th century, my grandfather Nathan and his younger brother Judah were standing in a railway station in the heart of Europe. They were seen by a group of anti-Semitic hoodlums who ran towards them waving clubs, screaming "Death to the Jews."
>
> My grandfather shouted to his younger brother to flee and save himself, and he then stood alone against the raging mob to slow it down. They beat him senseless, they left him for dead, and before he passed out, covered in his own blood, he said to himself, "What a disgrace, what a disgrace. The descendants of the Macabees lie in the mud powerless to defend themselves."
>
> He promised himself then that if he lived, he would take his family to the Jewish homeland and help build a future for the Jewish people. I stand here today as Israel's prime minister because my grandfather kept that promise.
>
> And so many other Israelis have a similar story, a parent or a grandparent who fled every conceivable oppression and came to Israel to start a new life in our ancient homeland. Together we've

transformed a bludgeoned Jewish people, left for dead, into a vibrant, thriving nation, defending itself with the courage of modern Maccabees, developing limitless possibilities for the future.

In our time the Biblical prophecies are being realized. As the prophet Amos said, they shall rebuild ruined cities and inhabit them. They shall plant vineyards and drink their wine. They shall till gardens and eat their fruit. And I will plant them upon their soil *never to be uprooted again.*[4] (emphasis added)

One should read the entire UN statement by Netanyahu (see the link in the notes) and not underestimate the national Jewish commitment to preservation, even if they have to go it alone. While President Obama has been steering the United States increasingly away from the stronger relationship Israel once enjoyed with previous administrations, France, one of the P-5+1 members (the five permanent members of the UN Security Council plus Germany), and Saudi Arabia recognize that the threat posed by modern Persia-Iran is not only prophetically against Israel, but holds global implications of a wider nuclear war and, if the U.S. will not stand in defense of God's land and people, the Saudis and France (for their own self-interests) will offer logistical support to Israel should they be backed into a corner and forced to strike the heart of the ancient enemy.

This recent development is but one scenario of what is timely and imminently important in *Cauldron*, a single example I have provided from among many that offer a unique evaluation of what is happening in the world and what lies ahead for the reader. You should pay very careful attention to this and other magnificently researched details by this veteran prophecy expert, Terry James, because what happens next in the Middle East will affect your life and future, as well as the lives of every person on earth. Understanding these events—"signs," as the Bible calls them—will empower you to take action for yourself and your family and to find peace that passes understanding, something that all of us will surely need in the immediate days ahead.

ACKNOWLEDGMENTS

MANY HAVE CONTRIBUTED to the making of this book, an in-depth analysis, review, and future outlook involving one of the most crucial areas of Bible prophecy for the so-called end of days. War and peace in the Middle East affect everyone on the planet in one way or another, and this volume has been made so much better in informing than if I, alone, had brought it to the attention of the readers who will turn its pages.

My deep love and thanks to my editor of many years, Angie Peters, for so masterfully shaping the book as no one else could.

My profound thanks to Tom Horn and the wonderful professionals at Defender Publishing for their superlative work in bringing the book to publication.

Thanks to Tom, personally, for the foreword that definitively frames *Cauldron: Supernatural Implications of the Current Middle East.*

To Dana Neel—who, as always, was so vitally involved as researcher, and ever an encourager—my love and most heartfelt thanks and appreciation.

Many thanks to my long-time friend and colleague, Daymond Duck, for his generosity in providing the graphic for chapter 14. Thanks also to his daughter, Karen Melton, who produced the effective illustration.

To Margaret, my wife, for again putting up with my sequestering myself for untold hours behind the keyboard of this computer, my undying love and devotion.

To you, the reader, my prayerful best wishes and my gratitude for reading this volume in your desire to understand where this generation stands on God's prophetic timeline.

INTRODUCTION

MIDDLE EAST TERRORISM hit Americans between the eyes on Tuesday, September 11, 2001, when two huge passenger jets slammed into the 110-story World Trade Center Twin Towers in New York City. Another was deliberately crashed into the Pentagon at Washington, D.C. Never before had people of the United States suffered such a devastating blow. Finally, Americans began to realize the importance of the issues of war and peace faced daily by those living in Israel and the whole Mideastern region of the world.

The horrendous attack set in motion the War on Terrorism, a growing conflict that seemed destined to involve every person on the face of the planet. United States military forces increasingly pursue elusive terrorist enemies around the world.

It might well be a war that cannot be contained.

Great upheaval exploded from the moment the Towers fell. America has spent more than $1 trillion in wars to liberate Iraq and control the spread of terrorism in Afghanistan and other places. Thousands of American soldiers have died in these wars, as have many more thousands in other nations as well.

The terrorist attack of September 11, 2001, on the World Trade Center buildings in New York
City thrust the spotlight on issues of war and peace in the Middle East and around the globe.
Source: The MachineStops

Iran has developed a nuclear program almost certainly designed to produce atomic weapons. Its angry leaders, all radical Muslims, want to completely destroy Israel, according to their own words. There are constant rumors that Israel could attack Iran's nuclear facilities and that war could break out at any moment.

Iran seeks to influence Syria and its leaders' hatred against the Jewish state. The Syrian dictators murder Syria's people in an effort to stay in power.

The Arab Spring, which was supposed to bring democracy to the whole Middle East, has proven to be the agent of the spread of deadly, Islamist terrorism.

Egypt has gone from being a fairly dependable American ally in the region, and at peace with Israel, to a state torn apart by turmoil caused by the Muslim Brotherhood. These radicals are determined, like Iran's leadership, to destroy Israel.

Only God's staying hand keeps a lid on the Middle Eastern cauldron.

Welcome to a look at what the Bible has to say about the end-times issues and events that rage within the Mideast today. This book will use God's Holy Word to explain what's going on—and what's been going on for centuries—in countries like Israel, Syria, Jordan, Iraq, Iran, Egypt, and that whole region called Palestine.

Not your usual geopolitical gobbledygook, *Cauldron: Supernatural Implications of the Current Middle East* will give you the straight scoop on the history, events, and prophecies relating to that important area of the world.

Earth's Belly-Button Battle

The region we know as the Middle East has been called "the Cradle of Civilization," because the first human beings came from the heart of that part of the world. It is truly "earth's belly button"—and there truly is a battle going on there.

Some today have rewritten the history books to say that Africa is the place where human beings first evolved. God's Word says otherwise. The Bible says God created man: first Adam, then Eve. They lived in the Garden of Eden, which the book of Genesis places in the area we know today as Iraq and Iran. Of the four streams Genesis lists as boundaries of Eden, the only two we know today are the Tigris and the Euphrates.

The Creator gave the land masses of the earth for all of mankind to settle and inhabit. He chose to use Israel, the Jews, as a people to bring the Messiah, the Savior, Jesus Christ, into the world. He chose, likewise, to give them a specific geographical area where they were to serve as an example nation of godly behavior for all peoples of earth.

God promised Israel the whole region from the Mediterranean to the Euphrates: "In the same day the LORD made a covenant with Abram, saying, Unto thy seed have I given this land, from the river of Egypt unto the great river, the river Euphrates" (Genesis 15:18). Yet, today, the area Israel occupies is not nearly as large as the original biblical description; it is now comparable in size to the state of New Jersey—a tiny space in the center of the region. This is the result of Israel's disobedience, but God's promises are still in effect.

Why the Middle East Matters

We are alive at the most exciting time in history! The nation Israel and events taking place in the Middle East are proof that God's great hand is upon this world today. Consider that:

1) **War and peace in the Middle East continually revolve around the Jewish race, God's chosen people.** (See Genesis 12:2–3; 22:17–18; 26:24; 28:13–15.) Many of those in the pulpits and seminaries of America today are deeply into teaching that the church—all who have accepted Christ as Savior—has replaced Israel in God's prophetic plan. This, in my view, is a part of the apostasy ("falling away," or rebellion against God) that is predicted for the last time (see 2 Thessalonians 2:3). God has *not* replaced Israel with the church (a fact that will be dealt with throughout this book).

All we have to do is keep an eye on news programs, newspaper headlines, and Internet news sources to see the stage being set for the fulfillment of prophecy. Israel always returns to the top of the news, no matter what other stories might temporarily make the front pages. Among the nations, Israel is the primary subject as far as prophecy yet future is concerned. In that regard, all else is periphery.

For example, all eyes turned to the very heart of the issues of war and peace in the Middle East on September 28, 2000, when Israeli Likud Party leader Ariel Sharon visited the Temple Mount compound, the holiest site in Judaism. Both the religious Jews and those who follow Islam claim the Temple Mount as central to their religion. Sharon's visit caused the Islamic world to explode in anger; ongoing peace talks continue to be affected by that event.

2) **Events occurring in the Middle East directly affect our wallets.** The availability of oil and the price we will pay for fuel in the future depend on whether there is war or peace there. We will look into this more deeply later in this book.

3) **Armageddon, the earth's final war, will take place in the Middle East:** "And he gathered them together into a place called in the Hebrew tongue Armageddon" (Revelation 16:16).

4) **The Bible says that Jesus Christ will come back to earth at Jerusalem** (see Zechariah 14:4). He will put an end to war by bringing true peace!

Psalms 122:6 states that God's children are to pray for the peace of Jerusalem. That means we are to pray for Christ, the Prince of Peace, to return. When we study the Middle East and the growing troubles there, we can understand why there is a need for things to be made better. Christ's return will make things better.

As Randall Price points out in his book, *Jerusalem in Prophecy*, "All Christians have a vested interest in Jerusalem because in its eternal form it stands at last as our heavenly home."[5] Believers in Jesus Christ are instructed to look for their Lord to return. One of the most profound signals they are to look for as the time of His return draws near is found in the following passage:

> And he spake to them a parable; Behold the fig tree,
>   and all the trees;
> When they now shoot forth, ye see and know of your own
>   selves that summer is now nigh at hand.
> So likewise ye, when ye see these things come to pass, know ye
>   that the kingdom of God is nigh at hand.
> Verily I say unto you, This generation shall not pass away,
>   till all be fulfilled.
> Heaven and earth shall pass away: but my words shall not pass
>   away. (Luke 21:29–33)

Current Turmoil Foretold

The 2003 war called Operation Iraqi Freedom didn't take God by surprise, nor have any of the great upheavals in the region since that time. That also goes for the man-made attempt at peace called the Roadmap to Peace. Nothing and no one can catch the Almighty off guard. The Lord had much to say about the future concerning the Middle East. He foretold that Mideast war and peace would affect the whole world, especially as the end of the Church Age approaches.

Here are four things Jesus predicted in a sermon He gave on the Mount of Olives:

1. False christs, false prophets, and false teachers will appear (Matthew 24:11, 24). We have seen many cults in recent times. Remember Jim Jones, David Koresh, and the people who committed suicide believing they would hitch a ride on the Hale-Bopp comet? But such cults are on the fringe. The one-world church (which, in my view, is the ultimate satanic cult) is on the move to bring all religions of earth together as one. Following the radical Islamic terrorist attacks on New York and Washington, D.C., there has been a significant movement proclaiming that all religions are the same in God's eyes. This, of course, is a false teaching. Islam is said to be related to Christianity in that both religions claim Jesus Christ. But true Christianity says that Jesus is the Son of God, while Islam considers Him as merely one of many prophets. Think about this: If Islam says Jesus is important in its beliefs, why are His teachings found in the Bible forbidden under punishment by law in most every Islamic nation—for example, Saudi Arabia? Why, in 2001, did the Muslim nation of Afghanistan, under Taliban tyranny, have eight Christian missionaries, including two young American women, held for months, planning to try them for preaching Christianity? Remember, this offense is punishable by death under the Afghan religious-judicial system. God will deal with the apostate church as outlined in Revelation 17. Let us study God's Word and pray for discernment, that we not be deceived in the last time.

2. There will be wars and rumors of wars (Matthew 24:6). Wars have always been a part of life on earth and especially in the Mideast. In fact, before 1991, Arab-Israeli wars broke out approximately every ten years. Rumors of wars have also played a big part in world politics, but especially in the Middle East. Whether it was the ancient Israelites guarding against invasion by the Philistines or modern Israel worrying about Syria, Iraq, or Iran, predictions of coming war have troubled people of all eras. And what about the constantly stated fear that one Mideast dictator or another is developing weapons of mass destruction—the most recent being the tyrants who run Iran? Osama bin Laden's henchmen proved that when the weapons exist in their hands, the madmen of the Middle East will use them. What greater proof do we need than to think on President George W. Bush's declared war on terrorism—Enduring Freedom—and all the tremendous turmoil that has taken place since to know that we are now deeply into the era prophesied by Jesus? Wars and commotion and rumors of wars have never been more in the headlines than today.

3. There will be great ethnic or racial upheaval (Matthew 24:7a). It is even more interesting to consider the words Jesus used to describe the wars that would come upon the world at the end of the age. He used the word that translated to the Greek word *ethnos* to describe "nation against nation." *Ethnos* means "ethnic" in English. More and more we hear the terms "*ethnic* cleansing" or "*ethnic* wars" used to describe the great racial and religious hatreds in India, Pakistan, Afghanistan, and other areas of central Asia. Ethnic wars have, of course, been going on for centuries in the Middle East. Practically every conflict today makes it look as though this prophecy is coming true before our eyes. That is because most every war between nations and every conflict between kingdoms involves ethnic or racial hatreds. World War II was centered on Adolf Hitler's hatred for the Jewish race. In the 1979 war between the Soviet Union and Afghanistan, race was at the core of the USSR's aggression. Soviets determined to tear apart Afghanistan culture in order to add that region to their domination. In 1980, the Iranians, who are mostly Persians, and the Iraqis, who are mostly Arabs, fought an eight-year-long ethnic war that caused the deaths of hundreds of thousands on each side. The Bosnian war in the 1990s was also a conflict of racial or ethnic origin. The Serbs and Albanians carried on a centuries-long hatred in their bloody war that started in 1991. Arabs hate Jews for the most part. The Jews hate the Arabs in return. The cause of the hatreds is sin in general.

4. **There will be an increase in famines, diseases, and earthquakes** (Matthew 24:7b). As in the case of ethnic troubles described above, there have always been famines, diseases, and earthquakes as part of the human condition. Unlike in centuries past, however, never have these things been so many or so great in scope as in our times. Famines engulf many African countries. Great numbers of earthquakes with large magnitudes are being reported regularly. We are familiar with the AIDS virus, the Ebola virus, and the E. coli bacteria, all of which literally devour the victim's body to one extent or another. These diseases seem unstoppable. But now there are threats of super-deadly gases, viruses, and bacteria such as anthrax, which terrorists threaten to unleash upon large-population areas of the United States and elsewhere. Many of those threats come from Middle East terrorists and dictators. The recent use of chemical weapons of mass destruction by Syrian dictator Bashar al-Assad or the fanatic Muslim rebels trying to take over Syria—no one knows for certain which—shows just how volatile the whole Mideast region is. The many dead civilians testify to the truth of Jesus' prophecies for the end of the age.

Exploring Mideast Excitement

There are two main reasons the Middle East causes worry for the entire world. One is a supernatural reason. The other reason is natural. The supernatural reason can be summed up in a single word: Satan. The natural reason also can be summed up in a single word: Oil.

This book explores both the supernatural and the natural reasons for the ongoing trouble in the Middle East. We will look particularly at what God says in His Word about this conflict and where it is leading, for He alone knows.

So, first we will investigate the supernatural reasons for problems in the region. Second, we will examine the natural reasons for Mideast troubles. And third, we will look at what the Bible says about where Mideast war and peace-seeking are taking our generation.

We will look at Mideast war and peace in three phases:

1. The beginnings of the conflict (Chapters 1–5)
2. The recent and current trouble (Chapters 6–10)
3. The prophetic-future era of terrors (Chapters 11–16)

The subject of the book involves many complex facets. For example, we must deal with Scripture; ancient, contemporary, and future history; and the concept of good and evil from God's perspective. Therefore, I've tried to address the subject more like an artist rendering a painting rather than a reporter laying down a straight story. My prayerful hope is that you will, by the end of the book, get the full picture God wishes to portray about these matters.

A Promised Blessing

God promises to bless the reading and study of His Word. We can examine this fascinating, often-thrilling subject with full confidence that God's Word "shall not return unto [us] void" (Isaiah 55:11). This is because God's Word is in reality a person, and His name is Jesus.

Warning

The Bible says in Revelation 21:18–19 that we must be very careful in how we treat the Word of God; to add or take away from His Word invites His anger. That's why it's important to do the following as you embark upon this study:

- Pray for understanding of God's Word (James 1:5).
- Pray for discernment during this last time (1 John 2:18).
- Trust that the Bible is absolutely true (2 Timothy 3:16).
- Treat prophecy in God's Word as literal unless the Bible specifically says otherwise (Revelation 8:10).
- Watch, listen to, or read about current events in the Middle East and the world while prayerfully thinking about prophetic implications.
- Get on mailing lists of biblically sound prophecy ministries.
- Remember at all times that the nation Israel is still God's chosen people. No one or nation has or ever will replace them.
- Remember that the Rapture of the church (the time when all believers are taken to heaven at Christ's return) might happen at any moment (see 1 Corinthians 15:51–52 and 1 Thessalonians 4:13–18).

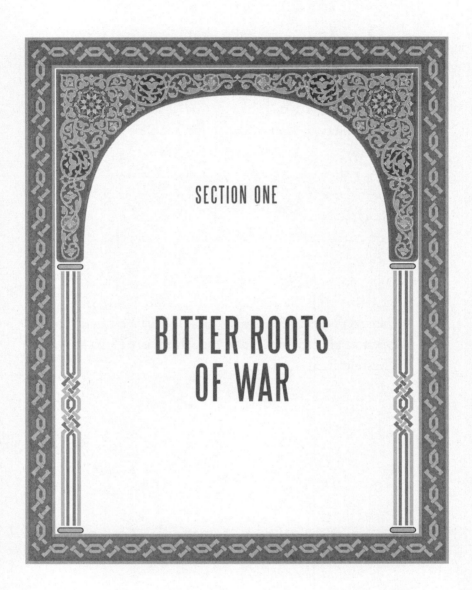

SECTION ONE

BITTER ROOTS OF WAR

CHAPTER 1

REBELLION RAGES IN HEAVEN

RECENT TERRORIST HORRORS that have come out of the Middle East turmoil tell us that we indeed live in a sin-filled world. Evildoings in that region surface daily in news reports. If God is perfect in every way, why did He let sin into His creation in the first place? God is omniscient (all knowing), omnipresent (always everywhere), and omnipotent (all powerful), so why didn't He prevent Eve, then Adam, from being tempted by the serpent? Why wasn't Satan kept out of the Garden of Eden?

All things were made by God, the Bible tells us: "All things were made by him; and without him was not any thing made that was made" (John 1:3). If God is perfect in every way, and if He created all things, who created sin? Who created evil? Where do these awful things come from?

The answer? I don't know.

Neither does anyone else.

These things are all wrapped up in what the Bible calls in the New International Version (NIV) "the secret power of lawlessness" and in the King James Version (KJV) "the mystery of iniquity" (1 Thessalonians 2:7–8). This powerful lawlessness is a big part of the cauldron in which

Mideast war and peace simmers. One story from some years ago illustrating that fact came across a world news wire:

> On Wednesday, the bodies of two Israeli boys, one an immigrant from Maryland, were found bludgeoned to death by rocks in a cave in the West Bank. The boys, Koby Mandell, 13, and Yossi Ishran, 14, had gone on a hike near their home in the West Bank settlement of Tekoa on Tuesday, and were seized, presumably by Palestinians, and killed. Newspapers quoted police as saying the boys' heads were so badly disfigured that facial identification was impossible.[6]

A Secret Power

When we look at twenty-first century earth and the troubles in the Middle East, one question that might arise is: Why can't people just get along with each other? The prophet Jeremiah spoke of the universal longing for peace:

> For from the least of them even unto the greatest of them every one is given to covetousness; and from the prophet even unto the priest every one dealeth falsely.
>
> They have healed also the hurt of the daughter of my people slightly, saying, Peace, peace; when there is no peace. (Jeremiah 6:13–14)

Just as in Jeremiah's days, many politicians have claimed they can bring peace, but news headlines prove every day that they haven't succeeded. Conflicts great and small continue to rage. The "secret" that the Bible calls "lawlessness" is present with us today and is on the increase.

Hatreds for each other within the Muslim faith as well as for Israel

Leaders throughout the centuries have attempted to restore peace to the Middle East, but without lasting success. Pictured here, a gathering of leaders at Camp David in 1978 included Menachem Begin (seated on left couch, in suit) and Anwar Sadat (seated on right couch, in dark suit), as well as other aides and dignitaries.

and the U.S. constantly fuel the drive to put the haters' various brands of Islam into practice to achieve supreme power.

> Al-Qaida's leader said Egypt's military coup that ousted Egyptian President Mohammed Morsi provides proof that Islamic rule cannot be established through democracy, and urged the Islamist leader's followers to abandon the ballot box in favor of armed resistance....
>
> "We have to admit first that legitimacy does not mean elections and democracy, but legitimacy is the Shariah (Islamic law)...which is above all the constitutions and laws," al-Zawahri said in comments addressed to Morsi's supporters....
>
> "You forgot that democracy is the West's monopoly and it is allowed for those who belong to the Islamists to benefit from

its fruits only on one condition—you be a slave for the West's ideology, action, policy and economy," he said....

Al-Qaida and other Islamic extremists roundly reject democracy as a Western-imposed system, and oppose it on the grounds that it puts man's laws above those of God.[7]

Crime and Punishment

A secret, of course, is something that hasn't been revealed. A mystery is something that usually becomes a known truth at the end of a story. In the case of "the secret power of lawlessness," we must wait until the greatest story ever told, the story of God's redemption, has played out on the stage of human history to find answers to the mind-boggling questions posed at the beginning of this chapter.

Looking deeper into the "secret" of the evil that invaded God's creation and continues to plague the Middle East today, let's consider the prophetic Scripture mentioned earlier written by the apostle Paul to the Thessalonians:

> For the mystery of iniquity doth already work: only he who now letteth will let, until he be taken out of the way.
> And then shall that Wicked be revealed, whom the Lord shall consume with the spirit of his mouth, and shall destroy with the brightness of his coming. (2 Thessalonians 2:7–8)

The prophecy is for a time that is still in the future. It involves the era when Antichrist will be earth's dictator. In essence, Paul was saying that the evil called "lawlessness" was going strong in the world during his day. It had power over people, over animal and plant life, and even over nature. It caused all of God's creation to begin degenerating. This great mysterious or secret evil, however, was prevented from exerting its full influence by an even greater power!

Paul wrote that this greater power is a person, whom Paul referred to as "he." This person will continue to hold back the full influence of this secret evil for a certain time, but then he will stop. Who is the power even greater than the mysterious power of evil? He is none other than God the Holy Spirit. So, even though the evil that was introduced into the creation—apparently when Lucifer rebelled in heaven, as described in Isaiah 14:13–14—is extremely powerful, God Himself controls its strength.

According to Paul, when the Holy Spirit stops standing in the way of evil, it will be hell on earth! Then the last and worst of all dictators will have a free hand to do as he pleases. He will be absolutely lawless, representing the mystery of iniquity in all its horror. Millions upon millions of people will die under his absolute rule over this planet.

But the good news, Paul writes, is that this tyrant will be destroyed when the Lord Jesus Christ returns (see Revelation 19:11–16). The glorious brightness of that moment will drive away the black clouds of the secret power of evil called sin. Before that happens, though, the world is in for a very rough ride indeed!

Lucifer's Fall

As mentioned earlier, the chief angel who rebelled brought to earth the sin that caused the troubles that rage in the Middle East to this day. Here's how it happened: Heaven was once filled with angelic spirit beings. Lucifer was perhaps God's most beautiful and powerful angel. Apparently no other created being in heaven enjoyed a higher ranking than did he, whom the Bible calls "son of the morning" (Isaiah 14:12). Ezekiel 28:14 tells us that he was a cherub, and he is also believed by some scholars to have been one of two archangels.

"The evidence shows that [angels] are organized in terms of authority and glory," explains Billy Graham in his book, *Angels: God's Secret Agents.* He continues:

It seems to follow this pattern: archangels, angels, seraphim, cherubim, principalities, authorities, powers, thrones, might and dominion (Colossians 1:16; Romans 8:38).... While Scripture designates only Michael as an archangel (Jude 9), we have biblical grounds for believing that before his fall Lucifer was also an archangel, equal or perhaps superior to Michael. The prefix "arch" suggests a chief, principal or great angel.[8]

The Real Star Wars

The pride in Lucifer's heart seemed to well up inside him when he, for some mysterious reason, developed "I" trouble, as recorded by the prophet Isaiah:

> For thou hast said in thine heart, I will ascend into heaven, I will exalt my throne above the stars of God: I will sit also upon the mount of the congregation, in the sides of the north:
> I will ascend above the heights of the clouds; I will be like the most High. (14:13–14)

Repeating the phrase "I will" five times in just two sentences, Lucifer let loose the lightning of his anger, jealousy, and lust in a fit of rebellious rage, telling himself that he would be like or equal to the Most High God Himself! As Bob Glaze notes in his book, *Angels: A Historical and Prophetic Study,* "God created Lucifer and his angels perfect. Satan and his fallen angels are the product of their own pride and disobedience."[9]

Evil Eviction

An angel's strength is awesome indeed. What a titanic struggle, therefore, must have taken place when Lucifer and his fellow rebel angels were tossed out of heaven. When the devil crossed supernatural swords and supernatural muscles with Michael the archangel, heaven itself must have flashed and crashed mightily with tremendous lightning and thunder:

> And there was war in heaven: Michael and his angels fought against the dragon; and the dragon fought and his angels,
>
> And prevailed not; neither was their place found any more in heaven.
>
> And the great dragon was cast out, that old serpent, called the Devil, and Satan, which deceiveth the whole world: he was cast out into the earth, and his angels were cast out with him. (Revelation 12:7–9)

Imagine! Thousands upon thousands of angels, good and bad, must have clashed in a way that would have stupefied us had we been there to watch the battle. Note that when God banished this magnificent angel from heaven, his name, "Lucifer," meaning "morning star," was changed to "Satan," meaning "adversary."

Warning

The Bible warns: "Woe to the inhabiters of the earth and of the sea! for the devil is come down unto you, having great wrath, because he knoweth that he hath but a short time" (Revelation 12:12). This verse refers to a future time that will be anything but good for those living on earth. Most likely it is referring to the time of great trouble Jesus predicted in Matthew 24:21: "For then shall be great tribulation, such as was not since the beginning of the world to this time, no, nor ever shall be." In my view, this time will be when Satan literally possesses the body of Antichrist. People will think he has been assassinated, then returned to life. It will be a false resurrection, however, for only Christ has the keys to death and to hell (see Revelation 1:18).

Satan's Insanity

Before he became the devil, Lucifer was possibly the most intelligent created being. Why, then, does he still believe he can overthrow the all-powerful Creator of all things? This seems to demonstrate a *lack* of intelligence, not great intelligence!

Satan's seeming stupidity must be a demonstration of the spiritually deranging effects produced by the sin of pride. Even though he knows that God knows the end from the beginning (Isaiah 46:10), that God cannot lie (Titus 1:2), and that God has prophesied Satan's judgment in hell (Revelation 20:10), this sin-darkened angel still believes he will win in the end. He has deluded himself beyond any sane reasoning (see Romans 1:21–22).

Along the same lines, world leaders continue to think they can produce peace. They believe people are basically good and reasonable, therefore, can be made to see the benefits of peace. However, the Bible says, "The heart is deceitful above all things, and desperately wicked: who can know it?" (Jeremiah 17:9). Fallen man has no peace. Man is sin-infected and has war in his heart.

Talk about a Wrestling Match!

Satan and his fellow rebels lost their fight against Michael and God's angels, but the devil is still looking for a fight. He will try to win at any cost, and his focus is on you and me.

The Bible says we are clearly in a wrestling match against supernatural forces, as described in Ephesians 6:12: "For we wrestle not against flesh and blood, but against principalities, against powers, against the rulers of the darkness of this world, against spiritual wickedness in high places." We can't see, hear, or feel these forces. For Christians who are spiritually attuned to God's will, however, it is possible to sense this struggle. The more the Christian tries to live in God's holy will, the greater this wrestling match is. But, as we have often heard, one plus God equals victory. We can't lose when we have God as a tag-team partner.

When Satan and his minions are cast down to this planet at the midway point of the Tribulation (after three and a half years of that seven-year period), the horror for people on earth will become unbearable. Millions will die in the struggle. The issues of war and peace in the Middle East have developed from this great cosmic wrestling match. In the next chapter, we'll look at what that struggle has meant to mankind right up to our day on this troubled planet.

CHAPTER 2

REVENGEFUL WRATH ON EARTH

HAVE YOU EVER known or know of a person who wants to get even for some wrong he thinks was done to him? More often than not, that anger causes bitterness in the person. If not dealt with, the inner rage will destroy the one holding the grudge.

The most angry, bitter, hatred-filled being ever is Lucifer. He hates everything and everyone—except himself. The Bible tells us that he will destroy many, many people before human history plays out. That hatred will also end in his own destruction.

This chapter deals with how the fallen angel deceived Eve and caused Adam to disobey God. That rebellious disobedience brought sin into the world. Sin, among other terrible things, causes man to hate his fellow man. Murderous wars have therefore raged throughout human history in the Middle East and around the world.

As we covered in the previous chapter, Lucifer's hatred, of course, stems from his prideful, sinful desire to take God's place. He blames not himself, but God, for his predicament. Since he cannot overcome the Creator of all things, Satan is bent on taking out his wrath on God's creation called mankind.

The devil has done a good job of venting his rage on the human race so far. But what he has already done is nothing compared to what he plans to inflict upon mankind during the Tribulation, a time more terrible than any before or any that will ever come.

Satan's war on man began in the Garden of Eden—the heart of the very region that is the focus of this book. His rage will conclude thousands of years from that time, at the end of Christ's millennial, or thousand-year, reign on earth.

Earthly Paradise—This 1657 map of actual and biblical geography indicates where most scholars agree the Garden of Eden was located.

Satan's most intensive war-making will continue to take place in the Middle East until he is cast into hell. That's why we give so much attention to that region and the issues of war and peace in this book.

Let's begin looking at the revengeful wrath of this one called Satan and the devil. It began very calmly and quietly in probably the most peaceful, beautiful place that has ever been on this planet…

Down-to-Earth Devil

I have to believe that, as early as the moment he entered Eden, Satan planned to use Middle East oil in his war against mankind. Geologists, mineralogists, and other scientists tell us that petroleum is largely decayed animal and vegetable matter that is compressed, or under great pressure, for many, many years. While there are varying theories and opinions regarding the origin of fossil fuels, Satan, I believe, knew this physical law concerning the great petroleum reserves very well. It seems more than reasonable that such lushness of life in the Garden of Eden, once dead and buried—if that process is the fossil-fuel source—would indeed produce great amounts of oil. It seems to be no coincidence that the Middle East, where the Garden of Eden was located, has the richest oil deposits on earth. (Chapter 9 deals more in depth with these matters.)

Satan must have known that man, woman, and everything in the garden would die if he could only seduce them to disobey their Creator. He knew this even though death had never before occurred. Oil is combustible—it burns! Fire can destroy as perhaps nothing else can. The Creator, after all, had prepared the lake of fire for Satan and the angels who rebelled with him. *How to use this…fire…against the Creator?* That well might have run through the serpent's thoughts as he moved close to quietly hiss to Eve: "Ye shall not surely die" (Genesis 3:4b).

(Think about it: Could the same question—*How to use this… fire…against the Creator?*—have been in the minds of the terrorists who thought up flying the big jets full of fuel into the World Trade Center towers on September 11, 2001? The planners of that horrific act deliberately chose planes headed from the East Coast to the West because they knew the aircraft would be carrying full loads of jet fuel. With a three-thousand-mile, transcontinental trip ahead of them, each of the planes could have been loaded with up to twenty-four thousand gallons of jet fuel. Certainly, never has petroleum-based fuel been used in a more destructive way!)

The man and woman *would* surely die, Satan knew, because God had said so: "But of the tree of the knowledge of good and evil, thou shalt not eat of it: for in the day that thou eatest thereof thou shalt surely die" (Genesis 2:17). Satan knew that all, in fact, would die…if he could just get the woman to fall for his seduction. Somewhere down the line in history, the tremendous amount of flammable petroleum that would result from all that death would explode in a fire that would not be quenched—at least not until this creature called man was no more…

The Snake's Sly Seduction

Mankind's introduction to the fallen angel was at first far from unpleasant. Eve didn't meet a roaring, devouring, lion-like beast; she met what was at that time one of the most beautiful of all God's creatures. Genesis 3:1a describes the being as a "serpent," one that "was more [subtle] than any other beast of the field which the Lord God had made." This doesn't imply that the serpent was sinfully deceptive at the point it was created. Rather, it indicates this creature was more intelligent and more attractive than all the others on earth that God had made—except for, of course, people.

We might have some reason to doubt that Eve was any more intelligent than the snake, considering the way she was taken in. However, I think her being so gullible was a matter of innocence as she stood before the already fallen, prideful, sinful Lucifer in disguise.

Rather than run away from the serpent like anyone might do today, Eve was fascinated by the creature's beauty, and she moved closer to hear what it had to say. The serpent's voice and the words it spoke were obviously at least as alluring as its beauty.

Today, people often don't recognize evil in the glittering things of the world that are bad for them. The serpent was beautiful and attracted Eve, but beneath the beauty was evil that took her in a direction away from God, who knew what was best for her. The snake's words embodied what we consider to be "speaking with a forked tongue":

And he said unto the woman, Yea, hath God said, Ye shall not eat of every tree of the garden?

And the woman said unto the serpent, We may eat of the fruit of the trees of the garden:

But of the fruit of the tree which is in the midst of the garden, God hath said, Ye shall not eat of it, neither shall ye touch it, lest ye die.

And the serpent said unto the woman, Ye shall not surely die:

For God doth know that in the day ye eat thereof, then your eyes shall be opened. (Genesis 3:1b–5a)

Satan's words were not total lies, but half-truths. Half-truths are usually worse than outright lies because they harbor greater power to deceive. In the first part of the conversation, the serpent asked a question that attempted to plant uncertainty in Eve's mind. "Did God really say…?" "Are you sure God said this?" is the tone in the hissing words. "I can't believe a good Creator would do that…deprive His creation of such things" is the even stronger implication. "A loving God, would He do such a thing? You must have heard His words wrongly," the seductive words implied.

The second part of the account, however, was an even better example of how effective half-truths can be: "Ye shall not surely die," the serpent must have hissed quietly.

It was partly true! Eve didn't immediately die when she took the first bite of the forbidden fruit. And, her eyes *were* opened! The serpent's words, though partially true, were deadly. Their poison far surpassed any snake's venom today in the deadly results they produced. When Eve, then Adam, ate of the forbidden fruit, all of mankind and all created things on earth began to die and degenerate. All things became sin-infected.

Eve and Adam became aware of the evil around them, and were terrified as well as ashamed. God's protective will had been to keep them from this mystery called iniquity, that secret called lawlessness. Their disobedience destroyed that protection, allowing the serpent's venom to begin its deadly work.

God Wannabes

"And ye shall be as gods, knowing good and evil" (Genesis 3:5b). The serpent's stern voice surely rang with authority to Eve's ears. Being "like God" was something she was meant to be in the first place! "You are something special!" Satan was saying. "You are a god!"

This is the same message that New Age philosophy tells us today: We are all gods and need no other god to tell us how to live and what to do. We are plenty smart enough to know good from evil. Psychology tells the same thing: All we need is a good dose of self-esteem. All we need is to feel better about ourselves. We've already mentioned how many of today's preachers and teachers feed their flocks this lie. We should just interpret the Bible any way we see fit, they proclaim. The main thing is that it makes us feel good about ourselves. We should consider ourselves as being like God Himself. Doesn't the Bible say that we're created in His image?

Wrong! That is another satanic half-truth! Certainly the Bible says man was created in the image of God. But all changed in that fatal second of disobedience. There is nothing God-like about man in the fallen state.

Woe Man and Woman

Genesis 3:6–10 provides a detailed account of the immediate consequences of the couple's action:

> And when the woman saw that the tree was good for food, and that it was pleasant to the eyes, and a tree to be desired to make one wise, she took of the fruit thereof, and did eat, and gave also unto her husband with her; and he did eat.

And the eyes of them both were opened. And they knew that they were naked; and they sewed fig leaves together, and made themselves aprons.

And they heard the voice of the LORD God walking in the garden in the cool of the day: and Adam and his wife hid themselves from the presence of the LORD God amongst the trees of the garden.

And the LORD God called unto Adam, and said unto him, Where art thou?

And he said, I heard thy voice in the garden, and I was afraid, because I was naked; and I hid myself.

What an eye-popping sight must have greeted this rebellious pair! Instantly, their surroundings must have changed from the most beautiful sights and sounds imaginable to a darkened, sin-filled scene. They now saw the evil as well as the good, and it must have frightened them out of their wits!

Even the voice of the one who had done nothing but loved and provided for Adam and Eve now frightened them. They were apparently afraid of their own shadows and everything else. Most of all, they realized they were naked. They apparently hadn't been wearing anything before. Why did they just now recognize this fact, and why did it frighten them so much?

Although it is not possible to know for certain, the answer might lie in their loss of protective innocence. God's glory had probably covered their nude bodies before their disobedience. The first man and woman had lost the glory of God, in whose image they were originally created. They had also lost a perfect, personal relationship with Him, so they were, at this time, lost. They would spend eternity apart from God, unless He sought them out, found them, and invited them back into His fellowship. Thankfully, He is a wonderful, loving God who seeks the lost so they can be reconciled to Him!

"The excuses men make to cover and lessen their sins, are vain and frivolous," says seventeenth-century Bible commentator Matthew Henry. "Like the aprons of fig-leaves, they make the matter never the better: yet we are all apt to cover our transgressions as Adam. Before they sinned, they would have welcomed God's gracious visits with humble joy; but now he was become a terror to them. No marvel that they became a terror to themselves, and full of confusion."[10]

The Blame Game

Sin was now out of its prison. Lawlessness had poisoned all of God's earthly creation. Everything had changed in a moment when Adam ate of the tree of knowledge of good and evil. The man and the woman in the cradle of civilization who had always a perfect, wonderful, personal relationship with their Maker now wanted to hide from Him.

Adam cringed in the bushes with Eve clinging to him and hiding behind her husband as God found them and talked to them. Adam acknowledged that he was afraid because he was naked (Genesis 3:10), then responded to God's questions demanding accountability with the finger-pointing words: "The woman whom thou gavest to be with me, she gave me of the tree, and I did eat" (3:12). Eve continued the blame game by charging the serpent with the responsibility: "The serpent beguiled me, and I did eat" (3:13).

Note that Adam used the words *"I did eat"* (emphasis added), not *"we* did eat," seeming to admit that the wrong that was done was his, not Eve's. That knowledge seemed to be instinctive with him. This is proven scripturally correct later because God's Word says that sin entered the world through the first man, Adam (see Romans 5:12).

Lord Pronounces Curse

After He had talked with Adam and Eve, God spoke to the serpent, pronouncing on him a severe curse:

Because thou hast done this, thou art cursed above all cattle, and above every beast of the field; upon thy belly shalt thou go, and dust shalt thou eat all the days of thy life:

And I will put enmity between thee and the woman, and between thy seed and her seed; it shall bruise thy head, and thou shalt bruise his heel. (Genesis 3:14–15)

Adam and Eve still had opportunity to repent of their sin. But Lucifer, who had been created knowing good and evil and who had chosen the evil, had no second chance. (Remember, he is bound for the lake of fire, along with all the angels who rebelled with him.) The curse not only embodies the physical condition of the snake and all of its offspring, but also, more importantly, it speaks of spiritual warfare that will rage until Jesus Christ restores all things to sinless perfection. This will take place when He remakes the heavens and the earth following His thousand-year reign on this planet. Jesus is ultimately, in physical and especially spiritual terms, the "seed" of the woman referenced here.

The record of that spiritual warfare is examined throughout this book alongside a discussion of the physical wars raging in the Middle East. The heart of the struggle is found in the last book of the Bible, Revelation.

Sin's Immediate Consequences

After God dealt with the serpent, He turned His attention to Adam and Eve. Sin's consequences were immediate and dramatic:

1) **For Eve and all generations of women to follow, childbirth would become extremely painful.** Feminist propaganda would have us believe otherwise, but the Bible says labor pains are a direct result of Eve's part in the fall from grace. (Interestingly, Jesus used similar terms when talking about the Tribulation period. He likened the end of the age and the Tribulation period itself to a woman in labor. As the end of the age approaches, mankind's troubles will become more intense and will come

with greater frequency. The blood, sweat, and tears of our present-day struggles will end with the glorious birth of an era of peace on earth when Christ returns.)

2) **Adam, Eve, and their descendants would be required to work just to make a living.** They would now have to till the ground, prepare the soil, and harvest the crops with great labor, clearing away briars, thorns, and weeds of all kinds before they could even prepare the dirt for planting.

3) **Animals would have to die to provide clothing for the first couple (Genesis 3:21).** In this, we see sin for what it is at this early point in the story: It is a bloody, destructive, deadly, horrible thing that requires a life to cover it so that God can again accept us into His fellowship. Sin, of course, meant that Jesus, God's only begotten Son, would have to die as a permanent covering for the sinner.

4) **Adam and Eve would be evicted from their lush garden home.** This was the first foreclosure. God did not do this out of hatred; rather, He did so because of His great love for man. God said that now, the man and woman knew both good and evil. If they had been allowed to have access to the Tree of Life, they would eat of it and live forever. But in their sin-filled condition, they would grow more and more grotesque—becoming monster-like because of the ravages of the sin infection. God could not and would not let this happen; therefore, He "drove out the man; and he placed at the east of the garden of Eden cherubims, and a flaming sword which turned every way, to keep the way of the tree of life" (Genesis 3:24).

Satan's Savage Assault

Mankind's time on earth has been filled with Satan's violence against him. Satan is described by John as "a murderer from the beginning" (John 8:44), and one of the best accounts of his hate-filled attacks is found in Jesus' words to the apostle Peter: "Satan hath desired to have you, that he may sift you as wheat" (Luke 22:31). Tracking through the pages of the Bible and world history, it's easy to follow the wrathful revenge of that old serpent, the devil.

The Bible says that people, before they are saved through the shed blood of Christ, are children of their father, the devil. The devil, the Bible says further, was a murderer from the beginning—and we certainly see that in our look at His first interaction with Adam and Eve in the garden. The historical record bears out that the fallen human race follows willfully in the murderous footsteps of the serpent.

We certainly don't have to go back as far as the Holocaust to find unbelievably terrible acts. Our headlines are filled hourly with vile human activity of every sort. Issues and events involving Mideast war and peace we see in our news today are foreshadows of things to come. Satan's wrathful revenge on planet earth will get worse, much worse!

CHAPTER 3

ABRAHAM'S COVENANT AND CONFLICT

TO THIS POINT, we have covered the spiritual roots of mankind's ongoing problems. Now we come to the specific, hard-core issues of war and peace in the Middle East and around the world.

Today's problems in the region we call the Holy Land cannot be ignored or put on the back burner. They are in-your-face, everyday news. Hundreds of reports coming from that area weekly could be used to make the point. Israel and its neighbors are rumbling toward war!

The following news excerpt vividly illustrates that fact. The report is from a former insider of the Iranian regime. Reza Kahlili was in the CIA directorate of operations working as a spy in the Iranian Revolutionary Guard. As of this writing, he serves on the Task Force on National and Homeland Security, an advisory board to Congress, and on the advisory board of the Foundation for Democracy in Iran (FDI).

> Iranian scientists are working on nuclear warheads—and trying to perfect them—at an underground site unknown to the West, according to a high-ranking intelligence officer of the Islamic regime....

The site, approximately 14 miles long and 7.5 miles wide, consists of two facilities built deep into a mountain along with a missile facility that is surrounded by barbed wire, 45 security towers and several security posts.

The new secret nuclear site, named Quds (Jerusalem), is almost 15 miles from another site, previously secret but exposed in 2009, the Fordow nuclear facility....

Quds, built about 375 feet under the mountain and accessible by two large entrances reinforced with concrete, has 12 emergency exit tunnels and spreads around the mountain.

The site has a capacity of 8,000 centrifuges and currently has three operational chambers with 19 cascades of 170 to 174 centrifuges enriching uranium....

One chamber is specifically allocated to laser enrichment research and development, and Iranian scientists have seen great progress, the source said....

Moreover, the source said, successfully making a neutron reflector indicates the final stages for a nuclear weapons design that would be a two-stage, more sophisticated and much more powerful nuclear bomb.

Regime scientists are also working on a plutonium bomb as a second path to becoming nuclear-armed, the source said, and they have at this site 24 kilograms of plutonium, which is sufficient for several atomic bombs.

The scientists are at the last stage of putting together a bomb warhead, he said, and the scientists in their design for a plutonium bomb are using polonium and beryllium, which would serve as the trigger for the bomb.

Iranian scientists, aided by North Koreans, are also working on new ways to have more miniaturized and more powerful atomic bombs, he said....

The regime is working on 17 Shahab 3 missiles in preparation of arming them with nuclear warheads, the source said.

The operational and technical aspect of the delivery system is 80 percent completed, he said.

The regime, aided by North Korea, is also working on neutron warheads that could be used as super EMP weapons for electromagnetic pulse attacks.[11]

Penalty for Premature Paternity

The prophetic issue of war and peace in the Middle East, as we have seen, began with the angelic rebellion in heaven. Sin then entered the human world at the Fall in the Garden of Eden. But the conflict really picked up steam when the great patriarch, Abraham, stepped onto the stage of human history.

God's plan is always the right plan. His is always the perfect plan. That was true when He created the angelic hosts. It was true when He created the man and the woman in Eden. It was also true when He promised Abram that he would father a great family through his wife, Sarai.

Sin is terrible because it altered God's perfection. The "lawlessness" we've been talking about has continued to interfere with God's perfect plan down through history. After Lucifer determined to do things his way rather than God's way and Adam disobeyed, choosing to do what he considered was best, the Bible record shows that mankind continued to grow worse and worse until the Lord had to destroy all but Noah and his family with the Great Flood. Abram and Sarai continued the long line of disobedient acts committed by fallen men and women. Rather than wait on God's precise timing to do its work, they acted on their own. We are living with the consequences of their sin thousands of years later. In fact, notes Hal Lindsey, "the current crisis in the Middle East originated in a feud that began in the tents of Abraham—the father of both Ishmael and Isaac."[12]

High Price of Disobedience

Jesus once said that among men, no one was greater than John the Baptist. Abram, who would later be renamed Abraham, surely was in John's class in God's view, because He trusted him to father God's chosen people, the children of Israel.

But even the greatest of men and women are fatally flawed because of their fallen nature. Such is the case of the great father of God's chosen people. Despite his deep love for God, Abram jumped the gun in the matter of God's plan for him and Sarai. The couple's disobedience was so serious that fighting and struggles have plagued the world ever since.

Journey for Jehovah

"Now the LORD had said unto Abram, Get thee out of thy country, and from thy kindred, and from thy father's house, unto a land that I will shew thee" (Genesis 12:1). When God gave Abram these instructions, the seventy-five-year-old man faithfully did as he was told. He always obeyed his much-beloved God, who had never failed him. He, Sarai, his nephew, Lot, and their families packed up all they possessed and went into the land the Lord showed him: Canaan. The images of the Middle Eastern landscape we see daily in news coverage of the region make it easy to envision the scenario as the ancient troupe set off on their journey:

> Shepherds looking north and east from what are now called the Golan Heights might have seen the first Hebrew scouts coming over a range of low hills. Herdsmen followed with sheep and goats, then came pack donkeys with the women and children, heading south towards Canaan. They wore brightly coloured tunics, knee-length for men, slightly longer for the women. Men

wore sandals or went barefoot, the women leather shoes. Most of the adult males had neatly trimmed beards and hair hanging to the neck; the women's tresses flowed down their backs.

When these nomads camped, they grouped round a tent belonging to…Abram, later to be known as Abraham. He was leaving behind the clan of his father and brothers at Ur in southern Mesopotamia and migrating into unknown territory.

Abraham's journey launched the history of the new Hebrew people, a moment of incalculable consequence for the world. Leaving the Euphrates valley with its dark, thick-walled houses, Abraham's growing clan moved to the dry but open wilderness and pasture land of Canaan.[13]

The journey, though monumental to the travelers in distance, scope, and risk, would eventuate in absolutely spectacular results. Genesis 12:2–3 records God's promise to make of Abram "a great nation." Further, God stated, "I will bless thee, and make thy name great; and thou shalt be a blessing: And I will bless them that bless thee, and curse him that curseth thee: and in thee shall all families of the earth be blessed."

Perhaps the most dramatic truth found in this passage is the prophecy that Abram's future family would affect the peoples of the whole world throughout the centuries to come. To know that God still curses those who curse Abram's offspring, we need only to remember what happened to Adolf Hitler and the Nazis of World War II Germany. Hitler committed suicide in total defeat. The Nazis were considered war criminals by the whole world, and most top Nazis were executed. This was the most hated regime of modern times.

And to know that God still blesses those who bless Israel, all we have to do is to consider that America, the nation-state that God used to help bring modern Israel to birth, is to this point in history one of the most spiritually blessed countries, and certainly the most materially blessed nation ever to exist.

Ultimately, Abram—whose name, of course, would later be changed to Abraham—is a blessing to the whole earth in that through his off-spring, God brought Jesus Christ, the Redeemer, into the world.

A Patient Heavenly Father

God had promised to bless the world through Abram and his descendants; however, he and Sarai obviously had tried to have children without success. They were very old—and getting older! The great man of God lamented the fact that he couldn't give God what He wanted: "And Abram said, Lord GOD, what wilt thou give me, seeing I go childless?… Behold, to me thou hast given no seed: and, lo, one born in my house is mine heir" (Genesis 15:2).

But, God wasn't worried. His plan hadn't changed. He patiently, lovingly took Abram aside and asked him to look at the heavens and try to count the stars. That mind-boggling number, the Lord said, would be the head count of his descendants one day.

Abram was still unsure about the matter and asked God for affirmation that He would possess the land. God gave that assurance through a covenant, which is a binding agreement of the most immovable kind. Like God instructed, Abram gathered animals for the covenant process. After putting Abram into a deep sleep, the Lord performed the covenant ritual. Abram had no part in agreeing to the promise, except to accept God's word on the matter. Then God gave a far-reaching prophecy explaining what would happen in the coming centuries:

1) Abram's descendants would be away from the Promised Land for four hundred years.
2) They would be greatly mistreated in foreign lands.
3) The Lord would punish the people who mistreated Abram's descendants.

4) After four hundred years, Abram's heirs would leave the land of their bondage with very great possessions.

5) Abram would live a long life, then die and go to heaven to join his forefathers.

6) Four generations later, Abram's descendants would come to the land of promise.

God concluded the covenant by describing the boundaries of the Promised Land as stretching from the river of Egypt to the Euphrates River. "The meaning to Abraham and the early readers of Scripture is clear," explains theologian John Walvoord in his book, *Armageddon, Oil, and the Middle East Crisis.* "The land promised was Palestine, stretching from the Sinai Desert north and east to the Euphrates River. This would include all the holdings of present-day Israel, Lebanon, and the West Bank of Jordan, plus substantial portions of Syria, Iraq, and Saudi Arabia."[14]

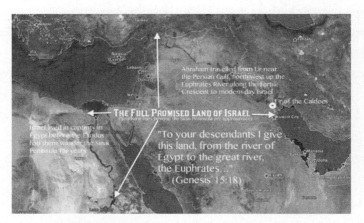

God outlined in great detail the land He promised to Abraham and his descendants.

Source: Endtimesanswers.blogspot.com

Unconditional Covenant

It's important to emphasize that this covenant God made with Abram was one that nothing and no one could ever break. The promise, or agreement, depended on God's absolute love and integrity alone and had nothing to do with Israel's performance.

Abram's Arranged Affair

Even with the covenant in place and God's assurance that He would fulfill His promise, the graying Sarai couldn't seem to ignore her ticking biological clock. Still, there was no child. Sarai began to wonder if she and her husband should put "plan B" in place by asking the couple's Egyptian handmaid, Hagar, to serve as what we would call today a surrogate mother. The practice was common and, while it does not excuse ungodly sexual activity during Abram's generation or any other, the culture at this time often called for such action when a couple couldn't conceive otherwise. Abram was quick to agree to Sarai's suggestion to do what they thought was best rather than what God wanted to do through them. Soon, Hagar had conceived a child with her master.

In the Middle East during these times, childlessness was regarded as the most dreaded misfortune a woman could experience. In fact, many believed that happiness could even be measured by the number of children, particularly sons, a couple had. For most women, much of their entire identity and sense of purpose was wrapped up in the ability to bear children. In light of this, Hagar displayed what would have been a typical attitude: Once pregnant with Abram's child, she haughtily looked down her nose at her barren—at least to this point—mistress. The beginning of the future troubles in the Middle East had begun!

Humiliated by Hagar's attitude, Sarai grew angry and took out her frustration, no doubt, on the ears of her husband. Abram acted less than a diplomat, telling Sarai to do with Hagar as she wished. Sarai did just that; in fact, she "dealt" so harshly with Hagar that her actions and words sent the pregnant woman packing (Genesis 16:6), foreshadowing things to come. The hostilities would build from this point to become full-blown wars that will continue to boil until Christ returns.

Heavenly Intervention

As Hagar was heading out of town, she had an unusual encounter. An "angel of the Lord" appeared to her in what many scholars believe was a theophany—a supernatural appearance of Christ before His birth to Mary in Bethlehem many centuries later. The angel of the Lord told Hagar to repent, or turn from her haughtiness, and trust herself and her unborn child to Sarai for safekeeping. He then made Hagar a great promise, a mixed blessing of great expectation and dire consequences. The great expectation was the promise that her offspring would grow to become a great number of people who would populate many nations. The terrible results of Abram and Sarai getting ahead of God's plan would be that the fruit of the sin would result in big trouble: Hagar's baby, to be named Ishmael, would be a "wild man" who would be "against every man," and "every man's hand [would be] against him." He would dwell among his brothers (see Genesis 16:7–12).

Hagar might not have realized exactly what all of the angel of the Lord's promises meant at this point. The promise of a wonderful future, however, convinced her to pick herself up and return to Abram's house.

The Birth of a Fierce Family

The description of Ishmael offered by the angel of the Lord quickly propels our thoughts to the Middle East today. What do we know about today's descendants of Abram and Hagar? Certainly the Arab people are descendants of that long-ago union. This is not a thought that is argued against by the Arab people themselves. They readily claim Abraham as their original father and Hagar as their mother.

That is the fact upon which they base their claim to the land now called Palestine. Many of the Arab authorities claim that Israel—that is, the Jews—is an illegitimate intruder in the area also called the Holy Land. That is why some of the terrorist organizations within the radical Islamic groups call for jihad (holy war) against the tiny nation of Israel.

Very interesting facts about recent history come to the surface when examining the words the angel of the Lord gave Hagar. The Israel-Arab conflict down through history is covered throughout the pages of this book. But we'll look at that trouble briefly here:

1) The Arabs have lived mostly as nomadic people in the arid lands of the Middle East since the time of Ishmael.
2) The Arabs have been in constant conflict, warring against other peoples and with each other during that history.
3) The Arabs continue to live much like their early ancestors in dress and cultural ways. They remain "wild" in the sense they have not, as a race, conformed to the modern, "civilized" way of life.
4) The Arabs now dwell among their brothers. The prophecy given to Hagar—"And he will be a wild man; his hand will be against every man"—means the Arabs and the Jews will live in the same region. They are, after all, half-brothers. They will quarrel over the same land, particularly as the end of the age approaches.

"The descendants of Ishmael have been at Isaac's descendant's throats for four thousand years now, and their blood feud has smoldered and frequently flamed into war during all that time," notes Bible scholar and author Hal Lindsey in *The Final Battle*. "No racial problem in the world can compare with this one in terms of duration and intensity of animosity."[15]

God Keeps Promise to Hagar

Not only have we seen the prophecy about Ishmael's descendants being "wild" come to pass; we've seen the prediction of their proliferation fulfilled as well. God has absolutely kept His promise to multiply Ishmael's seed; the great Arab race has exploded in population, dominating the Mideast region and beyond for many hundreds of years. Further, the Arabs have been blessed indeed with great riches. Petroleum brought from beneath the sands has made Saudi Arabia, Kuwait, and some other nations there the richest per capita countries in the world.

Sadly, because of the religious and governmental systems in most of the Arab-dominated nations, the masses of people enjoy few of those oil riches. Their dictator-leaders keep the great wealth for themselves.

God-Guaranteed Greatness

Abram had been eighty-six years old when his and Hagar's son Ishmael was born. Now, at ninety-nine years old, Abram was told an amazing thing by none other than God Himself. As recorded in Genesis 17:1–5, God said that not only was Abram to become a father again; he was going to be a father *many times over*—"I will multiply thee exceedingly" (Genesis 17:2). That is indeed enough to make a man fall on his face! And, that is exactly what Abram did. He lay flat on his face before Almighty God, who also told him many other wonderful things. For example, the name "Abram" was no longer significant enough to proclaim the greatness God was about to invest in him. From now on, he would be known as "Abraham," which means "the father of many nations." Kings and entire nations would be born from his line of descendants. The covenant between Abraham and the Creator of all things would, God promised, last forever.

It was a staggering promise Abraham's God made that day. More than that, the Lord guaranteed that Abraham and all of his descendants would own the land of Canaan forever. That includes all of what is called today the Holy Land.

God then made a second covenant between Abraham and himself, one made binding through the act of circumcision for Abraham and all his male heirs to follow (see Genesis 17:9–14). This covenant differs from the earlier one in that the first covenant was "unconditional"—Abraham and his heirs could do nothing to either keep or break it; God did it all. This later covenant was "conditional," one that must be entered by Abraham and his heirs. Circumcision also means that those entering that covenant must keep the requirements involved in obedience to God. To do otherwise brings certain judgments as corrective measures. In that sense, it is possible to break this covenant.

New Names for New Fame

Like the name "Abram," the name "Sarai" was not significant enough to reflect the powerful blessings God was about to bestow upon the couple. So God changed Sarai's name to "Sarah," promising to bless the woman who would not only become the mother of a son, but who would become "a mother of nations." The couple's new fame would become tremendous on the earth (see Genesis 17:15–16).

Ishmael's Mocking Brings Strife

Sure enough, twenty-five years after her son's birth was promised, Sarah became pregnant and delivered Isaac—and this is where we come to the beginnings of the strife between Abraham's sons. God's words recorded in Genesis 16:12 describing Ishmael's character were coming true: Ishmael was a wild young man looking for trouble, and he found it. Isaac was a very young child when Ishmael, about sixteen years old, began to mock the younger boy in threatening tones.

Sarah, obviously upset and angered, told Abraham that Hagar and her son would have to go. Abraham was extremely saddened about having to deal with the situation. The Lord talked with the old father of both boys and comforted him, letting him know that, in this case, Abraham should listen to his wife and do what she wanted him to do. Whether Sarah did it for the right reasons or not, or whether she knew it or not, sending Hagar and young Ishmael away from Isaac was the only way there would be any peace at all in Abraham's family.

God of Isaac Loves Ishmael

Genesis 21:14 and the verses following describe how Abraham gave Hagar and her son some provisions and sent them out as commanded. The old man's faith must have been tested greatly by having to watch the pair shuffle away from the protection of his home. But Abraham always believed God and trusted him completely.

The trip proved very difficult for Hagar and her son as they struggled to survive in the wilderness of Beer-sheba. When the supply of water Abraham had packed for them ran dry, just at the moment Hagar was about to give up on her son's survival—and her own, for that matter—she left the exhausted boy in the shade of a bush. "Let me not see the death of the child" (Genesis 21:16) wept the distraught woman, who was "seemingly alone and without help."[16] But she soon learned that she wasn't alone, nor was she without help. God, who sees all and who hears every cry, came to her, tenderly asked her what was wrong, reaffirmed His promise to make of her son "a great nation" (Genesis 21:18), and then miraculously provided a well of water in the wilderness. How wonderfully personal this time was between Hagar and the Heavenly Father! The God of Isaac also loves Ishmael…by this, we can know He loves us, too.

War Fever Not Forever

Sinful disobedience had set the wheels in motion that would cause Abraham to sire sons of strife. Peace will not come to either of Abraham's two families until the Prince of Peace returns to put down all war on the planet.

Thankfully, many prophetic signals, as we've already looked at in the introduction, let us know Christ's return must be very near indeed. Jesus is the only hope for mankind collectively, and He is the only hope for us individually as each of us passes through this life.

One day the great strife will end. There will be peace, not war, in the Middle East and everywhere else. Let us look further into Abraham's seed, through whom God brought Christ into this sin-troubled world.

CHAPTER 4

JACOB & SONS: GOD'S BUSINESS

PRESENT-DAY TROUBLES in the Middle East are nothing new. The troubles are due to man keeping God out of the peace process. Disobedience to God has always plagued the world. Satan makes the most of sinful man's opposition to God's perfect order. Satan's angry disorder can be witnessed in hourly news accounts around the globe. Recent upheavals include the violent Islamist revolutions in Libya, Egypt, Syria, and most all of the nations immediately surrounding Israel on all but the Mediterranean side. Luciferian rage threatens the Jewish state like it has since its ancient days as a nation.

Abraham Sires Problems

As discussed in the previous chapter, Abraham fathered Ishmael contrary to the Lord's will. Abraham and Sarah were then blessed with Isaac, the child God wanted born in the first place. Then, Abraham sired through Ketura, another handmaid, a huge family that has been in conflict with Isaac's children ever since.

The Arabs and Jews have been in an ongoing clash since Isaac came into the world. Today, the fiery relationship grows hotter by the day. Satan continues to use these families against each other. The struggle will grow worse until Christ returns personally to stop the conflict at the end of Armageddon.

Neither Isaac's family nor Ishmael's has fully received the great blessings God promised. There must first come an era ruled by the Prince of Peace. Both families of Abraham will receive everything promised them. That will come to pass during the thousand-year reign of King Jesus upon David's throne at Jerusalem.

Nonetheless, Abraham's seed has already been a blessing to the entire world through Jesus Christ. He is the Jews' Messiah and the Savior of the world who was born of Mary, a descendant of Abraham, Isaac, and Jacob. His birth is fulfillment of the prophecy in Genesis 3:15: "And I will put enmity between thee and the woman, and between thy seed and her seed; it shall bruise thy head, and thou shalt bruise his heel." The Bible says much about Christ's birth. One of the earliest foreshadowings of that wonderful event is the story of Abraham and Isaac, who were told by God to take a little trip.

God Says, "Take a Hike"

And it came to pass after these things, that God did tempt Abraham, and said unto him, Abraham: and he said, Behold, here I am. And he said, Take now thy son, thine only son Isaac, whom thou lovest, and get thee into the land of Moriah; and offer him there for a burnt offering upon one of the mountains which I will tell thee of. (Genesis 22:1–2)

It's impossible to grasp what the Lord was asking Abraham to do without understanding a little bit about sacrifices and offerings, a system very foreign to the thinking of twenty-first century Christians. When the sin of Adam and Eve—and, by birthright, their descendants—separated mankind from God, from that point on, "the only way for sin-tarnished people to approach a holy God was through the shedding of blood [remember the animals the Lord had slain to cover the first couple's nakedness?]. This was accomplished through the ritual of sacrificing animals" and involved a complex code, outlined in great detail in the book of Leviticus, that was "at the very center and heart of Jewish national life."[17]

So, the ritual of sacrifice itself would have been very familiar to a man as devoted to keeping the Lord's laws as Abraham. In fact, a man who loved the Lord as much as he did would have cherished every opportunity to draw closer to God through the privilege of worship and sacrifice. Yet this burnt offering would be like no other. The Lord wasn't asking Abraham to offer an unblemished bull, lamb, or goat; this was a radical instruction for a man to place his own long-awaited, beloved son on the altar.

"Abraham's previous experience of God would certainly not have led him to suppose child-sacrifice would please him," notes one commentary on Genesis. "Nor was this general practice in Abraham's time."[18]

Are you close enough to your Heavenly Father that you could hear instructions like these from Him without losing it? We can't know what doubts or fears began to rage inside Abraham's head or heart when he heard those words, but, according to Scripture, he didn't even question his Lord. He simply got right down to the business of obeying: He arose early and got his things together, then set out towards Moriah with his son as commanded on the three-day trip.

Although the King James Version of the Genesis passage states here that God "tempted" Abraham, we know that God doesn't tempt us to do wrong (see James 1:13). Temptation is Satan's territory. We saw that at its boldest manifestation during his temptation of Christ in the wilderness (Matthew 4:1–11). Instead, a word study reveals that the more accurate concept conveyed here would be "tested." We know from many places throughout Scripture that God does test His followers, and that is the case here. God was testing His servant—and what a severe test it was! Life and death hung in the balance. However, this was so much more than God testing a man. This dramatic event was the foreshadowing of God sacrificing His own Son for the awful thing called sin.

Trip to Moriah

The destination for father and son was Mount Moriah, a site aptly described as God's touchstone to humanity because of its great significance as a focal point of biblical history. More of an elongated ridge than a particular peak, it is clearly seen in many photos of Jerusalem. Stretching between Mount Zion on the west and the Mount of Olives on the east, Mount Moriah, often called the Temple Mount, is not only where this remarkable demonstration of Abraham's faith took place, but it is also the exact spot where the Holy of Holies sat within the Temple King Solomon would build many years later, in the tenth century BC. The Holy of Holies is the sacred area within the magnificent structure that housed the Ark of the Covenant, which was indwelt by God's glory until the moment of Christ's death on the cross.

Because of its sacred history, it's easy to see why this one spot on the globe is the focus of Satan's hatred. That hatred will continue to be at the heart of Middle East war and peace until Christ's return.

Mountaintop Experience

When Abraham arrived at the mountain as commanded by God, there seemed to be no weak-kneed wavering. He matter of factly told his servants to wait for Isaac and him to return after they had had a worship session: "I and the lad will go yonder and worship, and come again to you" (Genesis 22:5).

This offers a thrilling insight! There seemed no doubt in the old man's mind or emotions that both he and the son he had been commanded to sacrifice would return together, and that they both would be perfectly well when they did so.

Sons of Sacrifice

The biblical account of what happened next offers striking parallels to the last days of Christ's life on earth. First, Abraham put the wood for the fire upon Isaac, his son, for the boy to carry to the place of sacrifice, foreshadowing the way Jesus carried His own wood to Calvary for the cross upon which He was to be sacrificed. Next, Isaac called out to his father about the sacrifice that was to be made. Didn't Jesus call to His Father in the Garden of Gethsemane about the sacrifice He knew must be made for sin? Then, Isaac saw that there was no lamb. Have you ever considered that God saw no lamb that could adequately cover humanity's sin? Further, Abraham told Isaac that God would provide a lamb for what had to be done. Indeed, in His Son that day on Calvary, God did provide the "Lamb slain from the foundation of the world" (Revelation 13:8).

Finally, there is no record of Isaac protesting about what was going on; he went upon the altar willingly. He was bound by his father, but obviously he had obediently let the elderly Abraham tie him. In the same way, Jesus willingly and obediently laid down His life on the cross, led like a lamb to slaughter. He allowed His limitless power as God to be bound by and for God, His Father. He let Himself leave the power and the glory of heaven in order to die for our sin.

God's Great Intervention

As Abraham was about to plunge the knife into Isaac's heart, he was urgently interrupted:

> The angel of the Lord called unto him out of heaven, and said.…
> Lay not thine hand upon the lad, neither do thou anything unto

him; for now I know that thou fearest God, seeing thou hast not withheld thy son, thine only son from me. (Genesis 22:11–12)

This was the same angel of the Lord who would later be born through Isaac's bloodline. It was Jesus Christ who, before He ever came into the world to provide a once-and-for-all sacrifice, stopped Abraham from killing his son. We know this voice was of Jesus, not a created angel from among the many, because He spoke in the first person when commending Abraham for not withholding his son "from me." God honored faithful Abraham's absolute obedience to Him, and Abraham now trusted and obeyed His Heavenly Father completely. Imagine the overwhelming emotions Abraham must have felt as he then continued the mountaintop worship service with a ram that the Lord Himself provided (Genesis 22:13).

Covenant Includes Isaac and Kids

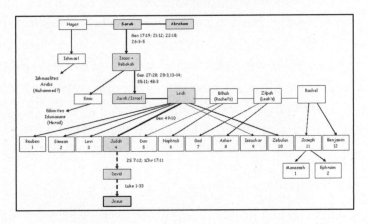

The blessings promised Abraham would extend to all of his descendants.

Source: www.SpiritAndTruth.org[19]

Isaac then began his own journey through life apart from his father and mother. God assured Isaac that He would be with him, and would give him the blessings He had promised faithful Abraham. True to God's Word, Isaac was indeed blessed. He became far richer than any of the people in the land he entered. But the Philistines, the nomadic people who roamed the land, were jealous of Isaac's great wealth. Isaac was forced to move from area to area looking for a well that could sustain his family, servants, and flocks. The Philistines threatened every time he and his people stopped to dig wells for water. Rather than fight them, Isaac picked up and moved along. He and his people moved three times. When he dug the third well, the Philistines stopped bothering him. Finally, he found a good water supply and settled near there.

Even the people who hated and harassed Isaac and his people finally admitted that he was blessed. In Genesis 26, we read of Abimilech, the Philistine king who came to Isaac wanting to make a peace agreement. Isaac at first asked why Abimilech came, considering that the Philistines had run them out of every place they had tried to settle. Abimilech insisted on a peace arrangement, most likely because of superstitious fear of a man as blessed as Isaac. Isaac made the agreement and the Philistines left in peace—for the time being.

We know the peace didn't last. Remember Goliath and that bunch? They were Philistines. So it has been in the Middle East in more recent times. Modern Israel in the land today faces constant envy, hatred, and harassment. There is no real peace between God's chosen people and the modern-day equivalent of the Philistines.

Battling Brothers

God's blessings upon Isaac were awesome. But with the blessings came a terrific increase in troubles. Satan worked overtime on him.

Genesis 25:19–26 tells us that when he was forty, Isaac married a woman named Rebekah who, like her mother-in-law, appeared to be childless. Isaac asked the Lord to do something about the problem, and his wife did become pregnant—with twins. The two children moved around uncomfortably within Rebekah's womb, prompting her to worry and then ask God about it. He told her the movement she was feeling was a battle for dominance; that is, she was sensing the wrangling of each baby pursuing his desire to be on top. The Lord said the children represented two nations to come that would be completely different from each other: one child would be stronger than the other. Also, He said that the first one born would someday serve the second born.

Even with the Lord's explanation of her discomfort, it is still very unlikely that Rebekah knew at this point what it would mean for generations to come. This battle she felt within would rage until the end of human history.

When the twins arrived, the first child was born with a ruddy complexion. Isaac and Rebekah named him Esau. The second child had his hand clamped on the heel of the first baby as they emerged in birth, as if he were trying to hold his big brother back. His parents named him Jacob.

If we were to pinpoint almost exactly the time the Mideast war began, we would see that the conflict started as a skirmish most wouldn't recognize as possible: Twin brothers seem to have started the fighting the moment when they began to battle it out in their mother's womb.

(Modern thinkers, scientists, politicians, and others would say this is not possible, because the unborn "are not people"—the fetus is merely a blob of flesh until the first breath. This is their justification, of course, for murdering children in the womb. They call it the right of the mother to choose whether to have the baby or to have an abortion. The claim that the unborn child is not yet a human being with rights is a false one—if one believes God's Word is true. Christians who believe that the Bible doesn't have anything to say about the fetus being a real person must face the account of this mother and her twin babies within her womb.)

The Birthright and the Blessing

The contrast between the twins born to Isaac and Rebekah couldn't have been starker. The Bible characterizes Esau as "a skillful hunter, a man of the field"—a "man's man," as we might say—and Jacob as "a quiet man, dwelling in tents" (Genesis 25:27). And, whereas the rough and ruddy Esau is many centuries later singled out as an example of ungodliness (Hebrews 12:16), Jacob is described in various translations of Scripture as "plain" (King James Version), "quiet" (New International Version), and "peaceful" (New American Standard Bible). He even earns the description "blameless and upright" from some biblical scholars who have studied the original translation of his story in its full context.

We learn of two key conflicts in the lives of the twins, once grown. The conflicts center on a birthright and a blessing.

The Birthright

As firstborn son, Esau possessed a special honor within the family, a double portion of his father's inheritance. This was his birthright. However, Esau apparently didn't value the importance of such a privilege; Genesis 25:27–35 tells of a time when, famished after an unsuccessful hunt, he sold his birthright to Jacob for a bowl of soup. In essence, he made this life-altering decision without a thought given to God or to his father… and all just to meet a temporary desire. Esau and all of his children for generations to come would pay the price for his sinful carelessness.

The Blessing

Sometime later, when her husband was very old, Rebekah hatched a plan to deceive Isaac so that her favored son Jacob, rather than Esau, would receive his father's blessing. In our day and time, to "bless" someone is a term of endearment or an expression of a desire for God's favor upon a person. We can all "bless" anyone at anytime, as often as we wish—even for a simple sneeze. However, the meaning of "blessing" in this account bears much more weight. For the ancient Hebrews, blessings (and curses) were "special categories of expression that were believed to have the power to determine reality. Once spoken, they could not be changed or repudiated."[20] This means that, once Isaac bestowed his blessing, he would not be able to amend it, retract it, or transfer it to anyone else. Jacob, whose name means "supplanter" or "one who takes the place of another," was so eager to receive the valuable gift of his father's blessing that he willingly joined Rebekah's plan of deception. She and her son arranged for Jacob to disguise himself, easily tricking the nearly blind Isaac into giving the blessing to Jacob rather than Esau.

Hate-Plagued History

The treacherous act of fooling Isaac and taking his blessing sent Esau into a rage against Jacob (Genesis 27:41). Knowing his aged father's remaining days were few in number, he vowed he would kill his brother as soon as he finished mourning his father. This was a threat Rebekah and Jacob took seriously; after all, Esau was a mighty hunter. They knew he had the ability to carry out his warning. Jacob's mother urgently talked to her favorite son and instructed him to take refuge at the home of her brother, Laban, in Haran. So Jacob did as his mother told him, and the brothers were separated.

About twenty years later, Jacob and Esau met again. All seemed forgiven, although Jacob was very afraid as he approached his brother. To Esau's credit, he held no grudge against his brother. He hugged Jacob enthusiastically and welcomed all of Jacob's family, which had grown enormous by that time.

Despite Esau's forgive-and-forget attitude, however, his many offspring through the centuries—the people called in the Old Testament the Edomites—have neither forgotten nor forgiven. Satan will not allow them to do so. It is a supernatural hatred that rages within the most fanatical of the Arabs.

And, Esau's bloodline became mixed with that of Ishmael in the eastern parts of the Middle East. The families intermarried, producing many generations of people who made up many great nations of the vast region. Theirs has been a hate-haunted history of vengeance against the Jews. That history is prophesied to get worse before it gets better.

Jacob's Ladder

After Isaac's death, when Jacob was escaping Esau's murderous rage by fleeing to the home of his uncle, Laban, he stopped to rest along the way and soon fell asleep. This is where we come to the familiar story of "Jacob's Ladder" that you might have heard in Sunday school. This isn't just a good story, however, and it wasn't just a dream Jacob had. It was a mighty vision of things to come.

As he was sleeping, Jacob saw a gigantic, escalator-like ladder, with many angels ascending and descending. They went up and came down between heaven and earth. Scripture says the Lord was standing above this ladder, and records His words:

> I am the LORD God of Abraham thy father, and the God of Isaac: the land whereon thou liest, to thee will I give it, and to thy seed;
>
> And thy seed shall be as the dust of the earth, and thou shalt spread abroad to the west, and to the east, and to the north, and to the south: and in thee and in thy seed shall all the families of the earth be blessed.
>
> And, behold, I am with thee, and will keep thee in all places whither thou goest, and will bring thee again into this land; for I will not leave thee, until I have done that which I have spoken to thee of. (Genesis 28:13–15)

Jacob named the place where he had the dream "Bethel," marking the spot with rocks for future travelers because he now considered this place the gateway to heaven. Indeed, the things the Lord spoke of to Jacob have come to pass; his descendants have been in the forefront of history.

Jacob vs. Jehovah

Many years later, after Jacob reached Haran, had married, and had become a father many times over, the Lord told Jacob to return to Bethel. A strange thing happened to the "supplanter" on his way: He got into a wrestling match with the Creator of all things (see Genesis 32:24–30). And here's the strangest part of all: Jacob won! Jacob wouldn't let go of his opponent, even after God had injured him. The Lord seemed impressed with Jacob's persistence and staying power, and He gave Jacob a new name. He went from being Jacob, the "supplanter," to "Israel," which means "he fights or persists with God" or "a prince who has power with God and with men." Thus, "Jacob and Sons" became "Israel"—a new name for a new business. The nation Israel is destined to be the head of all nations during Christ's millennial reign on the throne of David atop Mount Moriah in the Temple at Jerusalem.

Israel's Powerful Presence

One glorious day, when all things are made new by Jesus Christ, Israel will be at the head of all the nations. Until that time, the world continues to think of the tiny country as standing in the way of world peace.

A diminishing number of nations, including the United States, defend Israel today as a peaceful state wanting to get along with neighbors who only desire to drive it into the Mediterranean. The defenders are few and far between, however. Thankfully, America, despite the obvious dislike for the Jewish state by some at the highest levels of U.S. government, still seems, for the time being at least, determined to stick by Israel.

Israel is small, it is true. But, its presence is still commanding. It has one of the most potent nuclear forces on earth. That alone gives it a powerful influence. But it is Israel's sitting in the middle of the Middle-East powder keg that makes the nation the truly intimidating entity it is.

We will explore these modern-day facts later in the book. For now, let us consider how Israel is already beginning to fulfill the prophet Zechariah's forewarning:

> The burden of the word of the LORD for Israel, saith the LORD, which stretcheth forth the heavens, and layeth the foundation of the earth, and formeth the spirit of man within him.
>
> Behold, I will make Jerusalem a cup of trembling unto all the people round about, when they shall be in the siege both against Judah and against Jerusalem.
>
> And in that day will I make Jerusalem a burdensome stone for all people: all that burden themselves with it shall be cut in pieces, though all the people of the earth be gathered together against it. (Zechariah 12:1–3)

Jerusalem is already a trouble spot, which is what's meant by the phrase, "a cup of trembling unto all the people round about." The following news reports on tensions over the Temple Mount bear that out. (More about plans for the Third Temple atop Moriah is dealt with in chapter 15.) The cauldron is about to boil over in the matter of Mideast war and peace. The turmoil is sweeping the whole world toward man's final war, Armageddon.

> Israelis who believe the Temple Mount should remain in Israeli hands must take urgent action, Likud MK [Member of Knesset] Moshe Feiglin warned Thursday.
>
> Feiglin, who heads the Jewish Leadership faction of the Likud party, visited the Temple Mount on Thursday despite knowing he would find it locked to Jews, as a display of protest.
>
> In an "unprecedented" move, police on Wednesday informed Jewish groups that the Temple Mount will be closed to all non-Muslims until at least the end of Ramadan, on 11th August. The announcement has provoked renewed anger over

anti-Jewish discrimination on the Temple Mount, and sparked calls by activists for a mass-protest on 7th August, at the start of the Hebrew month of Elul.

Temple Mount activists had complained that for the past three days the Temple Mount—the holiest place in Judaism—remained inexplicably closed to non-Muslim visitors. The only "explanation" offered was a bland sign which simply read "Today the Temple Mount will be closed to visitors." Those restrictions did not, however, apply to Muslim visitors, who continue to receive unrestricted access....

The political right must realize that unless it is willing to sacrifice for the sake of Jewish access to the holy site, nothing will happen, he added. "I call for everyone who hears us to come here, to understand that they are giving the very heart of Jerusalem to foreigners, to Islam," he called.

Taking a conservative approach will not help, he said. "This isn't a matter of policy, of authorizations—we've already tried all the accepted routes. We need to understand that there needs to be sacrifice here, that one thousand people show up ready to make sacrifices, ready to be arrested," he explained.[21]

A Jewish website that aims to teach Israelis about the Temple has been met with an angry backlash from the Arab Muslim community.

The Har Hakodesh (lit. "The Holy Mountain") website includes educational material about the history of the Temple Mount, which was the site of the First Temple and Second Temple. The Temples were the focus of divine service for the Jewish nation.

The site also includes stunning photographs of the Temple Mount, including pictures taken by a non-Jewish photographer from parts of the Mount which Jews may not enter.

What has caused upset in the Muslim world is a representation of the Temple Mount as it would appear with a rebuilt Jewish Temple atop it rather than Al-Aqsa Mosque that currently stands there.

The site has been repeatedly targeted by hackers, and has been the focus of criticism in the Arab media. Sheikh Raed Salah, who heads the hardline northern branch of the Islamic Movement in Israel, has called for an "Islamic awakening" in response to the website....

The desire to see a rebuilt Temple is central to traditional Judaism, and the Amidah prayer, which religious Jews recite three times daily, calls for the Temple to be rebuilt.[22]

Judgment at Jezreel

The Bible says that the nation will be back in the Promised Land at the time of the world's final battle:

For I will gather all nations against Jerusalem to battle; and the city shall be taken, and the houses rifled, and the women ravished; and half of the city shall go forth into captivity, and the residue of the people shall not be cut off from the city.

Then shall the LORD go forth, and fight against those nations, as when he fought in the day of battle. (Zechariah 14:2–3)

Israel will be the trouble spot of the world, with Jerusalem at the center of the whole problem. More than that, the Temple of the Jews will be the one place Antichrist claims as his own as he declares himself to be God.

For hundreds of years, this idea was scoffed at by theologians and scholars. Israel was finished as a nation, they declared. The Jews would never return to the Middle East in large numbers. As a matter of fact, they questioned whether there was such a thing as a Jew left. The Jews were scattered and were lost, the great thinkers believed.

But the Jews did come back into the land. Modern Israel was born on May 14, 1948!

The Temple hasn't yet been rebuilt. But there are rumblings of a foundation stone possibly being laid at any time (read more about the subject in chapters 11 and 15). I personally don't think this will happen until a peace covenant is backed up by the power of the so-called international community we hear so much about these days. I believe it will take Antichrist to bring this about. He will do so because he will want to be like God, just as did his father, Lucifer. He will want people to worship him as God there on top of Mount Moriah.

Antichrist will first try to murder every Jewish person he can get his devilish hands on. It will be the time of "Jacob's trouble" referred to in Jeremiah 30:7. Again, we will look more at that later in this book. Jacob and Sons—Israel, the nation—will be at the heart of the most terrible time in human history. All nations opposed to Israel and Israel's God will gather to battle at a place called Armageddon, located north of Jerusalem near an ancient town named Megiddo. The battlefield will be on a large land mass called Esdraleon in a valley called Jezreel (which means "God sows") in northern Israel. That's where Middle East war will be at its worst. God's judgment will devastate the armies of the world on that spot.

CHAPTER 5

MESSIAH'S MISSION

THE HISTORY OF Jacob and Sons is a tale of many twists. This is not to say it is a fable or fairy tale. On the contrary, God's story of this sometimes-faithful, sometimes-wayward company called the house of Israel is absolutely true. And, of the whole house of Israel, just as in the whole family of man, no one is innocent but One. His name is Jesus Christ, the very Son of God!

Abraham, Isaac, and Jacob's descendants enjoyed times of great blessings when they were obedient to the Lord's directions. When they obeyed, they led peaceful, prosperous lives. But they spent more time than not in disobedience. The children of Israel paid the price and were corrected by the God of heaven who had made the covenant with Abraham. Every time they began to live in unrepentant defiance to the God who loves them, their enemy was allowed to come in and take them away to bondage in faraway lands. The Jews were removed to Assyria, Babylon, and Egypt.

As we begin to look at the time of Jesus' birth, earthly ministry, crucifixion, and resurrection, the Jews were again back in the land of promise. But so were the Roman oppressors.

Poor, Prophetless People

The Bible says that judgment begins with the family of God (1 Peter 4:17). He began cleaning house after His prophets had spent many years calling the people of Israel to repent of their sins. Even the priests had brought strange and forbidden practices into their ministry of God's law.

God said if the priests didn't change directions and begin doing things His way, He would curse the blessings He was giving them. He said further that He was already beginning to bring curses upon their blessings.

This was because the priests were supposed to put forth the pure word of God. They were God's messengers between Himself and the people of Israel. But they were profaning the holy name of the Lord by mixing the true law with the strange doctrines of the false religious practices of the time.

So God's people were not getting truth. And, it was tough enough getting them to live holy lives before God without adding in a watered-down or completely perverted message. God told the priests they were making Him tired with their words. When God gets tired, the sins must be very heavy indeed! The Lord said they were asking, "How have we wearied God?" God answered, in essence: "You have worn Me out by saying that those who do wrong are good and make Me happy" (see Malachi 2:17).

Does this sound like some modern preaching and teaching? "God loves everybody and wouldn't condemn anyone to an eternity in hell," many say. "God is love," they proclaim. These false teachers deny that sin must be dealt with by a Holy God. They, in effect, deny that sin even exists. In this way, they imply that God must be a liar, or that He doesn't exist at all.

God said the priests also wearied Him by asking, "Where is the God of judgment?" (Malachi 2:17). They were basically saying, "God doesn't care. He is not judgmental." Or, again, "God apparently doesn't exist!" (This is one reason we can know we are in the last time. Many preachers and teachers within Christianity today are smiling and declaring from their lecterns and pulpits that there is no coming judgment. They are scoffing and asking, "Where is the promise of his coming?" [2 Peter 3:4].)

The people of Israel were going deeper and deeper into sin because of those who were supposed to be teaching them the truth. God finally took them from the land, but He assured them that they would one day come back to the land of promise. The prophecy of their return is so accurate that Bible scholars have proven that the Scriptures pinpointed the precise day Jesus Christ would ride into Jerusalem, offering Himself as Israel's Messiah.

The Silence of God

God stopped talking to Israel through His prophets for four hundred years, a span called the Intertestamental Period. From what the Bible says, we don't know a whole lot about what happened during this time. However, we do know that during that era, Alexander the Great conquered the known world, including the land God gave the Jews. Alexander's four generals fought bitterly with each other to win territory for themselves following Alexander's death.

This violent struggle made it miserable for all people who lived in what we now call the Middle East. As a result of all the troubles in the region, Jews were forced from the land. Many more of God's chosen people lived outside the land of promise, in foreign nations, than in their own land.

The Jews were mainly scattered to the regions of Babylon, Assyria, and Egypt, although Jewish numbers grew in all the major cities of the then known world. Everywhere God's chosen were driven to live, those cities flourished because of the great contributions the Jews made in those societies and cultures.

Even though the Lord was silent in a way He hadn't ever been before, He was at work blessing the nations through the sons of Abraham, just as He had promised the old patriarch and his sons. God was preparing His people to return to the land to face the greatest decision they will ever face: whether to accept or reject their Messiah, the Lord Jesus Christ. At the same time, He was setting into place global alignments in preparation for the coming changes:

> God, in His Providence, was making ready the nations. Greece was uniting the civilizations of Asia, Europe and Africa, and establishing one universal language. Rome was making one empire of the whole world, and Roman roads were making all parts of it accessible. The dispersion of the Jews among the nations thus paved the way for the propagation of the Gospel of Christ in their synagogues and their Scriptures.[23]

And, finally, the Lord God was making ready the promised prophet through whom He would again begin speaking to His wayward people.

Promised Prophet Appears

Before God had turned off the intercom switch, He had given the people hope by telling them that a prophet would come on the scene to prepare the way for him: "Behold, I will send my messenger, and he shall prepare the way before me" (Malachi 3:1a).

That prophet's name was John, and we know him as Jesus' cousin, John the Baptist. His message was loud and clear: Israel's Messiah, the Savior of the world, was on His way. God Himself was coming to earth in the form of a man!

Caesar's Siege

Now let's look at the political landscape the Messiah whom John was proclaiming was about to enter. The Middle East under the Roman

Empire was at peace only in that there was an absence of open warfare. Every land the Romans conquered became peaceful, in that respect. It was called *pax Romana*, "Roman peace."

Discontent and uprisings were dealt with swiftly and harshly. The conquered people bowed to the Roman Caesar—or else. Alexander the Great conquered the lands of the Middle East around 332 BC. Surprisingly, he treated the Jews with consideration, refusing to destroy Jerusalem and allowing them to settle in areas he had conquered.

When Alexander died in 323 BC, two of his generals ruled the eastern part of the Greek Empire. Those generals were Seleucids, who held Syria, and Ptolemy, who ruled Egypt.

Palestine was the vast land of promise. It lay between Syria on the north and Egypt on the south. Syria controlled the region for a time, but was overtaken by the power of Egypt in 301 BC. The land remained under the Egyptian Ptolemy kings until 198 BC.

The Jewish people continued to live in relative peace under the Ptolemy kings. They built synagogues in the places they settled. In fact, Alexandria, the city in Egypt named after Alexander the Great, became a great center of Judaism.

Possession of Palestine then passed back to the Syrian Seleucids. The violent Antiochus Epiphanes reconquered the land in 168 BC and waged war on the Jews. Obviously Satan's man of the hour in the matter of Mideast war, he took the peace from God's chosen people. He did everything he could to kill all the Jews and wipe out their religion. He tore Jerusalem apart in 168 BC, went into the Temple atop Mount Moriah, and put a pig on the altar as an offering. The sacrifice to his god, Jupiter, made a mockery of the God of Israel. He outlawed Temple worship for the Jews and forbade, under penalty of death, the act of circumcision. He sold thousands of Jewish men, women, and children into slavery, and destroyed every copy of the Holy Scriptures he could get his hands on.

Is it any wonder this tyrant is considered a type of Antichrist by those who study prophecy and history? He tortured and murdered the Jews at every opportunity in an effort to make them renounce their religion.

Rome's Wrath

Rome, under General Pompeii, conquered the land mass today called Palestine in 63 BC. The Babylonian kingdom under the great King Nebuchadnezzar had laid siege to Jerusalem in 425 BC. Solomon's magnificent Temple was completely destroyed and burned, as was Jerusalem itself. Herod rebuilt the Temple atop Mount Moriah to keep the Jewish population happy, and therefore presumably avoid uprisings against Roman rule.

While the birth of the Messiah approached, there nonetheless grew resentment in the land. Most of the anger seemed centered among a few rabble-rousers who were considered the terrorists of the time. Some of these had a messianic message. That is, they mixed political aims with religious fervor and claimed to be the Messiah sent to deliver Israel from the oppressive rule of the Romans.

Talk of the prophesied Messiah particularly worried Herod. While he more or less dismissed the fear that one of the terrorists would be the promised deliverer of the Jews, he did worry about the rumored birth of a boy child who would be Israel's king. Fearing this predicted birth, he ordered the murder of all the male children born within a two-year period. Satan was again waging war in a big way upon the heirs of Jacob and Sons.

But despite the horror of the slaughter of babies, and in perfect fulfillment of prophecy, Jesus was born in the city of David, Bethlehem, a place that was in the bull's eye of great historic associations. For example, it was the place where Rachel, Jacob's wife, was buried, and it lay a mere fifteen miles from Hebron, the place Abraham, Isaac, and Jacob had called home. The site of King David's great defeat of the Philistine giant Goliath was just twelve miles to the west, and just a six-mile ride northward was Jerusalem, the splendid capital of Israel that had been established by David and that had flourished under the leadership of his son Solomon.

Jesus grew to manhood perfect in all ways and totally faithful to His Heavenly Father's will. He could be nothing less in order to fulfill God's requirement for the permanent solution to mankind's deadly sin infection.

Satan, when he couldn't prevent the birth of Jesus the Christ through Herod's order of infanticide, really stepped up his attack on Israel and the message being preached to the Jews. And there came upon the scene in troubled Judea a man—the promised prophet of Malachi 3:1—who indeed preached God's mighty message.

Baptist Beats the Devil

John the Baptist didn't surface as what we would imagine a prophet to be. He came on the scene like a circus sideshow freak. That's the way many in Judea viewed him, based upon Matthew's description: "And the same John had his raiment of camel's hair, and a leathern girdle about his loins; and his meat was locusts and wild honey" (3:4).

What a get-up! He wore an outfit made of camel's hair and lived among the thorns, dust, and critters of the wilderness hills surrounding Jerusalem. He ate bugs and honey stolen from the local bees. No doubt that, today, John would be rounded up as dangerous—if not to others, to himself. But there was nothing frivolous about this man or the message he proclaimed at the top of his voice: "Repent ye: for the kingdom of heaven is at hand" (Matthew 3:2). God's great kingdom was about to be offered to the Jews through Jesus Christ, their Messiah.

Don't forget: No one of Judea had ever seen a genuine prophet. This was a spectacle worth investigating, for sure. Hundreds upon hundreds did just that. People came from everywhere for many miles around to see and hear this wild man in the Judean wilderness.

The most curious of all were the so-called holy men of Jerusalem. John, it seems, was treading on their religious turf. He preached that the people must confess and repent of their sins. When they did, the wild man in the scratchy tunic dunked them under the waters of the Jordan River.

The Pharisees, an influential Jewish sect, and the Sadducees, the high-priestly families of Jerusalem, were at first merely curious about John the Baptist, most likely. But once he became the total topic of conversation in the big city, they hurried to the country to see what had so stirred the people, whom they considered theirs exclusively.

A Moving Message

The prophet's serious though no doubt joyous mood turned angry when he saw the stony-faced religious leaders watching the proceedings. He called them what they were—"vipers" (Matthew 3:7)—and said that they were facing the judgment of God Almighty if they didn't come with a heart seeking the Lord's forgiveness. He seemed to read their minds, which apparently were thinking that they were of Abraham's seed and didn't need this crazy, wild man telling them to repent, as he uttered the words: "And think not to say within yourselves, We have Abraham to our father: for as I say unto you, that God is able of these stones to raise up children unto Abraham" (Matthew 3:9). They were, after all, the holy men of Israel—who was this man, to be speaking to them like this? John said in answer to their thoughts that God didn't need them; they needed God. The Lord could turn the Judean rocks into the children of Abraham if He wished!

So began this stepped-up phase of war in the Middle East. There has been no peace to this day within or outside of the house of Israel. Satan continues the long trail of hate-filled aggression against the Jewish race that will come to full fury during the time of Jacob's trouble.

The majority of Abraham's descendants continue to reject the Messiah, the Lord Jesus Christ. It will take the last seven years of human history for God to gather to Himself and thus deliver a remnant of His chosen people. He will do it, just as He promised Abraham, Isaac, and Jacob.

Messiah Comes Forth

John the Baptist had been preaching his heart out, proclaiming One who was soon coming on the scene whose sandals he wasn't even worthy to carry. The Messiah was on His way! Yet, when Jesus came to John for baptism, John—obviously a bold, loud prophet who feared nothing—must have suddenly grown very shy and soft-spoken. Here was the Messiah standing before him…and the Lord wanted John to baptize *Him!*

John could but say—I believe in a reverential whisper—that the Messiah should baptize John instead of the other way around. But Jesus was there to be anointed by His Father in heaven. As an example to all who would follow, the Lord foreshadowed His own death, burial, and resurrection by the symbolic act of baptism. By this act, He was saying this was His Father's chosen way, and He agreed totally.

Jesus received the blessings of the Father when the Holy Spirit descended on Him as He came up out of the water. The Father was very pleased with his Son. Thus began Christ's earthly ministry.

Jesus Jolts Jews

Once Jesus' public ministry was launched—after His baptism and following the forty days He spent in the wilderness, where He was tempted by Satan (see Luke 4:1–13)—Jesus returned to His hometown of Nazareth. "As his custom was, he went into the synagogue on the Sabbath day, and stood up to read" (Luke 4:16). The words, which He read from the book of Isaiah the prophet, offered a stunning description of the ministry He Himself came to earth to accomplish:

> The Spirit of the Lord is upon me, because he hath anointed me to preach the gospel to the poor; he hath sent me to heal the brokenhearted, to preach deliverance to the captives, and recovering of sight to the blind, to set at liberty them that are bruised,
> To preach the acceptable year of the Lord. (Luke 4:18–19)

Surely silence weighed heavily in the synagogue as Jesus then "closed the book…gave it again to the minister, and sat down." We're told that all eyes were "fastened on him" when He said what His audience had probably already begun to realize: "This day is the scripture fulfilled in your ears" (see Luke 4:20–21).

The truth of what had just happened beginning to sink in, the religious men became furious. They were so mad they wanted to kill Jesus, a man they saw as a blasphemer who was declaring Himself to be God's Messiah.

Jesus is not only Israel's Messiah, but he is the very Word of God. This is important to know while we think about the subject of this book. It is important because Jesus made specific predictions about the Middle East that either have already come true, are in the process of coming true, or will come true in the future.

Popularity Panics Pharisees

Jesus got in trouble with the Pharisees because He claimed to be God. That assertion would seem blasphemous if not for one all-important thing: Jesus proved it, many times and in front of many people.

But the real reason the hypocritical Jewish religious leaders were mad was Jesus' popularity, which was growing by leaps and bounds. The Lord's following was taking attention away from them. Above all, they wanted to control the people for their own egos and their own gain.

"When Christ is close by, He has an uncanny way of making those people who don't know Him as Lord feel out of control," observes author Beth Moore. "Since they would rather maintain control over themselves and those around them, they would just as soon get rid of Him."[24]

Mighty Miracles Produce Powerful Proof

Jesus performed mighty miracles. His fame became so great that He often couldn't escape the vast crowds of people who wanted to see and hear Him. He made the lame walk normally. He made the blind see. He made the deaf and dumb hear and speak. Everywhere He went, Jesus did precisely what the Old Testament prophets and John the Baptist prophesied Israel's Messiah would do.

So, Jesus proved that He is God. He claimed to be Israel's Messiah, and even predicted His own people would reject Him. This was the same Jesus who, before He came to earth in the flesh, inspired the words of Isaiah 7:14: "Therefore the Lord himself shall give you a sign; Behold, a virgin shall conceive, and bear a son, and shall call his name Immanuel." He also is the author of the words of Isaiah 53:5: "But he was wounded for our transgressions, he was bruised for our iniquities: the chastisement of our peace was upon him; and with his stripes we are healed."

This book begins and ends, then, with belief that Jesus was and is Israel's Messiah. Only God Himself could know the future as Jesus did and perform the miracles He performed. No other person ever born has so profoundly influenced history as did Jesus Christ.

Jesus Is Israel's Messiah

"And the Redeemer shall come to Zion, and unto them that turn from transgression in Jacob, saith the LORD" (Isaiah 59:20).

"And his feet shall stand in that day upon the mount of Olives, which is before Jerusalem on the east" (Zechariah 14:4).

"He which testifieth these things saith, Surely I come quickly" (Revelation 22:20).

The Literal Truth

Today, a number of scholars believe that most prophecies about the return of Jesus are to be taken as spiritual or symbolic rather than as literal. They say, in some cases, that Christ has returned already in spirit and is here now in Christian believers. They write and teach that Israel has no future in God's prophetic plans. They say the church (all believers in Christ) has replaced the Jewish nation in the promises God gave Abraham, Isaac, and Jacob.

Others accept and believe the prophecies regarding Christ's Second Coming to be absolutely literal in their meaning. Jesus will literally return in His glorified body to a literal earth with His literal saints of His literal church in their literal, glorified bodies to put down the literal war of Armageddon. Then the literal King of Kings and Lord of Lords will set up His literal throne in literal Jerusalem, where He will literally rule and reign for, literally, one thousand years.

Jesus' Mideast Message

Jesus taught many good principles while He walked the earth. He healed hundreds of hopeless, hurting people. He performed spectacular miracles on many occasions. He even raised the dead! He also brought a message to the Middle East that He was the Jews' Messiah. He prophesied many things, including that the people of Israel would have to pay for the sin of rejecting their king when He presented himself to them.

But the most awe-inspiring message of all that Jesus brought was to the people of the whole world, not just to Jews of the Middle East. It was God's message of love to a lost and dying world: "For God so loved the world, that he gave his only begotten Son, that whosoever believeth in him should not perish, but have everlasting life" (John 3:16).

Christ Crucified

Satan hates the good-news message that Christ came to seek and save lost people from sin. The devil really threw Mideast petroleum-like fuel on the area of Jerusalem. He desperately wanted Jesus murdered, apparently thinking that would be the end of the matter. He still thought he could get the best of the God of heaven and of God's Son.

It is obvious that at this time Satan did not fully comprehend God's plan to redeem mankind. Satan is one of the smartest creatures God created. But, here, he didn't seem to understand the most important thing of all: Jesus had to die in order to provide the sin sacrifice God's righteousness required. Christ would then come back to life through resurrection, accomplishing God's perfect salvation plan.

But Jesus, when He said, "It is finished," while on the cross, meant God's eternal purpose had been served. From that moment, all people who have accepted God's great grace gift are covered for salvation under the shed blood of God's Son. He was the once-and-for-all sacrifice for the sins of man.

As mentioned several times now, Jesus is the "seed" referenced in Genesis 3:15, the one who has crushed the head of the deadly serpent, Satan. The end of Satan will come at the conclusion of Christ's thousand-year kingdom. But in God's prophetic foresight, the old serpent, the devil, was finished at the moment Jesus said so.

Meanwhile, we come back to the time during the last moments of the Lord's earthly ministry, when the devil began to arouse the Jews' hatred for Jesus.

Royal Reception

Jesus was famous. The great crowds gathered wherever He was. Many came to Him to genuinely repent. But thousands more came to seek healing or some other blessing, or just to be where the action was.

The religious Jews who were interested only in holding on to power over the people dared not try to do away with Jesus at this point. The crowds would have turned on them. Instead, they sought ways to get Him in trouble with the Roman authorities. They did this in secret meetings all over Jerusalem.

As outlined in the Gospel accounts of Matthew, Mark, Luke, and John, on a springtime Sunday when Jesus was in His early thirties, the Lord rode toward Jerusalem on a colt. He was coming to bring peace to the souls of people and free them from the painful bondage of sin. While He rode toward the city, the people who had gathered in large crowds for the annual Passover celebration spread palm leaves on which the colt could walk. They shouted "Hosanna!" while Jesus rode, indicating that they recognized Him as a royal representative of God. Some of the super-religious Jews in the crowd tried to quiet the enthusiastic people. They were furious that this man came claiming to be God's man of the hour.

Jesus said something tremendously important when He heard these men trying to keep the people from praising him as Israel's king. He said, "I tell you that, if these should hold their peace, the stones would immediately cry out" (Luke 19:40). All of creation knows that Jesus is the Creator! Even inanimate things would have literally exploded with recognition that Jesus was God come down to man if the people had held their praise at this time. But the praise would quickly turn to rejection as the time of Christ's crucifixion neared.

"The hostility of the religious leaders toward Jesus was now out in the open," points out John Walvoord. "Spurred by Jesus' popularity with the people, they began to plan for His murder."[25]

Interestingly, centuries earlier, Zechariah had prophesied this very day with mind-boggling accuracy: "Rejoice greatly, O daughter of Zion; shout, O daughter of Jerusalem: behold, thy King cometh unto thee: he is just, and having salvation; lowly, and riding upon an ass, and upon a colt the foal of an ass" (Zechariah 9:9).

Royal Rejection

The devil's drumbeat of hatred for God and man grew louder and louder. The religious Jews' evil plotting had gained the attention of the Roman rulers. Pilate, Caesar's representative for the territory now called Palestine, wanted to see if this man people believed to be king of the Jews was a threat to his authority.

Terrorism and rebellion were on the increase. Pilate had to put them down at any cost. His own head was on the chopping block, otherwise. His soldiers went to the place the betrayer Judas pointed out, where Jesus and His disciples often gathered, and arrested Jesus. The soldiers thought they captured Jesus there in the Garden of Gethsemane. But to be accurate, it wasn't a matter of the soldiers seizing Jesus; it was a matter of Jesus—willingly—allowing Himself to be taken. All of the angels in heaven were poised to strike if Jesus had but called upon them! Of course, He wouldn't have needed them had He chosen to resist the soldiers; He had escaped many times from those who wanted to harm Him simply by passing through their ranks without them ever knowing it. And, one word from His mouth could have destroyed them all. In fact, one account says that when Jesus spoke to the crowd of soldiers and the men who brought them to Jesus and the disciples, they all fell on the ground in a visible response to His power (see John 18:4–6).

The masses that had worshipped and praised Jesus while He rode into Jerusalem now rejected and reviled Him. Satan's work had done its job. When Pilate offered the crowd the choice of setting free either Jesus or Barabbas, a murderer and robber, the mob overwhelmingly cried out for Pilate to let Barabbas go. They shouted at the top of their lungs for Pilate to crucify Jesus.

It was as if the masses had become satanically possessed. They saw that Jesus wasn't the great king who had come to destroy Roman control over them. They thought He was an imposter, so they hated Him.

The pious Jewish leaders no doubt smiled their cunning smiles of self-satisfaction for the murderous work they had done.

But it wasn't just those Jewish "holy men" who were to blame. It wasn't just the masses who had turned so violently against the Lord who were at fault. It was the sin of all mankind that caused the Lord to willingly give up His life as the Lamb slain from the foundation of the world. It was also your sins and mine that brought the Lord Jesus Christ to the cruel cross on Mount Calvary.

Earth's Darkest Day

As the perfect Son of the Living God hung suspended between heaven and earth, becoming sin for the whole of humanity, black, rolling clouds gathered; satanic lightning flickered and flashed wickedly; and the very air exploded with crashing thunder. God turned His back on His Son in that awful moment. "My God, my God! Why hath thou forsaken me?" Jesus cried (Matthew 27:46).

God in heaven looked away from planet earth that afternoon, and the world became darker than it had ever been or ever would be again (see Luke 23:44–45). The moment Christ gave up His life—for no one took it from Him—the ground in and around Jerusalem split and broke apart. Corpses climbed from their graves and walked the streets. Every element in the heavens and on the earth quivered and shook, protesting that horrifying event. It was indeed earth's darkest day.

Glorious Sonrise!

Satan and evil seemed to have won the war against God and goodness that day and the following two days there in the Middle East. The Lord's disciples were devastated. They still didn't understand the plan of God for reconciling lost man to Himself. Yet, soon, the most inconceivable thoughts became reality: The tomb was empty! Peter, the big, burly fisherman who had defended Jesus by cutting off a man's ear when the Romans had come for Him…Peter, the one who then later denied Jesus before a young woman who identified him as a follower of the Lord, looked in the tomb. The grave wrappings were there. Jesus' body was not!

The risen Jesus spoke to Mary and told her to spread the word that He was alive. He then appeared to His disciples—and even ate fish with them. The Lord appeared to hundreds over the next days.

The Son had risen over the stormy, sin-cursed planet. It was a glorious victory over sin, death, and the grave. Jesus had assured a way for every person who would ever be born to live forever in perfect oneness with God! He had purchased their souls with His shed blood.

Christ's birth, life, death, and resurrection are the centerpiece of God's plan of redemption for Israel, the Middle East, and the entire world. Credit: Simon Speed

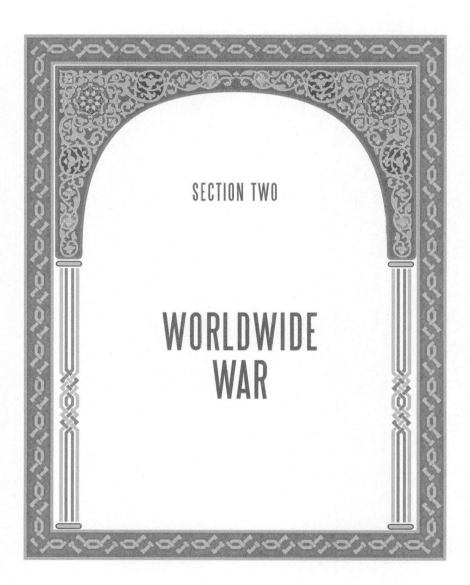

SECTION TWO

WORLDWIDE WAR

CHAPTER 6

DISPERSION AND PERSECUTION

LET'S RETURN FOR a moment to the hours just before Jesus went to the cross.

He sat upon the Mount of Olives with His disciples while the group looked down at the Temple sitting atop Mount Moriah. One of His disciples wanted Him to look at the beauty of the great structure. It was a magnificent sight. They were having a time of fellowship, and it must have seemed that nothing bad could come of their circumstances.

Jesus, however, knew what He faced. More than that, He was concerned for His friends and disciples. He knew they had to get a grip on reality as they faced the satanic war that lay before them. Very soon they would see Him die in the cruelest method known to man at the time. They must be given truth upon which they could reflect during the uncertain days ahead. Although they wouldn't understand for the moment, the prophecies Jesus gave that day in His Olivet Discourse would echo mightily through the centuries until the very end of the age.

"The Olivet Discourse forms Jesus' last major discourse and His most prophetic sermon," notes author and eschatologist Tim LaHaye. "While the message includes a prediction of the imminent fall of Jerusalem, it also looks to the distant future of the 'times of the Gentiles' (Luke 21:24), which will continue until the end of the Great Tribulation."[26]

Temple Toppled

Jesus told His disciples that the beautiful Temple they were looking at would soon be completely wiped off Moriah; its destruction would be so complete that "there shall not be left here one stone upon another, that shall not be thrown down" (Matthew 24:2). (The Temple Jesus was referring to was the Second Temple; the first, built by Solomon, had been destroyed by the Babylonians in 586 BC.)

Jesus' prediction of the destruction of the Second Temple came to pass some thirty-seven years later, when the soldiers under Roman General Titus not only toppled the Temple, but removed from the surface of Moriah every huge stone that had made up the building. Titus tried to stop the soldiers from destroying the structure, but Roman soldiers were often given the freedom to plunder any place they conquered, and they went into a frenzy. Going after precious stones and the gold and silver inlaid within the building, they set fires, causing the gold and silver to melt into the cracks and crevices between the stones. The greedy troops then tore the stones apart in order to retrieve every trace of the valuable metals.[27]

Later, after the scavenger soldiers had picked the site clean, the Temple Mount was leveled and smoothed, then salt was poured on top of the soil so nothing would grow. This, too, fulfilled Old Testament prophecies. But this was just the beginning of Israel feeling the chastening hand of God. He was going to use the Romans to drive most of the Jews from the land.

The words of Christ about the destruction of the Temple and Jerusalem would have been deeply troubling to the disciples.

"To the very end of His earthly ministry the apostles had been waiting for Jesus Christ to overthrow Roman rule in Palestine and to usher in the glorious Messianic kingdom," notes author Arthur Kac. "When, therefore, instead of fulfilling their hopes the Lord Jesus began to speak of his approaching death and the coming destruction of Jerusalem the apostles became deeply distressed."[28]

"Run for Your Lives!"

In the same Olivet meeting with His disciples, Jesus forewarned that the people of the area would have to run for their lives (Matthew 24:16). There was coming, He prophesied, a time of great trouble in the land. Jesus said the people who lived in and around Jerusalem shouldn't even take time to pack; they should just run for the hills of Judea when they heard of the Temple being attacked and the city being overrun.

The prophecy, of course, proved absolutely true. The Jewish population—and other people, too—were slaughtered if they stuck around once the looting and plunder started. Many soldiers for hire, along with the Roman forces, combined to massacre many. Hundreds upon hundreds were nailed and tied to crosses much like the one on which Jesus was crucified. The roads leading into and out of Jerusalem were lined with dead and dying people upon crosses.

The most infamous case of Rome crushing the Jewish rebellion is at Masada (Hebrew for "fortress"), which was the last Jewish stronghold in the Promised Land "located atop an isolated rock cliff at the western end of the Judean Desert overlooking the Dead Sea."[29] Several years following the destruction of the Temple, "after Judaea became a province of the Roman Empire...the last survivors of the Jewish revolt...chose death rather than slavery when the Roman besiegers broke through their defences."[30] The stand on the high plateau remains one of the greatest stories of courage in Jewish history.

The Jews' attempts to take the heavy yoke of Rome from their necks ended with thousands fleeing the land to stay alive. Many others were taken as slaves. Most everyone who was Jewish, whether those who converted to Christianity, those who practiced Judaism, or those who professed no religious affiliation, were either murdered or scattered to other parts of the Middle East and other lands beyond. Around AD 135, Rome dispersed the Jews because it considered the militant uprising against Roman authority a mostly Jewish rebellion. Many of Israel ended up in Rome, where the church of the Lord Jesus Christ would grow into a mighty movement.

"The Jew living now in the various parts of the Roman Empire was painfully aware of the fact that he had no National Home," states Kac. "And by this time the great bulk of the nation lived outside of Palestine. With the loss of the Jewish National Home in AD 70, the long exile actually began, and the Jews became wanderers over the face of the earth, a people without a country."[31]

God's chosen people were chastened by God for rejecting their Messiah. They were chased across the world by the forces of Satan. But the Jews had produced the most important gift ever given anyone: the Savior of the world. The Lord of heaven had already kept His promise to make Abraham, Isaac, and Jacob's descendants a blessing to all nations. He will yet make His chosen people the head of all nations as well.

While in Rome...

Meanwhile, Christianity was growing by leaps and bounds. The Jewish religious leaders had for many years persecuted Christians at every opportunity. The apostle Paul of Tarsus, a Christian-hating Jew before God changed his name from Saul, had been one of the worst of all persecutors of Christians.

Saul had held the robes of those who stoned to death the great hero of the Christian faith, Stephen. Saul had also gone into the homes of Christians and pulled them out so they could be imprisoned or murdered. This treatment, in the earliest time of the developing church, had been more the usual way of Jews treating Christians than the unusual.

When Saul saw Jesus in a blinding light on the road to Damascus, he was instantly converted to the Christian faith. Like Abraham, his name was changed to reflect the transformation of his life, and he became Paul, an evangelist for the gospel of Christ unlike any other who has ever lived. He then became the hunted and hated Christian whom the super-pious Jews wanted dead.

Over the hundred years following Paul's death, the Jews were absorbed into the Roman Empire and given the right to be citizens. But when the Jews found themselves at the center of growing rebellion against their Roman masters, they were scattered throughout the developing medieval states and persecuted almost everywhere they went. Christians, too, were greatly persecuted. Most Christians were Jews who had been converted from Judaism during this time. Satan's war-making in the Middle East and elsewhere appears to have been even more intense against Christian Jews than against the Jews in general. While in Rome, if Christians and Jews who held to Judaism didn't repent and do as the Romans did, there was a mighty price to pay.

Christians Forced into Catacombs

Christianity continued to grow tremendously during the second, third, and fourth centuries and beyond. Jesus' words, foretold to Peter and other disciples—"upon this rock I will build my church; and the gates of hell shall not prevail against it" (Matthew 16:18b)—echoed across the barren wasteland of the Middle East and regions to which God's children traveled.

Hundreds upon hundreds of Christians—including, many believe, Peter and Paul—died martyrs' deaths under Roman Emperor Nero and the Caesars who followed. They faced gladiators, bears, and lions in the Roman arenas to entertain Caesar and his mocking friends. Many Christians were set on fire and used as torches to light the night skies for the various sporting events. It was the bloodiest time of Christ's church. Thousands found shelter and safety in the catacombs, the underground tunnels that were Rome's cemeteries. Drawings on the catacomb walls tell a story of an underground church in the most literal sense of the word.

Modern Martyrs for Christ

Today in Nigeria, Kenya, Ethiopia, China, and many other places around the world, Christians are facing tortures and atrocities as terrifying as the horrors faced by the early Christians. The following reports offer striking proof:

Roadside Ambush in Nigeria Leaves Five Christians Dead and Four Wounded—On the evening of August 29, 2013, near Jos, Nigeria, Emmanuel Sunday was riding his motorcycle towards his village when the nineteen-year-old college student was stopped by an armed group of Islamic jihadists known as Boko Haram. The gunmen asked Emmanuel to identify his religion. He told them he was a Christian. As the young man looked ahead, he saw that the gunmen had detained a minibus and ordered a group of passengers who had also identified themselves as Christians to lie down on the roadside.[32]

As darkness fell, the gunmen robbed the Christians, and as the jihadists began shooting their captives, Emmanuel escaped by running toward a nearby maize farm. He then continued to run for two hours before finally reaching his village.[33]

Five Christians were killed in the attack, including two from Emmanuel's village. Four were wounded, including a pregnant woman.[34]

Boko Haram, whose name loosely translated means "Western education is sinful," so far is contained within Nigeria. Its leader, Abubakr Shekau, clearly states the group's mission: "Let the world know that we have been enjoined by Allah to kill the unbeliever."[35]

Seventy-two Civilians Killed in Mall Massacre in Kenya—Shortly after noon on Saturday, September 21, 2013, gunfire and grenade explosions erupted as Somalian Islamic militants known as al-Shabab launched a massacre at the packed Westgate Mall in Nairobi, Kenya, a mall frequented by expatriates and the rising middle class of Nairobi.[36]

According to Joshua Hakim, a born-again Christian, the terrorists shouted for all Muslims to leave the mall. When Hakim realized that the attackers were targeting non-Muslims, he pulled out his identification card and covered his first name with his thumb. Seeing only his Arabic last name, the terrorists let Hakim go; however, the Indian man next to him was not so fortunate: He was shot when he couldn't answer the question, "What is the name of Muhammad's mother?"[37] More than seventy-two civilians were killed and two hundred were wounded in the attack.[38]

Suicide Bombers in Pakistan Kill Nearly Ninety after Sunday Services—After services on Sunday morning, September 22, 2013, about 550 worshippers were exiting the 130-year-old All Saints Church, a Protestant congregation in Peshawar, Pakistan, unaware of two Taliban suicide bombers in their midst. The explosion killed nearly ninety, many of them women and children; more than 120 people were injured, and the church was destroyed.[39]

"I heard two explosions," said one parishioner who survived. "People started to run. Human remains were strewn all over the church." At the time of the interview, she was still searching for her sister.[40]

It is sad to have to say that while many of us here in America often will not let ourselves be inconvenienced enough to read our Bibles or pray, thousands of Christians are still laying down their lives for the Lord Jesus. According to the Ethics & Religious Liberty Commission, more than 200 million Christians are being persecuted worldwide; they are brutalized, sold as slaves, imprisoned, tortured, threatened, discriminated against, arrested, and killed—solely because they refuse to renounce or hide their faith in Jesus Christ.[41] And still the church survives and grows!

Medieval Meanness

The long history of persecution that continues into our time would soon enter one of its darkest, most vicious eras. The house of Israel had moved out of Jerusalem and Judea in many directions and into the Middle Ages. It was not a smooth trip. The Jews had enjoyed citizenship rights under Rome's authority for the most part. But now they were being put on the outer edges of the societies in which they lived and did business.

The Talmud—guidelines providing a reorganization of Jewish life according to rabbinic religious rules—was completed in AD 600, causing Jews special problems. While more and more of the western parts of the Middle East and Europe turned to Christian-type beliefs, the Jews turned more and more inward. That is, the Jews, under the Talmud, separated from non-Jewish peoples. They lived in their own communities and worshipped following strict, specific traditions and laws unique to them. At the same time, however, they were under the laws of the societies and governments where they lived.

It is proper to say "Christian-type" or "Christian-like" beliefs because, in many cases, people who claimed to be Christians obviously were not. Persecution of the Jews began to take place under the oppressive "Christian" societies. There were, of course, real Christians in these times, just as there always have been. The Jews weren't mistreated by the true Christians, but were loved by them—as compelled by the Holy Spirit and commanded by the Holy Scriptures.

Jews had been allowed citizenship under former Roman conditions, but now they were forbidden to participate in much buying and selling. They couldn't take "Christian" oaths required to do business under the feudal system, a perverted system of slave-based commerce. They therefore were excluded from all except some forms of craft work, money lending, and trading.

Governments and societies became more organized by the twelfth century. The use of money increased—as did its value. This meant that the Jewish artisans, traders, and money lenders grew in power and influence.

Just as God had promised, Abraham's seed took root and flourished wherever it was relocated. But the Jews were chastised for their disobedience to God. There began intense persecution because of jealousy and hatreds by the people around them. The first terrible massacres of Jews began in the Rhineland of Europe when the crusaders—knight-warriors of the Middle Ages—slaughtered many of God's chosen.

Satan's war room was no doubt electric with plans to murder as many of Israel as possible. And it was a devilish scheme indeed. He would get those who served him to kill God's chosen under the banner of Christianity.

A Plagued People

And they shall fall one upon another, as it were before a sword, when none pursueth: and ye shall have no power to stand before your enemies.

And ye shall perish among the heathen, and the land of your enemies shall eat you up.

And they that are left of you shall pine away in their iniquity in your enemies' lands; and also in the iniquities of their fathers shall they pine away with them. (Leviticus 26:37–39)

Although they lamented because of their removal from their home-land, Jews prospered in every area to which they scattered. Despite their neighbors' intense dislike for them as a race, those neighbors were forced to do business with them because the Jewish people provided the things other peoples wanted and needed.

Satan must have seen this as a good time to raise the temperature of hatred against God's chosen people. Just as in times before, Abra-ham's descendants became so disobedient and rebellious that God could no longer let them go their own way. He allowed satanic war against them to discipline and chastise the people He loves with all His great heart. Black Death fell upon mankind. It was unlike any other plague in recorded human history.

Ultimately, more than 20 million people in Europe reportedly died of this devastating disease, which was brought to the continent by sea in 1347. Historical records show that people gathering to greet twelve ships that had sailed through the Black Sea and docked in Sicily met crew members who were either dead or critically ill, with fever, nausea, pain, and strange black, oozing boils. [42] Superstition was a major part of life during this time, and it led to the growth of a rumor from the very mind of Satan. By the fall of 1349, the rumor had it that the plague was the result of a Jewish conspiracy. Lies were spread that Jewish leaders had plotted to send poison into France, Switzerland, and Italy. Particularly, so the lies went, the poisoners had poured vials into the wells of the regions where deaths occurred.

The count of Savoy, a Swiss aristocrat official, ordered Jews arrested in Geneva, Switzerland. They were tortured until they confessed that they had poisoned the water, even though they had not. These tortured Jews, under threat of death to themselves and those they loved, went along with their tormentors and pointed fingers of accusation at other Jewish people. The accused were rounded up and murdered.

The inquisitors, or medieval judges, sent the records of the false confessions from one town to another in Switzerland and down the Rhine River into Germany. Many thousands of Jews in more than two hundred towns and hamlets were hacked apart by sword and axe, and burned.

Also, the Jews were believed by many to be "Christ-killers." The Jewish people were attacked because of superstitions that said having Jews in their midst brought the Black Death. These superstitious anti-Semites didn't recognize their own sin, for which Christ had died.

With thousands upon thousands murdered because they were thought to be responsible for the Black Death, and because they were stripped of all wealth and livelihood, the Jews came to a catastrophic state of existence. It would be the seventeenth century before the Jews would again play much of a part in European society.

Of course, it wasn't the Jews who were responsible for the Black Death. We know now that it was the Bubonic Plague, which was caused by the bites of fleas infected with the disease. The fleas came from the tremendous numbers of rats that infested the region.

God Keeps Promises to Abraham

Throughout the Middle Ages, the Jewish people endured hatred and bigotry. Fear of the Black Death was just part of the violence against them. Economics played a major role in the torment of the Jews as well.

Merchants in the traders' guilds in such places as Strasbourg, France, led the way in butchering the Jews. They did so in the name of religious superstition, but actually these merchants owed the Jewish traders and moneylenders. It was a convenient way to get out of paying their debts.

The craftsmen and nobles did everything within their power to eradicate all Jewish influences out of a desire to do away with economic competition. Thus the biblical warning of 1 Timothy 6:10—"The love of money is the root of all evil"—was again proven true.

The people of Strasbourg who hoped that killing the Jews would protect them against the plague were in for a rude awakening. Rats soon overran the city, and more than sixteen thousand people died of Black Death. This, too, fulfilled God's promise to Abraham to "bless them that bless thee and curse him that curseth thee" (Genesis 12:3).

Just as the Lord promised in Leviticus 26, He remembered His covenant with Abraham, Isaac, and Jacob. While the land of promise lay fallow because Abraham's offspring had not honored God's Sabbath and other commandments, the chosen people were being prepared to once again begin entering the Holy Land.

Zion Calls to God's Chosen

Neither the Jews nor their enemies knew it, but their tormentors were used to drive Israel homeward. Christians—that is, those who were true believers—also played a part in nudging God's chosen back toward the region called Palestine.

These understood, through prophecy, that God would bring Israel back into the Promised Land to re-form a nation there. The

Christians worked and planned to see that Abraham's progeny again looked homeward.

A number of false messiahs also got in on the act. They came forward during the sixteenth and seventeenth centuries, doing their best to convince the Jews that they should return to the homeland. Each of these phonies wanted, of course, to personally lead in the return to Palestine.

But as persecutions lessened when the Middle Ages passed into history, the Enlightenment of the late eighteenth century urged the Jews to strive to become a part of European culture and forget about Palestine.

God again allowed persecutions of the Jews to turn their attention homeward. Eastern European Jews, in particular, refused to settle into that culture. The czarist pogroms of the nineteenth century brought in a serious Zionist movement.

Theodor Herzl, an Austrian- Jewish journalist, became one of Israel's modern heroes. At first he wanted the Jews to settle into the European societies. But with anti-Semitism on the rise, he became determined to urge the return to Palestine.

Theodor Herzl, founder of modern political Zionism, appears to be looking on (from portrait) as David Ben-Gurion, first prime minister of Israel, publicly pronounces the Declaration of the State of Israel on May 14, 1948, in Tel Aviv, Israel, some forty-four years after Herzl's death. Source: Israel Ministry of Foreign Affairs

Herzl believed that the Jews could live a peaceful existence only by concentrating in one territory. He brought together the first Zionist Congress at Basel, Switzerland, in 1897. The thrust of the meeting was summarized in the statement: "[Zionism] strives to create for the Jewish people a home in Palestine secured by public law." [43]

The Zionist Congress then met yearly until 1901. After that, they met every two years. The Ottoman Turkish government, which controlled Palestine during this time, refused to allow the Herzl-led Zionists to set up a region for Jews in the Promised Land. Herzl and the Zionist Congress then received backing by the British government.

Great Britain offered six thousand square miles of uninhabited land in the African area of Uganda in which to settle. But the Zionists would accept nothing less than to return to Palestine.

"Thus political Zionism was born," says scholar and author Arthur W. Kac. He continues:

It made articulate the millennial Jewish hopes and aspirations for a restored Zion. It brought the whole question out into the open and laid it at the doorstep of the Gentile world. Since the Gentile world did not want the Jew in its midst it was up to this same Gentile world to help the Jew find a place in this world, and this place is none other than Palestine. [44]

However, it's important to remember, as David Allen Lewis points out:

Zionism did not come into existence in 1897 when Theodor Herzl convened the first Zionist Congress in Basel, Switzerland. It begins in the opening pages of your Bible, in the twelfth chapter of Genesis. Moses recorded the unconditional promise of God in which the land is promised to the seed of Abraham forever. [45]

Further, Lewis states:

To Christians who agree with literal interpretation of the Bible, the words Zion and Zionist have special meaning. Zion, in Scripture, first meant the city of Jerusalem. Later it was expanded to include the Temple Mountain, then the expanded city of Jerusalem, finally the whole land of Israel (in some passages). Christians become a part of Zion by the new birth; that is, we become a part of the commonwealth of Israel.... The Church never replaces Israel, but our spirits are bonded to the spirit of Israel.[46]

Balfour Brings Jews Back

Theodor Herzl died in 1904 before seeing the fruits of his labor to return the Jews to their homeland. The leadership of Zionism, which represented only a very small part of the house of Israel, moved from Vienna, Austria, to Berlin, Germany. Zionism, before World War I, was made up mostly of Austrian, German, and Russian Jews.

The small number of Jews representing Zionism created a growing excitement about a possible return to the land by using propaganda using pamphlets, presenting passionate speeches, and publishing newspapers devoted to the return. Their efforts resulted in what is known as a "Jewish renaissance" in letters and arts, which marked a great increase in the use of the Hebrew language.

The failure of the Russian Revolution of 1905 and the wave of pogroms and repressions that followed caused growing numbers of Russian Jewish youth to emigrate to Palestine as pioneer settlers. By 1914, there were about eighty-five thousand Jews in Palestine; thirteen thousand settlers lived in forty-three Jewish agricultural settlements.

The Revival of the Hebrew Language

As mentioned earlier, the revival of Hebrew literature and language as part of the "Jewish renaissance" was a return to the ancient biblical Hebrew. But later on, there was a need to modify and expand Hebrew to accommodate modern usage for the twentieth century. In the 1880s, Eliezer Ben Yehudah led the movement to make Hebrew the official tongue of the Jews and the state of Israel.

The fact that Hebrew is now the official language of Israel and of most Jews living there is truly miraculous. Hebrew was virtually a dead language for almost two millennia. No other language has survived such a long span of time to then become a universal language again like Hebrew has. This is no accident. The fact that the Hebrew language was revived at the same time the Jews were restored to the land of Israel is another indication that God was at work. It is only logical that if God was bringing back the Jews to their ancient homeland, He would also restore the language He originally ordained His Word to be written in. Zephaniah 3:9 is a verse that some believe has been fulfilled with the restoration of Hebrew as the language of the Jews: "For then will I turn to the people a pure language, that they may all call upon the name of the LORD, to serve him with one consent."

Fierce, Fanatic Foes

In Ezekiel 36:1–10, God gave His prophet an unusual mission: Tell the "mountains of Israel" that the heathens who had treated the land brutally would pay a heavy price, because the Lord was furiously jealous about the land. The beloved land, God prophesied, would soon be occupied by His people, and it would again be tilled and sewn for bountiful crops that would spring up. God told the prophet to tell the mountains as well as the "hills…rivers…[and] valleys" that the people of Israel would build and inhabit cities throughout the whole region. Even the wasteland, He said, would blossom.

It seems that because the hard-hearted, hard-headed, hard-of-hearing people of Israel weren't listening to God during the time before their final return to the land of promise, God was talking to His geophysical creation! The land the world calls Palestine always becomes desolate when Israel is absent from it. An example of this is seen following Christ's crucifixion, resurrection, and ascension into heaven. After the AD 70 destruction of Jerusalem and the Temple atop Mount Moriah, the Jews began scattering into all surrounding lands. The Romans and others who ruled stripped practically all trees to make things such as buildings and ships, causing the land to erode. The topsoil washed away, and the ground beneath was not suitable for growing without considerable rains. That region, of course, goes through periods of drought. The land remains a desert-like wilderness to this day, except where the Jews in modern Israel have restored parts of it for agriculture. They are making great strides in improving the land. You have probably heard of the tremendous tree-planting program going on in Israel today. Everyone interested is urged to plant a tree there or pay a few dollars to have one planted. Desolation such as this will be the case when Israel begins to return to the land for the final time.

And so it was when the Zionists and others began making plans to return. The Promised Land was barren, and God almost seemed to feel sorry for it. Also, He had no good words for the heathens who falsely claim to have a right to the land He gave Abraham's descendants.

Today there is great argument and debate over the Middle East land called Palestine. War and peace are the issues that constantly trouble the people there. Nuclear war, diplomats of the world fear, could result if solutions are not found to the question: Whose land is it?

God has no trouble with the question or with the answer. The land belongs to Israel! Because of Israel's disobedience to God's instructions, the nation has always been taken to the woodshed by the Lord. It has always had troubles. But the resistance Israel has faced each time His people return to the Holy Land after being scattered is satanically inspired opposition.

God's chosen people faced devilish obstacles right from the start when they began coming back into the land just before the beginning of the twentieth century. The anger and hate-filled resistance grew worse—much worse!

Empire Umpires

Amos 9 prophesies that when the return of the Jews to the land comes to pass, nothing and no one will ever remove them from the land again (see verses 8, 14, and 15). The Middle East was inhabited by Arabs and other peoples until the earliest Jewish settlers began arriving in the 1800s. The land was desolate, with only a sparse scattering of primitive villages for the most part. Islam dominated the region and kept the population of Palestine in spiritual darkness.

Even under those primitive regional conditions, Jerusalem was a powerful magnet to all the world powers. Britain, France, America, Austria, and Russia opened consulates there.

Because of that interest by the powerful nations, there was tremendous development in the region. Steamships between Europe and the Middle East brought changes, as did the telegraph. The Suez Canal made the area a major trade route between Europe, Asia, and Africa.

Jews began coming back in waves, and by the middle of the nineteenth century, they had established large communities in and around Jerusalem. The Jewish settlers reclaimed the land from swampy soil. By the turn of the next century, the ground had been laid for a thriving agricultural economy to come.

However, the Jews met violence and resistance at every turn. It became obvious that someone would have to referee the situation to prevent constant warfare. The British Empire was up to the task.

General Assists in Birth

The early twentieth century was a time of great trouble for the Jews who continued to flock to Palestine. The Jewish population had reached eighty-five thousand by the beginning of World War I in 1914.

General Edmund Allenby most likely didn't know he was acting as a midwife to help bring forth the birth of God's nation. But his actions on behalf of Great Britain would result in the rebirth of Israel thirty-one years later.

The Balfour Declaration, mandating a Jewish homeland in Palestine, brought Allenby into Jerusalem with two legions of troops in December of 1917. Four hundred years of Ottoman control over the area had come to an end. In July 1922, the League of Nations asked Great Britain to work at establishing a homeland for the Jews in Palestine. Many Jewish immigrants flooded into the region between 1919 and 1939. The last wave brought one hundred sixty-five thousand, mostly from central and western Europe.

But the real force that moved the house of Israel was Almighty God. The heartbeat of ancient covenants pulsed within the Jewish breast and would not be slowed. God was bringing His chosen people home. The Holy Land was indeed about to leap to life!

CHAPTER 7

DRY BONES RATTLE AND SHAKE

A TRULY ASTOUNDING event took place on May 14, 1948. Modern Israel was born in a single day as prophesied in Isaiah 66:8:

> Who hath heard such a thing? who hath seen such things? Shall the earth be made to bring forth in one day? or shall a nation be born at once? for as soon as Zion travailed, she brought forth her children.

The miraculous rebirth of Israel in the twentieth century is covered in detail a bit later in the chapter. The regathering into the land in preparation for that birth is only slightly less astonishing. We will examine that era first.

According to many prophecy scholars, Ezekiel's account of the valley of dry bones is the most important prophecy for the twentieth century because it concerns modern-day Israel.

Babylonian Bullies

In 2 Kings 24, we read that Nebuchadnezzar, king of Babylon, personally came to Jerusalem while his armies were attacking the city. Jehoiachin, Judah's king, along with his mother and all of his government's top people, surrendered to Nebuchadnezzar. The great king, who had been reigning for eight years, took them all back to Babylon. He also took every piece of gold and other valuable articles from King Solomon's time. They took those things from both the Temple and from the royal palace, just as God's prophet had predicted. They also took all the top military fighting men and the people who had creative talents. Ten thousand in all were removed from their homeland. Only those considered to be the poorest of Judah were left behind.

Ezekiel lived during the same time as the prophets Daniel and Jeremiah. He was of the priestly line God had appointed to serve Himself and the people. Ezekiel never served in that office, however, because he was captured and taken to Babylon during the reign of King Jehoiachin.

Nebuchadnezzar's military forces took Israel captive in 597 BC. This was the second time the nation had been removed from the Promised Land. Daniel the prophet had been taken in the first removal and was serving at this time as Nebuchadnezzar's prime minister. Jeremiah, a very old man at this time, having been taken in the first captivity to Egypt, ministered to the remnant of Israelites in that land.

Daniel had been in Babylon nine years when Ezekiel arrived. The two may have met often. Jeremiah, much older than Ezekiel, may have been the younger man's teacher.

A Captive Audience

Ezekiel and the people of the second captivity were taken to the rivers of Babylon near a great canal that branched off the Euphrates. The prophet ministered to the people in that region. This captivity is recorded in

Psalm 137. Interestingly, ancient Babylon was much nearer the river Euphrates than present-day Babylon. The river and tributaries where Ezekiel and God's chosen people were exiled have changed course many times over the past centuries.

Judah Down in the Dumps

Imagine being forced on a long march after being pulled from your home—then being told you will serve your captors in a strange land for the rest of your life.

This was Judah's fate because of the people's sins and disobedience to God. They were indeed in the homesickness dumps. There was much lamenting and weeping during this period, as described by the psalmist: "By the rivers of Babylon, there we sat down, yea, we wept, when we remembered Zion. We hanged our harps upon the willows in the midst thereof" (Psalms 137:1–2).

Sin always comes with a high price, individually, nationally, and globally. But the Lord had not forsaken His people. Far from it! His loving, corrective hand was shaping attitudes toward their God and toward many other things. He had chosen Ezekiel for a very special prophetic purpose.

Dead Reckoning

While the Israelites in captivity along the river were in the depths of despair, Ezekiel supernaturally saw God's promises: "The heavens were opened, and I saw visions of God" (Ezekiel 1:1). God gave this prophet marvelous information about Israel that will come to pass at the end time. We find the most spectacular of those predictions in Ezekiel 37. Here the Lord set before His prophet a vision of a scene so eerie that he must have stood dumbfounded. Nothing but bones—human bones—filled the valley surrounding the prophet:

The hand of the LORD was upon me, and carried me out in the spirit of the LORD, and set me down in the midst of the valley which was full of bones.

And caused me to pass by them round about: and, behold, there were very many in the open valley; and, lo, they were very dry.

And he said unto me, Son of man, can these bones live? And I answered, O Lord GOD, thou knowest. (Ezekiel 37:1–3)

Ezekiel told the truth when he said that only God knew the answer to the question of whether the bones could live. However, these bones were so far from life because of their dryness, he surely must have thought they would never live again.

Then God's great voice must have thundered and echoed through the valley as He commanded Ezekiel to prophesy:

Say unto them, "O ye dry bones, hear the word of the LORD.

Thus saith the Lord GOD unto these bones; Behold, I will cause breath to enter into you, and ye shall live.

And I will lay sinews upon you, and will bring up flesh upon you, and cover you with skin, and put breath in you, and ye shall live; and ye shall know that I am the LORD." (Ezekiel 37:4b–6)

God was about to perform a miracle! Ezekiel, no doubt, still didn't know what was going to happen. But he believed with all his heart that his Lord was able to do what He said He would. Despite being dumbfounded, the prophet stepped from the sideline to the frontline: "I prophesied as I was commanded: and as I prophesied, there was a noise, and behold a shaking, and the bones came together, bone to its bone" (Ezekiel 37:7).

Tremendous rattling and shaking must have caused the prophet to gawk in amazement. The dry bones clattered together loudly as they joined to form many human skeletons. The prophet's words caused the valley to quake. It was Ezekiel's faith in God and faithfulness to God's instructions that the Lord used to produce this great vision.

Ezekiel's Zombies

Everywhere he looked, Ezekiel saw the skeletons' bones taking on muscle, tendons, and flesh (37:8). But once they were fully clothed in their skin, they appeared as dead people. There was no life at all in them.

The prophet would no doubt have been frightened out of his wits at this scene if God wasn't with him in the valley. These lifeless bodies were everywhere he looked. Ezekiel was about to prophesy the words that would bring life into these zombie-like people: "Thus saith the Lord GOD; Come from the four winds, O breath, and breathe upon these slain, that they may live" (37:9).

The wind, representing the Holy Spirit, breathed life into the corpses where they lay. They instantly stood surrounding the stunned prophet: a huge army of living, breathing people!

Who were these people miraculously brought back to life?

Ezekiel wasn't kept waiting for the answer to the question he probably asked himself. These who had been raised after being long dead were Jews, the whole house of Israel (37:11). They had been dead a very long time, murdered—beyond any hope. But they were now alive!

God's prophet wrote of things concerning Israel that are coming true today that began taking shape the moment the prophet was given the inspired word. Calling Ezekiel's vision of chapters 36 and 37 "unquestionably the monumental biblical fulfillment of the twentieth century," biblical scholar and author Chuck Missler observes:

Beginning in the last half of the nineteenth century, the regathering, which climaxed in the establishment of the State of Israel, is one of the most irrefutable evidences that we are on the threshold of God's climax for the nations.... There is even a possible chronological hint that is hidden in chapter 4 which seems to identify the reestablishment of the nation of Israel on May 14, 1948, and the regaining of the city of Jerusalem on June 6, 1967. [47]

The Jews' many wanderings throughout history brought God's chosen people to the twentieth century and the gathering of the dry bones. From that reentry into the Promised Land, a tremendous reassembly of Jews began. The miraculous rebirth of the nation in 1948 shocked even unbelieving historians. We see dramatic proof of God continuing to fulfill His promises to Abraham, Isaac, and Jacob today. Israel's future is brilliant above all other nations. From Jerusalem, atop Mount Zion, the Messiah, Jesus Christ, will reign and rule over a restored earth.

The Ultimate Promise Keeper

God used Ezekiel to tell the chosen people that He hadn't forgotten them. The Lord would not only bring them back from near extinction caused by genocide against them down through history, but He would put them back in the Promised Land. The people of Israel would know beyond any doubt that He was their God when He brought them back from death and put them again in the land. This would happen at a specific point in history:

> And I will pour upon the house of David, and upon the inhab-itants of Jerusalem, the spirit of grace and of supplications: and they shall look upon me whom they have pierced, and they shall mourn for him, as one mourneth for his only son, and shall be in bitterness for him, as one that is in bitterness for his firstborn. (Zechariah 12:10)

Since Israel has not yet turned to God in repentance, we know that the specific point in history has not yet been reached when they will recognize Him as their Lord. However, the Lord declared it. It will come to pass!

Time of Terrors

The facts cannot be easily disregarded: Many issues and events surrounding the troubled nation of Israel today are eerily like issues and events prophesied for end-time Israel.

Anyone who sees the Holocaust death-camp documentary films captured after the Nazis' defeat then reads Ezekiel's dry-bones prophecy should find troubling similarities. The hollow eyes and skeleton-like stick figures haunt their viewers.

While bulldozers push them into a mass common grave, the hundreds of Jewish corpses, whose bones are held together only by loose, clinging skin, twist and intermingle grotesquely. Ezekiel 37 should instantly connect in the prophecy student's mind when watching the black-and-white documentaries roll.

Emaciated victims of the Holocaust draw chilling comparisons to the lifeless bodies in Ezekiel's dry-bones prophecy. Source: Imperial War Museums

God's Echoing Forewarning

As discussed in chapter 6, the chosen people were scattered throughout the whole world. The Jews who remained in the land tried to fade into the other peoples who lived there, but were often found out, persecuted, and—in most cases—murdered.

God's warnings of judgment surely rang in the ears of those religious Jewish people. The preaching of the prophets must have haunted them while they fled, were enslaved, or were persecuted. Jeremiah's warnings on behalf of the Lord God sounded again as they did for Israel of earlier times:

> Therefore thus saith the LORD; Behold, I will give this city into the hand of the Chaldeans, and into the hand of Nebuchadnezzar king of Babylon, and he shall take it:
>
> And the Chaldeans, that fight against this city, shall come and set fire on this city, and burn it with the houses, upon whose roofs they have offered incense unto Baal, and poured out drink offerings unto other gods, to provoke me to anger.
>
> For the children of Israel and the children of Judah have only done evil before me from their youth: for the children of Israel have only provoked me to anger with the work of their hands, saith the LORD.
>
> For this city hath been to me as a provocation of mine anger and of my fury from the day that they built it even unto this day; that I should remove it from before my face. (Jeremiah 32:28–31)

Notice that in this judgment of that ancient time, God pronounced the punishment upon "this city." This referred to Jerusalem. Remember the words of Jesus while He looked over Jerusalem?

> O Jerusalem, Jerusalem, which killest the prophets, and stonest them that are sent unto thee; how often would I have gathered

thy children together, as a hen doth gather her brood under her wings, and ye would not!

Behold, your house is left unto you desolate: and verily I say unto you, Ye shall not see me, until the time come when ye shall say, Blessed is he that cometh in the name of the Lord. (Luke 13:34–35)

The Lord always considers His chosen people and Jerusalem in the same thought. The two are forever linked. This fact has been absolutely proven in our own time.

CHAPTER 8

FÜHRER'S FINAL SOLUTION FAILS

ADOLF HITLER, GERMANY'S Nazi führer, based his rage against the Jews on his past feelings about them just before and during World War I. Like other anti-Semitic thought, his theory put forward the lie that the Jew was the cause of most all struggle between good and evil. Therefore, Hitler blamed the Jewish race, which he called subhuman, for Germany's troubles. He wrote in his book, *Mein Kampf,* that the Jews caused World War I, Germany's loss, and the great economic depression that followed.

Satan's Sword against Israel

As emphasized throughout this book, Satan's all-out determination to destroy the Jewish race began right after he tempted Adam and Eve and they sinned in the Garden of Eden. Again, God foretold great hatred between mankind and Satan throughout history with the short but potent foretelling: "And I will put enmity between thee and the woman, and between thy seed and her seed; it shall bruise thy head, and thou shalt bruise his heel" (Genesis 3:15).

The apostle John's prophecy, through the vision he saw and recorded in Revelation 12, explains much about the troubles endured by God's chosen people:

And there appeared a great wonder in heaven; a woman clothed with the sun, and the moon under her feet, and upon her head a crown of twelve stars:

And she being with child cried, travailing in birth, and pained to be delivered.

And there appeared another wonder in heaven; and behold a great red dragon, having seven heads and ten horns, and seven crowns upon his heads.

And his tail drew the third part of the stars of heaven, and did cast them to the earth: and the dragon stood before the woman which was ready to be delivered, for to devour her child as soon as it was born.

And she brought forth a man child, who was to rule all nations with a rod of iron: and her child was caught up unto God, and to his throne.

And the woman fled into the wilderness, where she hath a place prepared of God, that they should feed her there a thousand two hundred and threescore days.

And there was war in heaven: Michael and his angels fought against the dragon; and the dragon fought and his angels,

And prevailed not; neither was their place found any more in heaven.

And the great dragon was cast out, that old serpent, called the Devil, and Satan, which deceiveth the whole world: he was cast out into the earth, and his angels were cast out with him.

And I heard a loud voice saying in heaven, Now is come salvation, and strength, and the kingdom of our God, and the power of his Christ: for the accuser of our brethren is cast down, which accused them before our God day and night.

And they overcame him by the blood of the Lamb, and by the word of their testimony; and they loved not their lives unto the death.

Therefore rejoice, ye heavens, and ye that dwell in them. Woe to the inhabiters of the earth and of the sea! for the devil is come down unto you, having great wrath, because he knoweth that he hath but a short time.

And when the dragon saw that he was cast unto the earth, he persecuted the woman which brought forth the man child.

And to the woman were given two wings of a great eagle, that she might fly into the wilderness, into her place, where she is nourished for a time, and times, and half a time, from the face of the serpent.

And the serpent cast out of his mouth water as a flood after the woman, that he might cause her to be carried away of the flood.

And the earth helped the woman, and the earth opened her mouth, and swallowed up the flood which the dragon cast out of his mouth.

And the dragon was wroth with the woman, and went to make war with the remnant of her seed, which keep the commandments of God, and have the testimony of Jesus Christ.

If that passage seems difficult to understand because of its highly symbolic descriptions, here is a list of some of the key words and phrases along with what many scholars agree is represented by each:

- "Wonder in heaven": supernatural vision in heaven
- "Woman": the nation Israel
- "Great red dragon": Satan
- "Third part of the stars": rebellious angels who fell with Satan
- "Man child": Israel's Messiah, Jesus Christ
- "Place prepared of God": a special hiding place God has provided (many believe this is Petra, in Jordan)

- "A thousand two hundred and threescore days": 1,260 days, the last half of Daniel's seventieth week (Great Tribulation)
- "Michael": one of two archangels mentioned in Scripture (Israel's defender)
- "Accuser of our brethren": Satan
- "Brethren": martyrs of Daniel's seventieth week (Great Tribulation)
- "Two wings of a great eagle": God's supernatural, protective power (Some prophecy students think these wings might mean, in part, the literal wings of aircraft.)
- "Time, times, and half a time": the last three and a half years of the seven-year Tribulation
- "Water as a flood": many people, probably enemy troops ("Waters" or "sea" usually means "many peoples," such as when Jesus prophesied in the Olivet Discourse that "the seas...will be roaring"; when John recorded the "sea of glass" in Revelation; and when he described in Revelation 13:1 "the beast out of the sea.")
- "Earth helped the woman": God's supernatural protection of Israel
- "Remnant of her seed": believing or saved Jews alive at that future time ("Her seed" refers back to Genesis 3:15; also, the "seed" is the offspring of Abraham, Isaac, and Jacob, from whom the house of Israel originated.)

All Middle East terrorism today can be understood by simply believing and accepting God's explanation about the satanic hatred that plagues Israel, the nation represented by the mysterious woman in this chapter. These verses give a 100-percent-accurate look into the future of where the world's current Mideast troubles are taking us.

Have you heard this question: Why would the terrorists kill so many innocent people by flying passenger jets full of fuel into the World Trade Center Twin Towers? Here's the answer: Because Satan directed the terrorists to punish and disrupt America for its support for Israel. It's just that simple. The devil wants Israel to be seen as the oppressor of its Palestinian neighbors. He wants the world to view God's chosen people as the reason there is no peace in the Middle East.

We've heard the news commentators and those they interview remark that terrorism is horrible. They usually tag on at the end of that statement, however, something to the effect that the United States must consider putting more pressure on Israel to stop its "terrorism" against the Palestinian people. By this reasoning, the pundits want us to infer that maybe the terrorists would stop their violence against the U.S. if America would stop supporting Israel.

More and more, the world will turn against God's chosen nation because the devil is in charge of this fallen world for the time being. We are told, through the Revelation account, that things will get much worse before they get better.

Hitler's Holocaust

We move quickly forward to the twentieth century. It isn't hard to follow the trail of the red dragon in the world of the 1930s and 1940s. Satan continues to stalk God's chosen people. Hitler's hatred turned up the heat of Satan's rage against the Jews. The hellish idea he called the "Final Solution" was aimed at killing every Jew in Germany, then in Europe, then in the whole world. This was to be the ultimate resolution to the "Jewish problem."

While many Jews from Europe reached Palestine, others did not. The British government, which had controlling authority in the region, attempted to block many Jews trying to reach the land of promise. The British did so because the government wanted to maintain a manageable balance in the region between Jewish settlers and Arabs.

So the Jewish people who did make it to Palestine found some degree of peace. But it was a peaceful life only when compared to their fellow Jews who did not escape the deadly Nazi regime or were turned back before the ships docked.

One of the most tragic events of that period is that American authorities turned back from our shores ships loaded with Jews fleeing the Nazis. There was great denial at the time, at least officially, that Hitler was trying to exterminate the entire Jewish race.

The Arabs' anger and resentments flared as they unleashed violent attacks against the Jewish settlers, torching their forests and fields and attacking and disrupting Jewish transportation. The Arab nationalists and the Jewish Zionists came to the point at which they would not discuss their differences. The problem threatened a much wider conflict. Seeing that the situation was hopeless, the British Authority in 1937 put forward the idea of dividing the area in question into two parts. While the Jewish leadership approved of the plan for the most part, the Arab leadership absolutely rejected it.

Arab violence against the Jews grew worse. Finally, in 1939, the British Authority issued a white paper that severely limited Jewish immigration to Palestine. But even that move to satisfy the Arab leadership did little to stop the violence against the Jewish settlers.

Literal Bones Begin to Show

Meanwhile in Europe, Hitler's terror against Jews got worse. At first, the Jewish citizens of the occupied countries were confined to ghettos. Eventually Heinrich Himmler, Hitler's SS chief, planned and implemented the concentration camps where millions of Jews, gypsies, and many other "undesirables" would be murdered.

The Final Solution, supposedly Himmler's idea, was meant to do away with the Jewish race to please Hitler. The Nazis began to ship Jews like cattle, packing them into train cars until there was no longer room for the captives to move. Then the doors slid shut and the trains began to roll, taking hundreds of thousands, day after day, from various locations throughout Nazi-occupied Europe to the death camps that had been built for the extermination of Jews. Upon reaching the death camps, the prisoners were forced to strip naked and led into showers to get rid of body lice. But, the showers were actually chambers where hundreds of prisoners at a time were killed by deadly gas fumes. Their bodies were then burned in massive ovens made just for that purpose. Jews and others the Nazis thought to be inferior beings, if they escaped the gas chambers, were worked and starved to death.

Death Train: Jews arrived at death camps by the hundreds of thousands.

The symbolic dry bones of Ezekiel 37 rattled and shook in the Holy Land. But in Germany and other Nazi-occupied countries of Europe, the literal bones of the house of Israel became visible as hundreds of thousands starved or were murdered. Soon the gas chambers and crematoriums were going full blast. The genocide had begun.

Many Jewish soldiers distinguished themselves during World War II on behalf of the Allied forces. When the war ended, they returned to the land of promise to defend their people's foothold in and around Jerusalem. Millions had died in Hitler's devilish attempt to complete his Final Solution. But the führer, not the Jewish race, passed into eternity apart from God; Hitler committed suicide in 1945. The Jews, although they didn't realize it, were being prepared for the great Ezekiel 37 prophetic fulfillment that is still in progress today. That prophecy continues to be at the heart of the issues of Mideast war and peace that will bring the armies of the world to Armageddon.

Rebirth through Blazing Battles

The house of Israel was "dead" because God's chosen people had been scattered and cut off from being a single nation. Now that symbolic corpse lay in the barren wasteland called Palestine. To the human eye, the long-vanished nation would appear to be a corpse. But in God's omniscient eyes, the chosen ones were like a precious fetus waiting to be born again. The bones were again gathered and joined together. Sinew and flesh now began to cover and complete the still, lifeless body of Israel.

The Birthing Begins

Before she travailed, she brought forth; before her pain came, she was delivered of a man child.

Who hath heard such a thing? who hath seen such things? Shall the earth be made to bring forth in one day? or shall a nation be born at once? for as soon as Zion travailed, she brought forth her children. (Isaiah 66:7–8)

When World War II ended, ancient hostilities flared into greater conflict than ever before. Militant Arabs demanded rights to Palestine and Jerusalem—rights they claimed were a thousand years old. Zionist leaders claimed rights even older, going back to the times of King Solomon and much earlier. The United Nations mandated that a Jewish state be created on May 14, 1948. This set in motion unparalleled Arab war making.

David Ben-Gurion, known as the George Washington of Israel by the Israelis, led the Jews to Israel's rebirth. The Arabs attacked at every opportunity, but Israel's forces carved out through tremendous battles new territories won from their enemies. The nation was indeed "born in a day"—May 14, 1948. And, when the smoke of battle cleared on May 15, Ezekiel's now fully fleshed-out house of Israel stood for the world to see. Isaiah's powerful words from the Lord must have thundered in each cannon fired and bomb that exploded. Thomas Ice of the Pre-Trib Research Center sums up the thrilling truth: "When the modern state of Israel was born in 1948, it not only became an important stage-setting development, but also began an actual fulfillment of specific Bible prophecies about an international regathering of the Jews in unbelief before the judgment of the tribulation."[48]

Awaiting the Breath of Eternal Life

The miracles that took place during this time of battle are legendary in modern Israel's history. God breathed into Israel the breath of its *national* life on May 14, 1948. Still, the breath of *eternal* life from God's own nostrils has not yet flowed into its people, as Ice referred to with his remark about the Jews' "unbelief" in the preceding paragraph. This is because the people of Israel have not yet recognized their true Messiah. But, it will happen: The Lord God will, at just the right moment in His perfect timing, breathe into His chosen nation the breath of eternal life. This will happen when Jesus Christ, the King of Kings, returns in power and great glory.

Mourning Time

And I will pour upon the house of David, and upon the inhabitants of Jerusalem, the spirit of grace and of supplications: and they shall look upon me whom they have pierced, and they shall mourn for him, as one mourneth for his only son, and shall be in bitterness for him, as one that is in bitterness for his firstborn. (Zechariah 12:10)

When repentance over their unbelief in Jesus as Messiah occurs, Israel will have endured the most terrible persecution in history. That time of great suffering will be many times worse than the Nazi Holocaust.

Antichrist, the most hate-filled human being who has ever lived, will be indwelt by Satan himself. All of the devil's hatred for the Jewish race will boil over. Adolf Hitler will seem like a little lamb by comparison to Antichrist.

By the time the Messiah returns at the end of Armageddon, there will be just a remnant of people who have not worshipped Antichrist as their god. This will be true of Jewish people as well as Gentiles. Particularly, the Jewish remnant will recognize Jesus as He breaks through the black clouds of that final day of the Tribulation.

A New Lease on Life!

This is the moment God's breath, through the Holy Spirit, will rush into the nostrils of all Israel, fulfilling the prophecy of Ezekiel 37:10: "And the breath came into them, and they lived, and stood up upon their feet, an exceeding great army."

The whole house of Israel (the Jewish people still alive) will instantly recognize that indeed Jesus Christ was their Messiah all along. They will know beyond any doubt that God's prophecies are absolutely true. They will indeed have a new lease on life! They will be a powerful army of God's chosen people, whom Satan and all of his forces, including Nazi Germany's führer and his Final Solution, couldn't destroy!

"This will be the fulfillment of the great Day of Atonement when they are going to look upon Him," states commentator J. Vernon McGee. He continues:

In that day they are going to look upon Him whom they pierced, and the question will be asked of Him, "What do these wounds mean? We didn't expect our Messiah, our King, to come with these wounds that You have in Your hands and feet and in Your side." He will say to them, "I got these wounds in the house of My friends. I came before, but you didn't accept Me or receive Me, and now I've come back." They will then mourn because of that.[49]

From Pentecost to Israel's Salvation

When God the Holy Spirit breathed eternal life into the believing Jews on the day of Pentecost, they became Christians (were saved from sin and death) in that moment. So, too, all of the house of Israel who are alive when Christ returns will be saved from their sins and from eternal separation from God the Father: "And shall put my spirit in you, and ye shall live, and I shall place you in your own land: then shall ye know that I the LORD have spoken it, and performed it, saith the LORD" (Ezekiel 37:14).

Meanwhile, Satan continues to stir trouble whenever and wherever he can. His deadly stirring is most visible in the cauldron of the Middle East. The old serpent is using ancient hatreds of religious and racial differences to keep the turmoil bubbling in and around Israel. Oil, petroleum, is the substance that continues to draw all other nations into the growing conflict.

The machinery of the industrial world demands more and more oil. World commerce is at stake. The love of money that commerce produces keeps the eyes of those world leaders fixed greedily on that whole region.

CHAPTER 9

MIDDLE EAST BOILS IN OIL

WHAT A TIME to be alive! Think of it: God chose for us to live at the time that is almost certainly the wind-up of human history. But this is not something the Christian needs to fear; this all means that Jesus is about to return!

All of the major signals that Jesus and Daniel the prophet foretold for the very end of this present Earth Age are in our headlines today. I firmly believe that the European Union, in combination with the international community, is the forming, final, one-world government of Daniel 2. The world's religions coming together in the name of unity and peace are shaping up to be the apostate harlot church that rides the "beast" of Revelation 17. Huge banking and commercial institutions merging into one economic power are fulfilling the description of the one-world, economic Babylon of Revelation 18. Great increases in technology, knowledge, and speed of travel exactly match things prophesied in Daniel 12.

We are also seeing the rise of false prophets. False teachers pollute our broadcast airwaves with their false doctrines. Wars and rumors of wars are a part of everyday life. We continue to witness famines and pestilences in the form of new, incurable diseases. Earthquakes are occurring often and everywhere. There are wondrous signs in the heavens, from man walking on the moon to unexplained UFO sightings and unprecedented solar flares recorded by astronomers and other scientists. All of these things are eerily like Jesus said it will be just before His return to earth.

Mankind demonstrates all of the wicked ways the apostle Paul predicted in 2 Timothy 3. As if all this weren't enough, Ezekiel's prophecies (see Ezekiel 37, 38, and 39) loom heavily over the Middle East.

What is the one thing that turns all news-gathering cameras and microphones toward Israel and her hostile neighbors? Oil! Because oil deposits drench the Middle East, world economies are tied to that region as no other. Therefore, all the leaders of the great world powers concern themselves with every bit of news about Israel and its Palestinian adversaries.

"Now, most of the world is involved in the conflict in the Middle East, and the prosperity of the world depends on some mechanism to guarantee peace and a continued flow of oil from the region," observes John Walvoord in his book, *Armageddon, Oil, and the Middle East Crisis*. "This is precisely what biblical prophecy predicts."[50]

The Middle East indeed boils in oil anxieties while the world storms toward an uncertain future. But God is not worried; neither does He want us to worry: "For God hath not given us the spirit of fear; but of power, and of love, and of a sound mind" (2 Timothy 1:7). He knows the end from the beginning and has reported, in advance, the conclusion of these matters in His Holy Word. Study it and believe it to be absolutely true, and you will find your frown of worry fading into a smile of anticipation. You will know that His Beloved Son, Jesus, is about to return to take God's children home with Him (read John 14:1–6).

God knew from before the Creation that oil would focus attention on the Middle East at the end of human history. He knew that the Garden of Eden's lushness of life would bring about the end-time energy source the nations would covet.

Eden's End-Time Energy

Let's travel for a moment back to the time God created everything described in Genesis 1:20–24 with one majestic sweep of His almighty hand:

> And God said, Let the waters bring forth abundantly the moving creature that hath life, and fowl that may fly above the earth in the open firmament of heaven.
>
> And God created great whales, and every living creature that moveth, which the waters brought forth abundantly, after their kind, and every winged fowl after his kind: and God saw that it was good.
>
> And God blessed them, saying, Be fruitful, and multiply, and fill the waters in the seas, and let fowl multiply in the earth....
>
> And God said, Let the earth bring forth the living creature after his kind, cattle, and creeping thing, and beast of the earth after his kind: and it was so.

This wasn't just a few scatterings of created beings and a mere smattering of vegetation. When the Creator of all things spoke, all of these things suddenly existed from what had been nothingness only a fraction of a second before. The vast ocean waters surged with life, from the smallest organism to the biggest whale. The brilliant, beautifully colored sky must have seemed suddenly cloudy while the flying, diving, soaring birds of every description tested their masterfully made wings. The dry land crawled, hopped, ran, leaped, and lumbered with marvelous reptiles and mammals of every sort. The sounds and sights must have been too incredible to take into the senses.

God's creation power, not evolution, produced abundant life in that electrifying second of early earth time. Nothing crawled from primordial soup to change over the next zillion or so years. Everything popped into existence under the hand of the Living God. There were no accidents or errors in the Lord's action. He knew exactly what He was doing. In the process, Eden's potential end-time energy source—oil—was produced.

Lush Garden Slush

God is omnipotent (all powerful). He is omniscient (all knowing). He is omnipresent (everywhere, all the time). Through His omnipotence, He created the abundant and vast array of life in one split second. He knew all about, in His omniscient foreknowledge, the Fall of man through sin. The Lord was, in His omnipresence, already forward in time when oil was formed from the dead, decaying things He was creating. He is already in the future when the last great battle of history is being fought in the Middle East at Armageddon.

The rage in the Middle East today, the hateful conflict between Israel and its radical neighbors, points to the reality that things are aligned precisely as God foretold. Oil is certainly the ingredient that makes the great world powers look toward that region with concern.

So the present Mideast problems involving war and peace that tug the world toward Armageddon again go back to the Garden of Eden and the Fall of Adam through willful disobedience. God didn't cause this calamity. In His love and concern for us, He simply reported, through prophecy, the end of the matter. Is all of this about oil's connection to the creation scientifically possible? I believe it is more than that.

Let's look closer at what the scientific study of petroleum says. Then let's look at what the Bible says about the catastrophic deluge God used to judge sin and cleanse the earth of sin's corruption.

Today's scientists believe that crude oil was formed over millions of years from the remains of small plant and animal life in the ancient seas. As this life—primarily plankton and algae and other organisms—died, it sank to the sea floor, where it was buried with sand and mud.

Heat, pressure, and bacteria compressed and "cooked" the material until it formed a thick liquid called oil. Over time, the oil traveled upward through the earth's crust until its path was blocked by dense rocks. It's under these rocks where we find most of our oil today.

The Bible says in Genesis 6 and 7 that God sent a great Flood because of sin upon the earth. The water covered everything, including the highest mountaintop, by at least fifteen cubits (a cubit is believed to be about eighteen inches).

So you can see that this catastrophe involved an incredible amount of water. This wasn't just some local flood, as some would have us believe. The Bible says that all flesh and plant life on the earth's ground portions died in the overwhelming surge. When the water receded, many of the various forms of life in the rivers and the seas were left to flounder and die on the drying ground. This included, of course, the plankton, algae, and other vegetation of the rivers and seas.

The fossil record shows this was true. Evidence of seashells and other residue of sea life has been found on some of the highest peaks in the world. When the waters swiftly withdrew, huge chunks of dirt, rock, and other material broke off and became massive mudslides. Many believe this is the reason the Grand Canyon was cut from the earth as it was.

The dead, decaying animal and sea life, as well as the birds that drowned, were covered by the mud. People, also, according to the Bible, died by the millions and their bodies became a part of the mixture that formed within the pockets where oil is now found.

Nowhere on the globe was there more lushness of plant and animal life than in the region where God had planted the Garden of Eden. It is sensible to think that the area would have the largest deposits of oil. At present, two Middle Eastern nations, Saudi Arabia and Iran, are ranked as among the world's top five oil producers. With a daily production of 10.7 million barrels and a proved reserve of nearly 267 billion barrels, Saudi Arabia leads the list, and Iran—with daily production of 4.1 million barrels and a proved reserve of 132.5 billion—is ranked as the fourth-largest oil-producing nation in the world, with the third-largest proved reserve.[51] (Nations rounding out the top five include Russia, second; the United States, third; and China, fifth).

There are some today who say that the Middle East having the lion's share of all known oil in the world has changed because of new drilling techniques such as fracking, which can force oil from previously unreachable rock layers into retrievable quantities at an economically feasible cost. The United States would, if this is true, have as much in potential oil reserves as the Middle East. Still the region surrounding Israel is the main attraction to those who lust after the black, liquid gold.

Oil Ignites Tensions: A Navy fighter flies over a burning, Middle Eastern oil field.

Oil Eases Toil

When Noah and his seven other family members stepped onto dry land from the ark (see Genesis 8), they faced the curse God had pronounced because of sin—the curse of having to work for their food. They had to raise the animals, cultivate and sow the ground with seed, and "toil" by the sweat of their brow to make a living.

Hard labor isn't fun for most people. It certainly has never been fun to me! While there is usually a sense of accomplishment after a job well done that makes us say as God said when He looked upon all He had created, "It is good," the actual work can be back breaking.

Throughout history, society has tried to come up with ways to create labor-saving devices. For example, the aqueducts of ancient civilizations saved people from the hard work of hauling water by bringing it directly into the cities. In more recent times, the hand pump to get water from deep wells became an important part of early American life, even in frontier towns. And automated looms saved time and energy in weaving cloth for clothing and other things.

Even these earliest labor-saving inventions required human power, except in the few instances in which the mechanisms could be driven by the wind or running water. But the fantastic energy stored underground around the world soon completely changed everything. The advancements that the discovery of the power of oil inspired are nothing short of phenomenal.

Think of the progress! Until the late nineteenth century, we could travel on flat land no faster than the fastest horse could run. With the coming of the steam engine and other inventions of locomotion, travel became much faster—and made it possible to move forward for a much longer time before having to stop. Petroleum and its byproducts were at the heart of producing advances that are truly astonishing. It all happened, basically, within only a century.

The twentieth century saw mankind go from the steam engine to the computer-directed, solid-rocket engines that let man exceed twenty thousand miles per hour. And man walked on the moon!

All of this happened in about the last 120 years. Before the discovery of the power potential in petroleum, we remained basically unchanged in our ability to progress, as far as labor-saving devices were concerned.

Not only did oil bring the electricity that powers the washing machines, refrigerators, vacuum cleaners, and all the rest, but it also created a tremendous economic base that in turn brought about a leisure class. Now, there are those who laugh when they read that they are part of a "leisure" class—we still work pretty hard! Compared to our ancestors, however, we Americans live like royalty. As a matter of fact, when you think about it, with our modern conveniences and our ability to travel to and from most anywhere in the world in only a few hours, we live far better than did Solomon.

Most stunning of all is the communication technology we enjoy. Like the prophet stated in Daniel 12:4, knowledge has increased beyond anything previously imagined. We have only begun to realize the things that harnessing oil has made possible.

Need Feeds Greed

The more work-saving devices, the better. This is the attitude of the people of the industrialized world. And, more and more nations are moving toward becoming industrialized.

People in general, especially spoiled people with all the modern conveniences, want more and more free time to play rather than work. Vacations, or even weekends on the lakes with powerboats, are much more fun than working 8 to 5 to buy those luxuries and pay the bills.

Despite the mega-trillion-dollar debt facing Americans nationally and personally, the unquenchable need to buy more and more is on the increase. The compulsion to buy things is one form of greed that seems to be like a virus in the American economic bloodstream. With national credit card debt at a staggering $849.8 billion and the average household owing $15,185 to credit card companies, that greedy addiction cannot be denied. [52]

The apostle Paul wrote in 2 Timothy 3:1–4 that in the last days, people will be covetous and love pleasure more than they love God. Does that describe America today? Everyone wants "stuff"—homes, cars, boats, etc.—at least as good and, hopefully, even better, than what the Joneses have. When the warm days of springtime come, even the true Christian churches seem to empty into the lakes and other playgrounds on Sundays.

The plastic credit cards, themselves petroleum-based items, drive Americans deeper and deeper into debt. The greed factor gets much bigger, growing like a snowball rolling downhill. Companies rush to fill the consumers' desires. Their own covetousness demands more and more production, with manufacturing processes depending upon more and more petroleum.

This is where Mideast war and peace come into the picture. As mentioned earlier, most of the world's easily accessible (cheap-to-extract) petroleum is in the land God promised Abraham, Isaac, and Jacob—not the tiny strip of land occupied by Israel today, but the complete land of promise.

Today, Israel's neighbors claim the majority of the world's petroleum, and most of them are in an undeclared war against the tiny state. As a matter of fact, the enemies of Israel are blood vowed to push Israel into the Mediterranean Sea.

The mostly Arab governments who, when combined, control the vast oil fields of the Middle East, are in a sense an economic superpower just as surely as America is a nuclear superpower. They can bend the will of the rest of the world by raising—or simply threatening to raise—the price of oil. The lust for oil is probably the major factor that will bring an invasion into the Middle East. But more about that a bit later.

The industrialized Western nations have been lucky so far. The Arab countries are too busy fussing and feuding with each other to get together and make demands so far as prices of petroleum are concerned. They more often than not undercut each other's prices and keep the costs relatively low.

A time is coming, no doubt, when they will put aside their continual fighting and get together on a greatly increased price per barrel of oil. When the greed overcomes their feuding, something will have to give. Most likely, that something will be Middle East peace…maybe even worldwide peace.

Oil, then, is the factor at the very heart of concern for world leaders. This group, referred to by news media as "the international community," will do all within its power to put a permanent peace into effect in that region where the greatest oil supplies have been stored since the Flood.

Pact with the Devil

One of the things we are to look for as a signal of the end times is the formation of a one-world government, what some call the "New World Order." The Bible says that at the end of this present age, a powerful group of world leaders will imagine to take over the world in all of its aspects: economically, governmentally, technologically, religiously, etc. (Read Revelation 17:12–13.) That is what happened when Nimrod and his fellow one-worlder friends wanted to establish a single government, economic, and religious world order (see Genesis 11). Humanism, the religious philosophy that drove Nimrod and the builders of the tower of Babel, is still around, and growing as a philosophy through which to bring about total control over all peoples and all the world's wealth. Oil has a very high place in their big plans.

God came down to earth and scattered the tower builders to all parts of the globe, confusing the language so they could no longer communicate well enough to continue their satanic building project. Today's similar engineers are aided by the computer, which is helping them get around the language barriers. God will again have to intervene, this time at Armageddon.

Today's would-be one-world builders probably think they are doing a great service by trying to bring everyone together in peace and unity. The Bible says, however, that such a last-days effort to do as Nimrod tried to do at Babel will end up bringing about Antichrist and the worst time in the history of man. Humanism says man himself can do it all apart from God. This always has been a formula for utter destruction. Only God can take the war out of the Mideast war-and-peace equation.

Derricks Dot Desert

Some very good students of prophecy believe the following passage concerning "oil" and "Asher" to have reference to petroleum and the Middle East in the last days:

And of Asher he said, Let Asher be blessed with children; let him be acceptable to his brethren, and let him dip his foot in oil. Thy shoes shall be iron and brass; and as thy days, so shall thy strength be. (Deuteronomy 33:24–25)

Other students, equally qualified, believe the "oil" strictly refers to olive oil, the highly valued natural extract produced in the Middle East. Still others believe there is a double reference in this passage: They think it could refer to both olive oil and petroleum, which is in even greater abundance in the Middle East than olive oil.

I haven't made an in-depth study in this, so can't even venture a good guess as to whether "oil" here might refer to one, the other, or both. I do believe, though, that this passage is prophetic. The land given to Abraham's descendants is guaranteed by God Himself to receive a profound blessing.

It is true that Israel and the area given the tribe of Asher have been blessed in the ancient past. But these verses represent a great blessing at some future time, the likes of which have not yet occurred. Olive oil is a well-known product of the region, to be sure. But it is not of enough significance in quantity or as a contributing factor to promise tremendous blessings to either Asher or its neighbors, as this prophecy seems to suggest. Neither can we conclude that petroleum has been the kind of blessing implied in this passage. To the contrary, oil has been more a reason for conflict than for blessing in the region.

This passage seems to mean that, at some future time, this area will be a genuine blessing to all of Israel and all of Asher's other neighbors. The oil referred to will be of such great benefit that everybody will love the tribe of Asher.

The tribes haven't occupied their God-appointed territories in modern times. The people of that tribe will not occupy that land until the Millennium. Therefore, the promise of great blessings involving oil must be for the time when King Jesus rules and reigns from Jerusalem.

There is no way we can even imagine the things God has planned for that wonderful era. But it is reasonable to wonder if the great petroleum reserves there now might be used in some marvelous way to bless the nations one day.

I can hear the environmentalists screaming, "There will have to be some miraculous system to keep that stuff from polluting our air, if it's going to be a blessing rather than a curse!" I can hear some commuters hollering, "Prices will have to be better, or it won't be heaven on earth!"

Regardless, the oil is there, and in great abundance. This is not by accident. "Given the oil reserves of this area and the economic power that comes from the redistribution of the world wealth to this region, it is not hard to imagine the prophecies of the ancient seers coming true," notes Paul Feinberg. "Though many regimes seem grossly out of step with our modern, high-tech societies, there is wealth and power enough to send all the nations of the world there to protect that they see as their own self-interests."[53]

There since Babel

Middle East soil can't contain the petroleum substances that boil just beneath its surface. The tower of Babel builders found the sticky stuff— a thick, asphalt-like material they found in abundance on the plain of Shinar—to be a devilish blessing rather than a curse. They used it to paste together the bricks they made to build the ungodly structure Nimrod was determined to complete (see Genesis 11:2–3).

The boiling petroleum broth has been a constant part of some areas of the regions throughout recorded history. The south end of the Dead Sea was said to have looked like a boiling cauldron of asphalt as recently as the late nineteenth century.

Towers of Power

A number of years ago, Saddam Hussein, dictator of Iraq, left Kuwait in a hurry when the Desert Storm coalition forces pulverized much of his military. Before he left that small country he had invaded for its oil riches, he set the oil wells on fire.

Millions of petrodollars went up in black, sky-darkening smoke. Oil fire specialists were called in to douse the flames. The Iraqi dictator knew exactly where he could hurt the Western industrial nations the most. The money lenders of the world—the great financiers who control world economies—were, for the moment, helpless to stop their losses. One big part of their tremendous power seemed to be literally going up in smoke.

Those black towers of steel represent, at least symbolically, the modern-day tower of Babel. The structures, looking like small Eiffel towers on the desert sand, serve as monuments to the one-world, gigantic monetary power structure being built today. As stated before, this was the primary reason all of those nations, including Saddam Hussein's frightened neighbors, got together to stop the rampaging tyrant.

We watch and complain about the rising fuel prices. Oil and its costs affect us in so many ways that the topic itself would provide enough material to make a book. Gasoline is only one facet of oil-price considerations. Electricity and all that involves, plastics for every manufacturing process you can name, communications and its many aspects…all these and many more things are impacted by the price of petroleum. The United States is particularly a sitting target for price-increase tyranny. The American people will yet suffer the consequences of the one-world controllers' intentions to gather to themselves the wealth of the world.

The vast riches of the Middle East must be preserved at all costs, even to the destruction of national economies and of human life. The Middle East is the one area of the world the one-world tower builders will control, no matter the price. Armageddon will be their final attempt to stop God from establishing Jesus Christ's throne in the heart of that land.

Real Rags to Riches

As demonstrated in recent years, the economic well-being of entire nations depends upon availability of reasonably priced energy. California, itself having an economy as large as many nations, is a prime example just within the United States.

Political environmental extremists, by forbidding the building of new power plants and prohibiting the development of energy resources, have greatly affected California's way of life. Rolling brownouts and blackouts of electricity in recent years have caused problems from inconvenience to hardship on many Californians.

OPEC (Oil Producing Exporting Countries) has the power to cause all nations to bend to its will in a similar and more troubling way. Its power is based upon the ability to control production, prices, and embargoes.

It is, in effect, a collective superpower, even despite the recent tremendous upheavals in the region. National economies rise and fall based upon the petroleum they can distribute and withhold. Oil is the lifeblood of the developed and developing nations of the world.

Even rumors of supply shortages threaten the lifestyles of people in America, Europe, and Japan, the nations having the most to lose. This is seen in recent years when Iran's leadership threatens to block the Strait of Hormuz if Iran's nuclear development facilities are attacked, or when OPEC threatens to turn down the flow of petroleum. Energy, far and away fueled by oil more than by any other source, is at the heart of the developing one-world order's ability to control the citizenry.

Energy is at the center of the power and wealth that provide livelihoods—and luxuries. The book of Revelation has much to say about the end-time Babylonian system of economic control over people, as the following passage indicates:

And the merchants of the earth shall weep and mourn over her; for no man buyeth their merchandise any more:

The merchandise of gold, and silver, and precious stones, and of pearls, and fine linen, and purple, and silk, and scarlet, and all thyine wood, and all manner vessels of ivory, and all manner vessels of most precious wood, and of brass, and iron, and marble,

And cinnamon, and odours, and ointments, and frankincense, and wine, and oil, and fine flour, and wheat, and beasts, and sheep, and horses, and chariots, and slaves, and souls of men.

And the fruits that thy soul lusted after are departed from thee, and all things which were dainty and goodly are departed from thee, and thou shalt find them no more at all.

The merchants of these things, which were made rich by her, shall stand afar off for the fear of her torment, weeping and wailing,

And saying, Alas, alas that great city, that was clothed in fine linen, and purple, and scarlet, and decked with gold, and precious stones, and pearls!

For in one hour so great riches is come to nought. And every shipmaster, and all the company in ships, and sailors, and as many as trade by sea, stood afar off,

And cried when they saw the smoke of her burning, saying, What city is like unto this great city!

(Revelation 18:11–18)

The very souls of men, women, and children are at the mercy of the elite who control buying and selling. That system of commerce depends upon the ability to deliver the goods. Therefore, those who control the oil used in the manufacturing and delivery of merchandise are the masters of this world system. The sheiks and leaders of the Middle East are in a commanding position as they deal with the one-world builders.

From Tent to High Rent

Although much of the tremendous oil riches lie beneath the land promised to Abraham's bloodline, Israel has refused to fully claim that Promised Land. Worse, God's chosen people have disobeyed God's loving instructions on a number of occasions. When they do so, they are put out of the portions of the original land grant territory they have occupied.

Other peoples have moved in and occupied the area; in fact, intruders still hold on to the majority of Israel's property today. But, their land grab will always be illegal in God's perfect sight. Just as Jeremiah prophesied, the land has yielded its "substance" and "treasures" to those other than God's disobedient people (17:3–4). Oil is the "substance" and "treasure" in our day. The mostly Islamic Arabs now have the riches, as foretold in that passage.

With the second industrial revolution in the mid-1800s to mid-1900s came an explosion of wealth for many of the tent-dwelling Arabs and others in that land of oil. The most powerful of those people suddenly found themselves among the richest in the world because their petroleum was needed to run the motorized machinery of industry's production lines. The sheiks and kings of the Middle East literally did go from rags to riches…from "tent" to "high rent."

At the same time however, despite their nations' riches from oil sales, the majority remains under the oppressive, dark force of Islam. Most of the Arabs and other populations of the Middle East live as poorly as their ancestors. Royal families and other privileged people in high places enjoy the limousines, the jet planes, and palaces. You might say, "That's the way it is in America, too. Only the few have the wealth." But the difference is that Americans—at least for the moment—have the opportunity to work and worship as they please. Anti-Christian religious unity, under the umbrella of government, doesn't yet hold an iron grip around the throats of our people (although the trend in that evil direction is becoming more and more evident). Our heritage is filled with rags-to-riches stories concerning men and women who have achieved great wealth.

The right to worship without fear of having our heads chopped off for believing in a way different from the state religion is at the heart of our true wealth. This is a right we must not take for granted. There will come a time when the whole world will be forced to live as many of the poor unfortunates in much of the Middle East live today. The story of that future horror can be found in Revelation 13.

Blessings Cause Curse

Riches seem to most of us a blessing. We think of how wonderful it would be to come into a lot of money. This covetousness is easily seen in the popularity of such past and recent TV programs as *Who Wants to Be a Millionaire?* and *The Million Second Quiz.*

Daydreaming about lots of money has not just recently become part of our culture. Some of us remember a program that aired in the late fifties called *The Millionaire.* In this series of stories, an unknown donor gave away a million dollars each week to a very surprised person. It was, of course, fiction, but it was a very popular show. The stories sometimes portrayed that the million-dollar gift ended up being a source of unhappiness rather than joy.

Ishmael—remember him? Abraham's son by Hagar, Sarah's handmaid, was promised great blessings by God. Many of the Arab people today legitimately claim Abraham as their father. Some prophecy students believe that because the Arab nations have the greatest amount of oil, that fact is fulfillment of God's promise to bless Abraham's descendants—in this case, his descendants by Keturah, whom the patriarch married following Sarah's death.

But we must look at the truth of the matter. The oil riches cannot be a blessing from God. He didn't promise this part of Abraham's family the land they presently occupy. Much of that land is rightfully the Jews' land; it belongs to Israel because God promised it to them. Abraham's family by Hagar and Keturah will come into their full blessing during the Millennium. They will then become a great nation just as the Lord promised. Today, however, they are under a curse, not a blessing. The Arab people today continue to live under the curse of radical Islamic fundamentalists, who would just as soon murder their own as the Jews they hate so much.

The one-world builders more often than not look the other way when these poor, hapless people suffer atrocities by those over them. The world wants the vast oil deposits the Islamic tyrants hold in their bloodstained hands.

Is Oil Gog's "Spoil"?

War has been the way of life for people of the Middle East for centuries. We know from news reports that the people there live every day under threat of a breakout of fighting. Many times the fighting involves gunfire, and people are killed. Or, terrorist bombs are used to murder both Arabs and Jews who only want to live in peace.

There is coming a time when God Himself will intervene directly into this matter of Mideast war and peace. Ezekiel foretells this coming time:

> And the word of the LORD came unto me, saying,
> Son of man, set thy face against Gog, the land of Magog, the chief prince of Meshech and Tubal, and prophesy against him,
> And say, Thus saith the Lord GOD; Behold, I am against thee, O Gog, the chief prince of Meshech and Tubal. (Ezekiel 38:1–3)

> Thus saith the Lord GOD; It shall also come to pass, that at the same time shall things come into thy mind, and thou shalt think an evil thought:

And thou shalt say, I will go up to the land of unwalled villages; I will go to them that are at rest, that dwell safely, all of them dwelling without walls, and having neither bars nor gates,

To take a spoil, and to take a prey; to turn thine hand upon the desolate places that are now inhabited, and upon the people that are gathered out of the nations, which have gotten cattle and goods, that dwell in the midst of the land. (Ezekiel 38:10–12)

The prophet predicts the reason the festering boil of hostility will come to a head. God will allow the leader of those who hate Israel, "Gog, the chief prince of Meshech and Tubal," to "think an evil thought" that will involve some sort of "spoil." What is a "spoil"? This particular meaning of the word refers to the material rewards of victory in war. Gog will lust after something in the heart of Palestine that will promise him great riches as his reward for victory.

The Land of Magog

There is some disagreement among biblical scholars as to the exact location of the land called in the Ezekiel passages "Magog." For example, some believe it to be in Russia: "'Magog' is a real nation occupying a territory that was known to Ezekiel and his Jewish readers in the fifth century before Christ," notes biblical prophecy scholar and author Grant Jeffrey. "I believe the evidence supports the conclusion that Magog refers to the territory that is currently occupied by the present nation of Russia, including several of the southern republics of the Commonwealth of Independent States (formerly the USSR)."[54]

Jeffrey notes that others challenge this identification of Magog's location as being in Russia, however:

Some scholars suggest that Magog was connected with some small tribal groups in ancient Mesopotamia in the area presently occupied by Iran. Others suggest Magog is connected with the tribes led by an ancient king known as Gyges in the area of ancient Lydia (present-day Turkey) to the south of Russia. The ancient historian Pliny claimed the Syrians thought the name God was the same as Gyges, a king of Lydia whose country was named from him—Gygea, or Gog's land.[55]

It is my belief that Russia does seem to be at the center of the military force prophesied to invade Palestine. Do we have any indications today that Russia and its surrounding neighbors might invade the Middle East? One thing for sure: Russia is certainly in great need of some things.

The seventy-four years of Communist rule following the 1917 Bolshevik Revolution were bad enough. Russian people were either murdered by Vladimir Lenin, Joseph Stalin, and their successors, or were nearly starved due to wars, failing agriculture, and other Soviet socialist policies. Sadly, the fall of the Soviet Union in 1991 didn't bring much better prospects for the Russian people.

Today, the Russians, although somewhat better off than in the days of Stalin and his immediate successors, still are not happy and fulfilled under the oppression they continue to endure. They want the things the Western nations have. Getting these things for the huge Russian population will involve money—lots of it.

Presently, Russian leader Vladimir Putin is on the hot seat. He has conducted his grip on power in Russia in ways that could easily be construed as god-like. He no doubt realizes he must produce, and soon, or he will find his *dacha* (country house) on the Black Sea and all other perks given to someone who will produce the improved conditions the Russian people demand.

Despite hype to the contrary by the Russian propaganda establishment and some Western journalists' willingness to parrot those lies, Russia is in ruin. Its military men and women are living at the poverty level. A number of Russian officers have committed suicide because of alcoholism and the despair of not being able to adequately feed, clothe, and house their families.

The top generals become more anti-West and anti-Israel as their economic plight becomes worse and worse. Many of the highest leaders in the military want to get back to the glory days when they were admired by their people and feared by the rest of the world.

Surrounding peoples who populate the region within what the Bible calls Magog are in similar circumstance to the Russians. They need food and want material things they have no hope of getting short of conquering some who do have these things. The history of that area is one of plunder. Throughout the ages they have taken what they want, when they wanted—if and when they became strong enough to do so.

When God told Ezekiel to prophesy against Gog, the chief prince of Rosh (Russia), He indicated that the leader's "evil thought" would be in the "latter days," or the end of the time just before the climax of human history. At that time, all the people surrounding Palestine and other people throughout the world will question Gog and those of his coalition forces. They will ask: "Have you come to take great spoil?" Some think this indicates there will be no more resistance to this force than that of a formal diplomatic note of protest.

Ne'er-Do-Well Neighbors

The invasion will be massive, according to Ezekiel's prophecy:

> And I will turn thee back, and put hooks into thy jaws, and I will bring thee forth, and all thine army, horses and horsemen, all of them clothed with all sorts of armour, even a great company with bucklers and shields, all of them handling swords:
> Persia, Ethiopia, and Libya with them; all of them with shield and helmet:
> Gomer, and all his bands; the house of Togarmah of the north quarters, and all his bands: and many people with thee....
> Thou shalt ascend and come like a storm, thou shalt be like

145

a cloud to cover the land, thou, and all thy bands, and many people with thee. (Ezekiel 38:4–6, 9)

Some prophecy students believe the words "like a cloud to cover the land" mean flight after flight of Russia's air force, along with paratroopers. That description, plus the words, "shalt ascend," provides good evidence to back up such thought. Gog's military will be like a storm.

The tremendous Russian mechanized army (tanks, etc.) will thunder toward Palestine, with greedy hearts and eyes on the riches of the Middle East. Combined with all of its partners in crime from Magog and many neighboring nations, the thousands upon thousands of vehicles and ground troops will no doubt raise a huge, boiling amount of dust. It will indeed look like a "cloud to cover the land"!

Some say this invasion has already occurred. Others believe it is not to be taken as literal, but as a spiritual invasion of some sort. I believe this will be a literal invasion by literal military forces—something far beyond the scope of the 1991 Desert Storm military action. How do we know this will be literal?

Such a thing has never happened in the Middle East on this scale. Individuals in their own nations and regions have always been too busy warring with each other to mount such an attack. It is said this will be in the "latter days." All other signals show that we are most likely in that predicted time today. Most importantly, God said He Himself will bring this great mass of humanity into the Middle East, where He will destroy all but one-sixth of them. He will do so for a very special purpose.

"Here we have Russia moving with powerful forces in a program of conquest of the South," says Dave Breese. He continues:

We also learn that Russia will take to itself certain allies who will be a part of this attempted program of conquest. Especially we note that Persia will be an ally of Russia [Ezekiel 38:5]. One of the frightening developments of our time is the furnishing of nuclear weapons and materials to modern-day Iran—once known as Persia. The recent leaders of Israel have frequently said, "Our real concern in the Middle East is not with Syria or Lebanon or the Saudis but with Persia. Persia, or Iran, is considered a rogue nation steeped in Islamic fundamentalism and led by near-insane leaders who would stop at nothing."[56]

The Invasion Equation

Ezekiel's prophecy reveals that we can be certain of one thing: This attack is specifically on the nation Israel. It is a satanic attack, bent on once and for all ridding the world of the chosen people of God. The Lord will bring things to a head, as described here:

> Therefore, son of man, prophesy and say unto Gog, Thus saith the Lord GOD; In that day when my people of Israel dwelleth safely, shalt thou not know it?
> And thou shalt come from thy place out of the north parts, thou, and many people with thee, all of them riding upon horses, a great company, and a mighty army:
> And thou shalt come up against my people of Israel, as a cloud to cover the land; it shall be in the latter days, and I will bring thee against my land, that the heathen may know me, when I shall be sanctified in thee, O Gog, before their eyes. (Ezekiel 38:14–16)

The prophecy foretells in no uncertain terms that the Lord Himself will completely defeat Israel's attackers, proving beyond any reasonable doubt that He is God—and that Israel is His chosen.

This attack will come when Israel is at peace—or, at least, when the Jews are living as if they are at peace. Do we see a peace process in the Middle East today? Yes! We have witnessed the peace process for decades; it has really become intense in the past several years. But it is a false peace the haters of Israel seek.

The current efforts to bring an end to hostilities in the Middle East might very well bring about the "covenant made with death and hell" of Daniel 9:26–27. The Antichrist could be waiting in the wings of world diplomacy, ready to come forward when the false peace process is ripe.

The Ezekiel 38 and 39 prophecy about the Gog-Magog invasion also indicates that Israel will have little or no defense. That is certainly not the situation at present. Most geopolitical observers say Israel's military is the fourth, maybe the third, most powerful in the world today. Its nuclear-weapons capability gives the small nation that status.

Israel's "Samson Option," well known by Israel's enemies, is the vow of the nation's military leaders to bring everybody and everything down around Israel, should it be attacked by overwhelming force. Israel will use its nuclear arsenal. Ezekiel's prophecy states that, sadly, like Samson, the immensely strong judge of Israel, the nation will be seduced into letting down its great military strength. Israel will be shorn of its nuclear force at some point.

When the false-peace, diplomatic Delilahs get through, Israel will be "without bars or gates" and an "unwalled village." The nation will be a sitting duck.

The invasion equation involves the following:

1) Israel must be back in the land of promise.
2) Its neighbors, especially Russia, must be in need and full of greed.
3) Israel and the land it occupies must have "spoil" of a significant nature.
4) There must be some sort of peace that puts Israel at ease.
5) Diplomats and others must be able to realize that an attack is about to take place (perhaps through spy satellite technology).

While the Middle East boils in turmoil, it is reasonable to guess that lust for the riches oil can provide will bring the "evil thought" into Gog's mind. However, that turmoil proves that Israel is not at rest or at peace, as Ezekiel's prophecy says it will be at the time of the attack.

Watch the peace process and other developments in the region. Know that the satanic aim is not to bring true, lasting peace, but to give Israel a nuclear-arms haircut.

CHAPTER 10

ANCIENT ANGERS TAKE AIM

NO OTHER PEOPLE, as a race, have been in the Middle East region now called Palestine longer than the Jews. At times, they have been there in large numbers, and at other times they have been there in very small numbers. But, despite the fact that the race has been scattered into the entire world several times, at least a few Jews have been living in the area for more than three thousand years.

People who have been around for a long time usually have made many friends. But they've also met some unfriendly folks along the way. Quite possibly, they've made an enemy or two as well.

Israel has very few friends today; in fact, it seems to have more than its share of unfriendly neighbors and violent enemies, as reflected in news reports on the ongoing Israeli-Arab troubles that dominate international headlines. Many accounts, such as the excerpted news item that follows, point to the hatred of and anger at Israel that are at the center of the matter of Mideast war and peace.

Israel is widely believed to possess the Middle East's only nuclear arsenal, drawing frequent Arab and Iranian condemnation. It has never acknowledged having nuclear weapons.

Israel is not a signatory of the Nuclear Non-Proliferation Treaty and, as a result, is not obligated to allow IAEA [International Atomic Energy Agency] inspectors into its nuclear facilities, or abide by the international body's mandates regarding plant function.

Ambassador Ramzy Ezzeldin Ramzy, head of the Arab League group at the IAEA, insisted that the resolution would be brought up for a vote on Friday, despite US pressure to withdraw it.

"The world has to know that Israel is not playing a constructive role, that Israel has a (nuclear) capability," Ramzy told Reuters.

Arab diplomats said that they refrained from putting forward their resolution on Israel at the 2011 and 2012 IAEA meetings to boost the chances of the Middle East conference taking place last year, but decided to table the resolution this year when that did not happen.

Arab delegations have tried to focus attention on the Dimona reactor in southern Israel, which they claim has been "overlooked" by IAEA inspectors for decades.

The Arab League has unsuccessfully tried to convince the US and European nations to join a campaign to end Israel's policy of nuclear ambiguity. It has, however, received some support at the United Nations.

In 2010 a UN resolution calling for a nuclear-free Middle East singled out Israel for criticism, while ignoring Iran, which is suspected of developing a nuclear weapons program, and whose former President Mahmoud Ahmadinejad constantly threatened to wipe Israel off the map.[57]

Unwelcome Wanderers

Sin is of deadly importance in God's holy eyes. It is, after all, what separated His highest creation from Himself and polluted His entire created universe. Sin also separated God's chosen people from Himself. The Lord likens this tragedy to one particular aspect of the curse following the Fall: Eve and all of her daughters throughout human history endure pain and discomfort in birth. Their wombs weep through menstruation, pointing back to that act of disobedience by Eve.

The following passage describes how He considers Israel's disobedient dealings with Himself:

> Moreover the word of the LORD came unto me, saying,
>
> Son of man, when the house of Israel dwelt in their own land, they defiled it by their own way and by their doings: their way was before me as the uncleanness of a removed woman.
>
> Wherefore I poured my fury upon them for the blood that they had shed upon the land, and for their idols wherewith they had polluted it:
>
> And I scattered them among the heathen, and they were dispersed through the countries: according to their way and according to their doings I judged them.
>
> (Ezekiel 36:16–19)

Because of their sin of disobedience by worshipping idols and refusing His direction, the Israelites polluted the land. Both the people and the land are unclean in God's eyes. God mentions blood in the pollution process. This refers to the fact that He compares man's righteousness (idol worship and all other false attempts to be religious) to filthy rags (Isaiah 64:6). The chosen people's attempts to be blameless in their own eyes and through their own ways made Him look upon them as used menstrual rags. Therefore, He would kick them out of the land, as He had kicked Adam and Eve out of the Garden of Eden. They had polluted the Promised Land!

Trouble followed the people no matter where they went in their scattering. The ancient satanic hatreds follow the Jewish people to this day. Wherever they have wandered throughout the world, they have been victims of anti-Semitism to one degree or another. They've been unwelcome almost everywhere they have tried to settle.

"Why has human history been inundated with hatred of the Jews and a drive to crush Jerusalem?" asks Jack Van Impe. "Because God loves Jerusalem—and the Jewish people—and Satan hates both."[58]

Hatred Pushes Jews Homeward

Jews living in parts of the world other than the Promised Land, "scattered…among the heathen, and…dispersed through the countries" (Ezekiel 36:19), were no better off than their brothers and sisters in Palestine. They, too, were persecuted without letup.

There is perhaps no more terrible hatred than that of someone because of his or her race. This type of loathing, which has caused more massive wars and deaths than any other, will be at the heart of the Tribulation. Jesus said in Matthew 24:7 that "nation shall rise against nation, and kingdom against kingdom." As mentioned in an earlier chapter, the word "nation" is from the Greek word *ethnos*, and is similar to the word "ethnic" in the English. We hear even today of "ethnic cleansing." Racial hatred is prophesied by Jesus Himself to get much worse as the end of the age approaches. We are certainly experiencing an increase of such hatred in our world today. Israel will again be at the center of the racial hatred during the last seven years known as Daniel's seventieth week.

A Poor Witness

Whenever the Lord has judged Israel and sent His people into other lands, they have made a cursing mockery of His name by claiming to be His chosen, yet living as though He doesn't exist. The people of the other nations look at the Jews throughout history and think that either these are not God's elect, or else God isn't much of a God. In other words, the Jews' disobedience causes the world to doubt God and His truth—a poor witness indeed from the people chosen by God to be His own.

God, as we have learned, has selected Israel as an example of how He deals with His children. That is, people who belong to Him can know, through His dealings with the Jews, exactly how He wants us to conduct our lives. Those who are His own, like the house of Israel, can expect correction when they stray from His loving will.

Jews have been the most hated, hunted, and persecuted people on earth since the time of Christ's crucifixion and resurrection. Early in this new century, anti-Semitism is once again on the rise across the world.

Here are some thoughts on these matters by two of my now-deceased friends and colleagues, both of whom loved Israel with all their spiritual hearts.

David Allen Lewis wrote the following:

What a perverse joke it is when present day replacement theologians accuse their premillennial brethren of being socially irresponsible in the face of the drastic, crisis needs of our world, and yet they themselves are provoking an evil hatred for the nation of Israel through their tired, old, worn-out anti-Semitic theology. How have they managed to resurrect these ancient errors and breathe such new vigor into them until they are now sweeping like an "ill wind that bodes no good" throughout the ranks of the Church? The two major anti-Semitic Christian doctrines are replacement and the theology of contempt.

What is being preached in certain quarters today is exactly what both the Protestant and Roman Catholic teachers were promoting in pre-Nazi Germany. We had better be alert to these alarming facts. Don't ever say, "It cannot happen here."

I hear from some of my brethren that God no longer has any use for natural Israel. The Church has taken the place of Israel in God's economy. That is called the Doctrine of Replacement.

Then there is the Doctrine of Contempt. Simply stated it claims that since the Jews killed Christ they are worthy of any punishment that falls upon them. The Holocaust? Good enough for them....

We still have time to speak out and prevent another Holocaust in our times, but the handwriting is on the wall. If we are silent, history will repeat itself. The Holocaust is not mere history, it is potential.[59]

Zola Levitt stated further:

Why is all this happening to Israel? The best of all reasons is that prophetic Scripture says it will happen. While the world press dithers over Israel's supposed intractability with the peace process or bad treatment of the Palestinians or a wrong-headed prime minister, the real reason is that Israel must be maneuvered into a position where it will be "hated of all nations" (Matthew 24:9).

It is well to remember that close to 100 percent of end times prophecy concerns that tiny nation, and the biblical signs of the end pertain especially to Israel. The Olivet Discourse of our Lord—His answer to the disciples' question, "What will be the sign of Your coming and of the end of the world?" (Matthew 24:3)—details phenomena that are global in scope but of particular concern to those in the Holy Land. The Lord addresses His disciples as Israelites in particular when He observes, "He that shall endure unto the end, the same shall be saved" (verse 13).

It is the Jewish people gathered in Israel at the time of Armageddon who must endure "unto the end"—that is the second coming of the Lord—to be saved. At the time, "they shall look upon me whom they have pierced, and they shall mourn for him as one mourneth for his only son" (Zechariah 12: 10).[60]

Readying to Reenter Promised Land

God used tough love to prepare His people to return to the land He gave them. Although Jews have been returning to the land of promise a few at a time since their last scattering, it wasn't until the 1800s that they started going home in significant numbers. We have looked in previous chapters at that Zionist movement founded by Theodor Herzl. Many Jewish people were inspired by Zionist ideas, and some Jewish settlers purchased considerable plots of land around Jerusalem for farming.

Soon, new Jewish communities were springing up. Due to over-crowding of the immediate land in and around Jerusalem, eight new Jewish neighborhoods were built just outside the walls of the city.

Jews were in the majority in the area by 1880. Large portions of land were purchased, bringing about more and more rural Jewish communities. As the Zionist movement gained backing, plans were made to return on a widening scale.

Two sizeable immigrations of Jews soon came from Eastern Europe. They worked hard to homestead the swampy areas of the regions, turning the territory into farmland. By 1900, they had built new settlements on the reclaimed land.

This laid the groundwork for the thriving agricultural economy to come. The new Jewish population was opposed at every turn. To begin with, the terrain was at first hostile. Mosquitoes infested the swampy areas, and it took extremely hard work to make things grow as they should.

The Turkish Ottoman Empire's governing authority also did all it could to make things difficult, imposing restrictions on completing paperwork necessary to allow cultivation of the land and to do other things necessary to make progress.

The Jewish population reached eighty-five thousand by the time

World War I began in 1914. This compared to only five thousand populating the land early in the previous century.

Balfour Brings Bullies

God had laid the groundwork for the return to nationhood of His chosen people. "Miraculous" is the term used—in some cases by even nonreligious historians—when considering how Israel was reborn as a country in the twentieth century.

The Jews had been totally scattered, then suddenly, in terms of the centuries of history, they were back in the land of the Bible. This took many by surprise, including preachers and religious scholars who didn't think there was such a thing as a Jew left on the planet.

Arthur Kac, in his book, *The Rebirth of the State of Israel,* observes:

The survival of the Jews is the world's most unique and baffling historical phenomenon. The uniqueness of the Jewish people is their survival in spite of the fact that their homeland had been destroyed twice and the people dispersed from their country.

As a rule, when people leave their home country and emigrate to a foreign land they become thoroughly assimilated with the people of the host country after one generation, if not sooner. The Jews as a group are a notable exception to this rule.[61]

The treacherous teaching that God was through with the Jews as a race had grown greatly during the years they were living outside of the land of promise. But now, they were back, just as the Bible said. God was preparing to prove the world and the false teachers wrong. The chosen people would yet be used to glorify his Holy Name!

The British Empire, upon whom the sun was said to never set, was in the process of moving into its twilight hours. Nonetheless, even though no one realized it, God was using Britain's government to help bring about the rebirth of Israel.

As stated earlier, there were only about eighty-five thousand Jews in the land by 1914, when the First World War began. The British government, needing money to fight the war, wanted to make friends with the Rothschild banking house and other Jewish money interests.

On November 17, 1917, British Foreign Secretary Arthur J. Balfour issued, on behalf of England, the Balfour Declaration, which indicated approval of the Jewish goal of bringing about a Jewish state in Palestine. The document read, in part: "His Majesty's government views with favor the establishment in Palestine of a national home for the Jewish people."

Arab zealots reacted angrily to the British declaration, stepping up their violent terrorist activity whenever possible. Finally, Arab pressures caused the British to back away from their Balfour Declaration promises. But, the seed of desire to establish a Jewish state was deeply planted. There hasn't been a moment of true Mideast peace since that troubled time.

Unsettled Settlers

I sense that Israel's plight in its early return to the land and its subsequent ordeal in surviving to become the modern Jewish state requires reiteration. Thus, at the risk of being annoyingly repetitive, I again present here some earlier facts about the Jewish people coming back into the land.

The great hatred Satan has for God's chosen began to boil within the minds of the anti-Semite Nazi thugs and others. The increased persecutions and murders of Jews in Europe soon made those who were once reluctant to leave their homes and businesses flee for their very lives.

The last great wave of immigrants of 165,000 entered the land of promise before Adolf Hitler and his demonic henchmen began to shut off the flow of fleeing Jews. Tragically, the British authorities, following the large influx into Palestine, began turning back thousands of would-be Jewish immigrants. Those authorities didn't want the Arabs to become even more upset at the imbalance in numbers between Arabs and Jews in the region.

Adolf Hitler's reign of terror put Jews through indescribable horrors. Source: German Federal Archive

Even more tragically, other nations, including the United States, refused to let shiploads of Jews get off in their ports. The Jewish people had no choice but to eventually be returned to the Nazis.

The Jewish people who made it safely to the land of promise found it to be far less than paradise on earth. Although it was a thousand times better than the horrors being endured by Jews under Hitler's control, life was hard.

Hate-filled, fanatical Arabs attacked the Jewish settlers at every opportunity. Their anger exploded. They burned forests and fields belonging to the Jews. Jewish efforts to transport people and materials such as building supplies, agricultural implements, seeds, and other things were viciously attacked. The tactics were effective at delaying the settlers' getting a firm toehold in the land. But God was with them, and their return to the land was well underway.

God had said through Ezekiel that He would return the chosen people—not for their sakes, but for His Holy Name's sake (Ezekiel 36:22). There would come a time when the world will know that He, alone, is God!

Palestine's Puzzle Pieces

"And the heathen shall know that I am the LORD, saith the Lord GOD, when I shall be sanctified in you before their eyes" (Ezekiel 36:23b). Satan's hatred fanned the Middle-East anger into white-hot rage. At the same time, European Jews were undergoing persecution as great as any the chosen people had ever endured. They were caught, as they say, between a rock and a hard place.

While Hitler and his propaganda minister Joseph Goebbles revved up the anti-Jew campaign in Germany and other parts of Europe, Arab nationalists increased anti-Jewish activity in the land of the Bible.

It came to a point that Arab nationalist leaders would not meet with Zionist leaders, and violence threatened to explode in all-out war. The British controlling authority determined something had to be done, and in 1937 recommended dividing the region into two states: They wanted to partition an Arab state from a Jewish state.

Jewish leaders approved of the concept, but the Arab leadership absolutely opposed it. They wouldn't accept partition of the land in any form whatsoever. Arab terrorists stepped up violence against the Jews. This greatly worried the British government and the response of the controlling authority—as stated previously—was to issue a white paper. This document, issued in 1939, imposed harsh restrictions upon Jewish immigration. It seemed that the Jews were being punished for the terrible wrong the militant Arabs were committing!

About that time, of course, Adolf Hitler's aggression brought the world into the widest war ever. For the time being, the attention of the Arabs, Jews, and all others turned to matters of the developing World War II.

The puzzle pieces of partition recommended by the British through their anti-immigration white paper would have to be put together at some other time. Nonetheless, Jewish leader David Ben-Gurion, who would later become Israel's first prime minister, was determined to fight on two fronts. Regarding the white paper and the Holy Land Jews' involvement in the coming war, Ben Gurion said: "We will fight the war as if there were no white paper, and the white paper as if there were no war."[62]

Volunteer Jewish forces from the Palestinian region fought hard against the Axis powers throughout the war. Many won medals of valor.

When World War II ended, the flames of ancient hatreds burst violently to the surface again. Militant Arabs demanded rights they claimed were a thousand years old to the land in and around Jerusalem. Zionist leaders claimed the Jews' rights to the land and Jerusalem that were even older—dating to the time of King Solomon and earlier.

The God of Israel had His all-powerful hand on His returned people, even though they were back in unbelief. He will follow through on His word. He will make His Name great through Israel in spite of the Jews' opposition to His direction for the nation.

United Nations' New Notion

God most often has performed His miraculous works with the close involvement of men and women, boys and girls. The human element was always involved in one way or another when Jesus performed such wondrous acts as healing, feeding the five thousand men and their families with the few fishes and loaves, and raising the dead. That is, everything God has done in accounts of miracles has been for and through people—usually the meekest of people.

God also uses others to accomplish His will. The United Nations is a worldly—earthly rather than godly—group of people the Lord used in such a way. Of course, UN members had no idea they were being used by Him to fulfill end-time biblical prophecy.

The British turned the Palestinian territory, along with its problems, over to the United Nations in 1948. Violence became widespread and threatened a much larger war. The UN stepped in, deciding to divide the land of Palestine into an Arab and a Jewish state. It was determined to make Jerusalem an internationalized city.

Most Jews agreed. The Arabs fought against division bitterly.

Just before Ben-Gurion announced the declaration of Israel's independence, some three hundred thousand Arabs fled the area. The Arab forces prepared to attack, and another three hundred fifty thousand fled from the coming war zone. These six hundred fifty thousand refugees refused settlement anywhere other than the land that had been their homes. They were welcome to stay within their regional homeland, according to the declaration of Israel's independence—which might accurately be called, "Israel's rebirth certificate."

———

Declaration of Israel's Independence

Read by David Ben-Gurion in Tel Aviv on May 14, 1948 (5th of Iyar, 5708).

The land of Israel was the birthplace of the Jewish people. Here their spiritual, religious, and national identity was formed. Here they achieved independence and created a culture of national and universal significance. Here they wrote and gave the Bible to the world.

Exiled from Palestine, the Jewish people remained faithful to it in all the countries of their dispersion, never ceasing to pray and hope for their return and the restoration of their national freedom.

Impelled by this historic association, Jews strove throughout the centuries to go back to the land of their fathers and regain their statehood. In recent decades they returned in masses. They reclaimed the wilderness, revived their language, built cities and villages and established a vigorous and ever-growing community with its own economic and cultural life. They sought peace yet were ever prepared to defend themselves. They brought the blessing of progress to all inhabitants of the country.

In the year 1897 the First Zionist Congress, inspired by Theodor Herzl's vision of the Jewish State, proclaimed the right of the Jewish people to national revival in their own country.

This right was acknowledged by the Balfour Declaration of November 2, 1917, and re-affirmed by the Mandate of the League of Nations, which gave explicit international recognition to the historic connection of the Jewish people with Palestine and their right to reconstitute their National Home.

The Nazi holocaust, which engulfed millions of Jews in Europe, proved anew the urgency of the re-establishment of the Jewish state, which would solve the problem of Jewish homelessness by opening the gates to all Jews and lifting the Jewish people to equality in the family of nations.

The survivors of the European catastrophe, as well as Jews from other lands, proclaiming their right to a life of dignity, freedom and labor, and undeterred by hazards, hardships and obstacles, have tried unceasingly to enter Palestine.

In the Second World War the Jewish people in Palestine made a full contribution in the struggle of the freedom-loving nations against the Nazi evil. The sacrifices of their soldiers and the efforts of their workers gained them title to rank with the peoples who founded the United Nations.

On November 29, 1947, the General Assembly of the United Nations adopted a Resolution for the establishment of an independent Jewish State in Palestine, and called upon the inhabitants of the country to take such steps as may be necessary on their part to put the plan into effect.

This recognition by the United Nations of the right of the Jewish people to establish their independent State may not be revoked. It is, moreover, the self-evident right of the Jewish people to be a nation, as all other nations, in its own sovereign State.

ACCORDINGLY, WE, the members of the National Council, representing the Jewish people in Palestine and the Zionist movement of the world, met together in solemn assembly today, the day of the termination of the British mandate for Palestine, by virtue of the natural and historic right of the Jewish and of the Resolution of the General Assembly of the United Nations, HEREBY PROCLAIM the establishment of the Jewish State in Palestine, to be called ISRAEL.

WE HEREBY DECLARE that as from the termination of the Mandate at midnight, this night of the 14th and 15th May, 1948, and until the setting up of the duly elected bodies of the State in accordance with a Constitution, to be drawn up by a Constituent Assembly not later than the first day of October, 1948, the present National Council shall act as the provisional administration, shall constitute the Provisional Government of the State of Israel.

THE STATE OF ISRAEL will be open to the immigration of Jews from all countries of their dispersion; will promote the development of the country for the benefit of all its inhabitants; will be based on the precepts of liberty, justice and peace taught by the Hebrew Prophets; will uphold the full social and political equality of all its citizens, without distinction of race, creed or sex; will guarantee full freedom of conscience, worship, education and culture; will safeguard the sanctity and inviolability of the shrines and Holy Places of all religions; and will dedicate itself to the principles of the Charter of the United Nations.

THE STATE OF ISRAEL will be ready to cooperate with the organs and representatives of the United Nations in the implementation of the Resolution of the Assembly of November 29, 1947, and will take steps to bring about the Economic Union over the whole of Palestine.

We appeal to the United Nations to assist the Jewish people in the building of its State and to admit Israel into the family of nations.

In the midst of wanton aggression, we yet call upon the Arab inhabitants of the State of Israel to return to the ways of peace and play their part in the development of the State, with full and equal citizenship and due representation in its bodies and institutions—provisional or permanent.

We offer peace and unity to all the neighboring states and their peoples, and invite them to cooperate with the independent Jewish nation for the common good of all.

Our call goes out to the Jewish people all over the world to rally to our side in the task of immigration and development and to stand by us in the great struggle for the fulfillment of the dream of generations—the redemption of Israel.

With trust in Almighty God, we set our hand to this Declaration, at this Session of the Provisional State Council, in the city of Tel Aviv, on this Sabbath eve, the fifth of Iyar, 5708, the fourteenth day of May, 1948.

United Nations leaders thought they were assuring peace in the Middle East for the future when they backed up the formation of the Israeli state. But it wasn't their notion that performed the miracle of Israel's rebirth; it was the great God of heaven—the miracle-working Lord God of Abraham, Isaac, and Jacob, to whom the promises of nationhood were made—who did it all.

Truman Trumpets Return

Thus saith the LORD, which giveth the sun for a light by day, and the ordinances of the moon and of the stars for a light by night, which divideth the sea when the waves thereof roar; The LORD of hosts is his name:

If those ordinances depart from before me, saith the LORD, then the seed of Israel also shall cease from being a nation before me for ever. (Jeremiah 31:35–36)

How anyone can read the portions of Scripture above with a heart desiring understanding, then think that God is through with the Jews and the nation Israel, is far beyond my amazement. Add to that Scripture what the historical record in recent times has dramatically displayed for the whole world to see about Israel and the Jews, and it seems insanity to think that God is through with His chosen people.

Can, for instance, it be just coincidence that the most powerful nation at the time of Israel's rebirth threw its might behind the right of the tiny nation to come forth? Can it be mere coincidence that the president of the United States just happened to have as a personal friend a Jewish man with whom he at one time ran a clothing business? The business failed miserably, but the friendship succeeded to such an extent that it, in my view, helped bring prophecy to pass.

Harry S. Truman, thirty-third president of the U.S., didn't talk publicly to the pre-government leaders of Israel just before it won its statehood. He refused to agree with the very insistent advice against supporting an Israeli state given by his secretary of state as well.

Instead, historians report that Truman's decision was based upon his many conversations with his former business partner in a haberdashery they once ran together. Those discussions, along with Truman's apparent personal religious beliefs about Israel, reportedly helped him make up his mind to throw America's great influence behind Israel's rebirth.

U.S. Supports Struggling State

The American president was up to his ears in diplomatic and military problems at the time modern Israel was about to be born. The Soviet Union (USSR), as Russia was then called, threatened all of Europe. It had already begun tightening its stranglehold on Eastern Europe and threatened West Berlin with starvation.

The USSR's blockade of West Berlin made world peace questionable. Soviet dictator Joseph Stalin took advantage of Western Europe's war-fatigued economy to flex his military muscles.

President Truman was worried with the task of asking the U.S. Congress to reinstate the military draft. Britain's Winston Churchill was warning of the menace of war from Stalin's forces. The fighting and turmoil in the Middle East wasn't at the top of the list for the president's attention. The people about to declare Israel's independence, thus its nationhood, didn't have Truman's ear.

But an historian and researcher recently found that there was bitter debate within the Truman administration about the matter of the founding of the Jewish state.[63]

George C. Marshall, the powerful U.S. secretary of state, and those within the U.S. State Department were absolutely against America's support for establishment of the Jewish state. Marshall and the State Department bureaucrats, whom Truman called with both irritation and amusement "the striped pants set," were so angry about Truman's possible support of Israel that Marshall threatened to quit the administration. Not only that, he told the president he would vote Republican for president next time rather than Democrat.

Marshall and the others argued that the oil-rich Arab countries would react to such action by cutting off relations with the United States. That would mean the oil flow from the Middle East would stop or be severely slowed.

Marshall, a former top general of the Army, argued that the Arabs would join with the Soviets against America, using the refusal to sell oil as a powerful weapon. He also argued that forty-four thousand Jews facing more than 3 million angry Arabs while holding no strategic military positions in the land couldn't survive.

But despite opposition by the State Department and Secretary of Defense James Forrestal, President Truman recognized Israel as a nation. He gave America's official recognition only eleven minutes after Israeli prime minister-to-be, David Ben-Gurion, gave the address declaring Israel's independence from the former British territory of Palestine.

According to the research, Truman kept quiet about the fact that he had made up his mind to support the establishment of the Israeli state two months before the May 14, 1948, birth of the nation. The president, in telling why he came to that decision, said: "Historical claims, and claims of humanity, both pointed in the same direction."[64]

The decision was made, the research shows, during a meeting with future Israeli president Chaim Weizmann. The meeting was arranged by Eddie Jacobsen, Truman's former partner in their failed haberdashery store in Missouri. Reportedly, Truman told Weizmann that he favored partition of Palestine in order for Israel to create a state and that Jacobsen's longstanding friendship with Truman was the key to the successful meeting. Truman had previously refused to meet with American Jewish leaders to discuss the issue of a future Israeli state.

The recognition of Israel passed the U.S. Congress with ease. George C. Marshall never made his angry opposition public and stayed with the Truman administration, later becoming the U.S. secretary of defense. According to the researcher, Truman reacted to the founding of the nation of Israel and his part in it by saying it was "one of the proudest moments of my life."[65]

Bedeviled Birth

Arab countries surrounding the newborn state declared war the moment they learned of the nation's announced independence. Despite the fact that Israel defeated Arab military forces in a number of successive battles, the oil-rich Arab leadership cut off neither diplomatic relationships with nor petroleum flow to the United States.

As the billowing clouds of war began to thin out, modern Israel stood like the prophet Ezekiel's dry-bones vision. The date was May 15, 1948. Still, the nation's freedom was not secured.

The nations of the Arab League were blood-oath vowed to do away with the infant state. Egypt, Syria, Jordan, Lebanon, Iraq, and Saudi Arabia positioned military forces for an all-out assault. The courageous, battle-hardened Israeli people, though outnumbered six nations to one and by millions of troops, took up arms and fought back valiantly.

Even seasoned reporters of the scene were dumbfounded by what happened next. The Israeli forces counterattacked on all fronts. Not only did Israel defend its territory, but won half again as much land through victory after victory. Many strange battlefield incidents have been reported and retold about the time of Israel's rebirth. Some call what happened coincidence. Others call it miraculous!

Refereeing the Ruckus

Things quickly worsened for Israel's enemies. Within less than a month, the Arab League forces were in full retreat on all fronts. Israel was gobbling up more and more of the land of those who had attacked. Of course, it was really Israel's land.

The United Nations got into the act, calling on Israel to cease pursuing its backpedaling, sometimes fleeing, enemies. The situation had gotten totally out of hand, and there was uncertainty about the security of the oil fields. The internationalist powers that be managed to bring about a sort of calm. Finally, the UN brokered a truce, sparing the Arab League loss of territories and greater humiliation.

Peace the Issue

The one great issue in the world today is the cry for peace (see Jeremiah 8:11). Leo Tolstoy's epic novel *War and Peace* laid out the horrors of war suffered by the Russian people during the Napoleonic wars. This was the era not too long before the Bolshevik Revolution of 1917. His was, of course, also a great though tragic love story of a young woman named Natasha. The book contrasts the two opposite states of the human condition: love and war.

It's interesting that Tolstoy's story addresses themes somewhat like truth God portrays in his Holy Word: the love of God, through the perfect peace He offers the human race, as contrasted against Satan and sin's murderous war against the creation called man.

Russia is the region north of Israel from which, as we've seen before, the Gog-Magog attack will come, according to Ezekiel 38 and 39. At that time, peace will be taken from Israel, and all mankind, in a big way.

It's more than just interesting that 1917 is the year that both the Bolshevik Revolution in Russia and the Balfour Declaration involving the land of promise took place. Lenin, then Stalin, brought the Soviet

Union onto the world stage of power. Modern Israel, at the same time, was conceived as a future major player on the stage of human history.

War-Making Machinery

It must be more than mere coincidence that at the same time oil came into the picture in a big way, the machinery of industry developed a tremendous thirst for the black liquid gold called petroleum.

So, too, the machinery of war began making demands for oil to fuel the killing capability that war requires. With oil's discovery and the wartime machinery that uses the fuels that came out of petroleum developments, man could rain down death on his fellow man as never before. Love and peace have, from that time to this, taken a far-distant second place to the petroleum-fueled wars that continue to plague us. Indeed, it seems petroleum has poisoned peace.

Western World Woes

The discovery of huge amounts of oil in 1908 would, in the future, bring tremendous change to the Middle East. Indeed, as we discussed in chapter 9, petroleum and all the things it would bring radically altered the whole world.

Drilling for oil began immediately following World War II. The region was not at first a matter of world attention. But as automobile production and aviation transportation began to call for greater and greater fuel supplies, the Middle East deposits turned the eyes of the world in that direction.

Factories of many sorts, especially in America, sprang up or were converted from war-time to peace-time production. United States industry demanded a large portion of petroleum. Europe and other areas recovering from the destructiveness of war soon needed ever-increasing supplies as well.

The Arab nations whose oil deposits were in abundance were for a time unorganized. Their ancient ways and customs limited their ability to make the most of the liquid riches beneath their sands.

OPEC was formed in 1960. Its member countries, however, were not united in pricing and petroleum policies. The full impact of what they owned hadn't yet hit the oil sheiks and royal families, but that changed in a big way in 1973. The Middle East had previously supplied only about 5.5 percent of total oil output. The United States, on the other hand, supplied as much as 52 percent of the world's crude oil production around 1950. But by 1973, the Middle East was supplying 40 percent of total world needs, while U.S. production had slipped greatly.

Ages-old hatreds flared. The Arab nations, still simmering with hostility from their overwhelming defeats by Israel in 1948, 1956, and 1967, again attacked the Jewish state. Egypt and Syria attacked Israel on October 6, 1973—Yom Kippur, Israel's holiest day of the year, the Day of Atonement.

Israeli forces beat back the aggressors, advanced to within twenty miles of Damascus, the Syrian capital, and crossed the Suez Canal to penetrate into Egyptian territory. As in previous such wars won by Israel, the UN intervened and most of the aggressors' land lost in the battles was returned.

Still, the Arab nations were vengeful. They clamped an embargo on oil and created a real crisis, particularly in the United States. Long gas lines and high prices threw many American commuters into panic. The point was made dramatically. Middle East oil reserves were now something that had to be recognized and dealt with by the world community. Israel was seen by many as the stumbling block in the embargo crisis. Israel would have to be dealt with in a different light, too!

Jihad Jitters

Arab anger against Israel is not what we normally think of as being mad about something. For the most part, Arab anger is tied to Islam. To the

Arab, government, society, culture, personal daily life—indeed, every-thing—is tied to the Islamic religion.

Muslims are the believers in the religion of Islam, which was founded by Mohammed, the man considered the major prophet of the god Allah. The Muslims believe that Jesus was but one of many prophets of Allah, along with Adam, Noah, Moses, John the Baptist, and others.

Islam claims 23 percent, nearly one-fourth, of the global population, with an estimated 1.6 billion of the world's peoples practicing belief in Allah.[66] To be fair, many Muslims don't call for jihad, or holy war, against Israel. But the militant, radical, or fanatic Arab Muslims do demand that Israel be wiped from the face of the Middle East, and particularly from Palestine and Jerusalem.

Those who promote and recruit for Islam claim in their literature that jihad is a last resort. They say violence must always be in the name of Allah's righteousness. The terrorism that comes out of the fanatical Islamic camps, however, is brutal. It makes no distinction between sol-diers and innocent men, women, and children.

The Islamic promoters claim, too, that the Koran (Islam's holiest book) doesn't forbid the freedom of worship to those who don't believe in Allah. Their literature says Islam is tolerant of all other religions, and even claims that Islam has much in common with Christianity and Judaism. The facts say otherwise.

It is true, the Jews and the Arabs have a common father, Abraham. That's where the similarity ends. The fact is, also, that hundreds of thou-sands of Christians have been slaughtered and many others are still being tortured in the name of Allah for their crime of belief in Jesus Christ as Lord and Savior. At the same time, Jews are reviled and, when the opportunity comes, are murdered by radical Islamic terrorists.

Again, many Muslims are not a part of the murderous behavior. But, most are, possibly out of fear, silent on the matter when it comes to try-ing to stop the atrocities.

Remember Salmon Rushdie, the author of *The Satanic Verses?* He pointed out the deadly aims and goals of fanatical Islam. Then he had a multi-million dollar hit contract put out on him by Ayatollah Khomeini, the Iranian Islamic cleric. This sounds more like the way organized crime acts than the way a religion that only wants to do good acts!

The tyrants in power in Arab nations seem in most cases to be in league with the radical, fanatic Islamic religious leaders. Yasser Arafat was infamous for calling for jihad. His Palestinian Liberation Organization (PLO) has long had as its aim bringing all Arabs against Israel in a holy war that will forever end the Jewish problem, as they see it.

Because Middle East oil deposits are so important in its eyes, the possibility of jihad makes the whole international diplomatic community nervous. The jihad jitters must be calmed at all costs. The diplomats, mostly through United Nations actions and recommendations, therefore have seemed over the years to look the other way when Palestinian terrorists and other jihadist-type entities, in the name of Allah, murder Israeli civilians and attack Israeli military personnel who have done nothing to provoke the attacks. Israelis, on the other hand, come in for severe criticism by the internationalists and world news media, even if they defend themselves.

Holy Hotheads

Religion, then, is the central rallying point for fanatical Arabs who want Israel destroyed. We know, from what we have looked at so far, that the war against God's chosen people is not of God, but of Satan.

Even small children have been sent into battle to die for the fanatics' religious causes. One example is during the war fought between Iran and Iraq in the 1980s. Iraq's President Saddam Hussein sent children to fight the Iranians in some cases, and the Iranians sent children to fight the Iraqis in some cases. Both sides believed in Allah as their god.

Radical Muslims believe that by dying for Allah in a "righteous" cause, a person goes directly to heaven. The person will be greatly rewarded, they believe, with harems and other great rewards.

The questions arise: Whose Allah is the right Allah? Which Allah was the "righteous" Allah in the Iranian-Iraqi war? The very fact that the fanatics are so unreasoning makes the possibility of Mideast war a worrisome threat. They need no cause other than to attack in the name of Allah.

A news item of some years ago provides a record of such unreasoning devotion to the god of Islam.

Although he has been condemned in much of the world as a murderous criminal, in the West Bank town of Kalkilia, at least Saeed Hotari is a hero. His face is plastered on posters everywhere. He's a legend. The children, especially, idolize him.

"When I grow up, I want to be just like him," said Hosni, a 9-year-old Palestinian boy.

But Hotari was not a rock star, famous athlete or a movie star. What makes him famous is what he did on the last night of his life—when he killed 21 people and himself at an Israeli disco.

On the night of Friday, June 1, Hotari stood in line at the Dolphinarium, which was one of the most popular Tel Aviv discos. The 22-year-old Palestinian had turned himself into a human bomb: Strapped to his chest was a deadly mix of powerful explosives and hundreds of steel ball bearings. At 11:26 p.m., he triggered the bomb, killing himself and leaving 21 others, mostly young girls, to die in one of Israel's worst suicide bombings ever....

After the attack, Hotari's father Hassan was congratulated by the community.

"I am proud and I will never forget it until the last day of my life," he said. "This kind of death is better than any other kind of death. Thanks to God."

The younger Hotari was described by friends and relatives as devoutly religious, quiet and ordinary. And now, it is believed that as a martyr he is awarded a special place in heaven, the highest level of paradise, where some say 70 black-eyed virgins await him....

Hotari did not leave behind a farewell. But he has left a legacy.

"I want to join an operation attack just like Saeed," said 9-year-old Hosni, a cousin of Hotari.[67]

Zionist Zealots

Israel, even as a nation back in the land of promise in unbelief, has seen God's mighty, miraculous hand at work in all of the wars the Arab forces have brought against the modern state. Against overwhelming odds, the Israelis have pushed the holy hotheads of radical Islam back to where they came from, and have won new territories—territories that are theirs by divine right in the first place.

Zionists might believe it was their planning and might alone that brought modern Israel the victories of 1948, 1956, 1967, and 1973. They are very wrong. It was the God of Abraham, Isaac, and Jacob who protects His chosen nation.

"There is only one sound and logical view by which to account for the indestructibility of the Jews," states Arthur Kac. "This view is set forth in the Bible where the survival of the Jews is attributed to the unchangeable will of God, and where the preservation of the Jews is part and parcel of their national destiny as a people chosen of God to fulfill a certain mission in the world."[68]

Peace Police

Pressures are mounting on Israel. The Bible says the pressures will become so great from the nations of the world that Israel will give in and sign a covenant or agreement with what God calls "death and hell" (Isaiah 28:15, 18). God warns about this false peace the world diplomatic community wants to force upon His nation, and as described in

Nahum 1, there will come a leader, a "wicked counselor" (verse 11) from the nation who will sign the covenant with the prince who is to come. The Antichrist will convince this Israeli leader or his representative that he, the Antichrist, and his forces can protect the Jewish people and give them a lasting peace at last.

The international community today is counseling the Israeli government leaders to give up land for a comprehensive peace treaty. The UN and the coalition of forces within its body will assure that the peace will be secure.

But God says it is wicked counsel and against God's will...evil against the God of heaven. The Lord says that although many voices are giving such advice, they all will be cut off at some prophetic point. The Lord tells the nation that He will break the world system of control from off the back of his people (Nahum 1:13).

Today's international community peace police speak with soft, supposedly reasonable, voices. When Antichrist comes onto the scene in full power, the voice of his regime will become a raging, bloody scream of demands that will make Adolf Hitler's rantings seem pleasant by comparison.

Ancient angers are taking aim. Prophecy impacts this generation like no other.

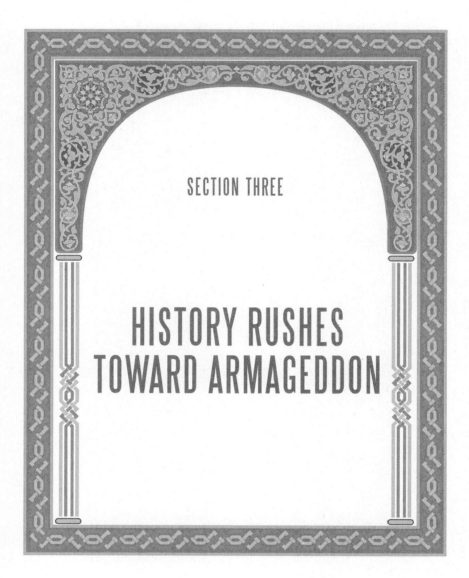

SECTION THREE

HISTORY RUSHES
TOWARD ARMAGEDDON

CHAPTER 11

THE TEMPLE TEMPEST

A STORM IS BREWING. That storm will grow to be much more powerful and more destructive than the EF-5 tornado that hit the Oklahoma City area in 2013. But it's not a natural storm involving the weather. It is supernatural! Pre-Armageddon clouds in the Middle East are now churning up fearsome winds of war directly over one particular spot on the planet: the Temple Mount in Jerusalem.

God's house on top of Mount Moriah has always involved matters of war and peace. When the people of Israel have done what God wanted them to do, there has been peace—and the people have lived calm lives of worship and contentment for the most part. When they have disobeyed to the point that they no longer hear God's instructions, war has come upon them. They've been taken from the land and had their temples destroyed. In this chapter, we'll be looking at the Temple and all the storms that have blown against it in the centuries long past. We'll look also at dangerous winds that are blowing around the Temple Mount today.

Tumultuous Temple History

God is no jack-in-the-box! Stephen, the first Christian martyr recorded in Scripture, said to an angry mob, quoting Isaiah 66:1–2:

> But Solomon built him an house.
> Howbeit the most High dwelleth not in temples made with hands; as saith the prophet,
> Heaven is my throne, and earth is my footstool: what house will ye build me? saith the Lord: or what is the place of my rest?
> Hath not my hand made all these things? (Acts 7:47–50)

And Solomon himself said in 1 Kings 8:21: "And I have set there a place for the ark, wherein is the covenant of the LORD, which he made with our fathers, when he brought them out of the land of Egypt."

King David, in a rare moment when he wasn't fighting Israel's enemies, thought about how God had no place to call home. The Ark of the Covenant, the holy vessel that was built during the Israelites' wanderings in the desert and that "served as the only physical manifestation of God on earth,"[69] surely needed a solid house of cedar wood. After all, David had the very finest home of his day. But the ark in which the glory and power of God dwelt had been kept in tents of cloth in the tabernacle, because it had to be easily moved while the children of Israel moved about.

David considered how Israel was now in a more settled condition. Under his leadership, the nation's borders had been expanded and secured and a capital had been firmly established in Jerusalem. Therefore, he wanted, on behalf of God, to build a permanent home where the Lord could live on earth.

When the king presented the idea to the prophet Nathan, Nathan told David it sounded like a great idea to him. He said for David to go ahead with his plans. But, as man's ideas usually are when it comes to self-realized religious thought, David's idea to build a Temple and Nathan's go-ahead to begin the project were wrong, for a couple of reasons.

1. *God told Nathan in a dream that David was not to build the Temple for the ark because God could not be contained.* The Lord instructed the prophet to ask David:

> Shalt thou build me an house for me to dwell in?
>
> Whereas I have not dwelt in any house since the time that I brought up the children of Israel out of Egypt, even to this day, but have walked in a tent and in a tabernacle.
>
> In all the places wherein I have walked with all the children of Israel spake I a word with any of the tribes of Israel, whom I commanded to feed my people Israel, saying, Why build ye not me an house of cedar? (2 Samuel 7:5–7)

Imagine thinking that the God who created all things needed mere man to build Him a house! God said to tell David that the Lord would build David a house, instead of the other way around.

2. *God told David he was not to build the Temple because his hands weren't clean enough to build such a holy house.* David, a mighty man of war, had blood on his hands after fighting the many righteous battles against the Philistines and others who invaded Israel. But the house of God was to be a place of peace. The only bloodshed permitted there would be through the worship of animal sacrifice, foreshadowing the sacrifice for the atonement of sin of God's only begotten Son, Jesus Christ.

Although God didn't want David to be the one to build the Temple, He did give the go-ahead for a Temple to be built, hand-picking from among David's sons Solomon, a man blessed with "rest" or "peace"—we might read that "clean hands"—for the task. In fact, Solomon wouldn't merely build the Temple, he would become David's successor as king, foreshadowing the time when Jesus would one day sit on the throne during His millennial reign.

David Obeys

In spite of God's thumbs-down to David being the one to wear the supervisor's hat on the job site of the Temple project, David, as always, humbled himself and acknowledged that the Lord was right. He jumped in and did all he could to help *within the boundaries of what God would allow him to do*. As it turns out, his God-sanctioned involvement was extensive. David is the one who received the plans for the project from the Lord, and he also gathered materials, recruited craftsmen, and outlined in great detail how worship would be conducted once the Temple was complete.

Sharon Stirs Islamist Hatred

Palestinian Liberation Organization (PLO) leader, the late Yasser Arafat, once stirred Jewish anger by saying that the Jews have no connection to the Temple Mount. This was in response to Ariel Sharon's September 28, 2000, visit there. Sharon's action caused thousands of Arab Islamic people in and around Jerusalem to demonstrate against Israeli interest in the area where the Dome of the Rock stands today.

Some archeologists believe that many artifacts of the Temple built by Solomon are sealed in tunnels and underground rooms inside the Temple Mount. They think the tabernacle items and perhaps even the Ark of the Covenant itself might be hidden there (read more in chapter 15). However, the Palestinian Authority, which controls access to the site, forbids all but a very limited number of archeological digs inside the mount. At the same time, Jewish people interested in getting at the truth accuse the Palestinian authority of digging beneath the Temple Mount in order to find and destroy all artifacts that might add to the proof that Solomon's Temple sat there. Until the last few decades, there were only biblical records to show that any temples sat on Mount Moriah. More and more extrabiblical and archeological proof is now confirming the absolute truth of what the Bible says on these matters. This apparently worries the anti-Israeli forces to the point they feel they must destroy any potential proof of Jewish claims to the site.

Solomon Succeeds

Solomon was wise indeed! He was quite smart even before asking the Lord for wisdom. It seems like he followed his own advice about the wisdom of seeking advice (see Proverbs 20:18) when he looked to a friend of his father to give counsel and help in getting ready to build. Hiram, the king of Tyre, loved David and eagerly answered Solomon's call to help, once he knew David had named Solomon his successor. Hiram had all the know-how and means to transport the building materials Solomon's workforce would need. Also, Hiram's kingdom had many expert craftsmen who could do the job in top fashion.

With David's help in preparing and Hiram's help in supplying a great team of workers, Solomon was ready to begin the project, and ordered its construction to commence when his father died four years after the younger man had taken the throne. The task before the king was tremendous, and he needed much help. He hired highly skilled Phoenicians to do the work, with the help of thirty thousand workers recruited from his nation. Solomon also picked out another seventy thousand men to carry the heavy loads of building materials, and he chose yet another eighty thousand to cut stone from the mountains, with thirty-six hundred appointed to oversee the effort.

God had stipulated as part of the plans He gave David for the Temple that no noise from equipment such as hammers, chisels, or iron tools of any sort should be heard from the construction site (1 Kings 6:7). This greatly increased the complexity of the project and the craftsmanship required, because the stones at the off-site quarry had to be precisely finished *before* being brought to the Temple Mount. The measurements had to be executed with such perfection that they would fit together exactly in the structure. No tools could be used at the construction site to chisel or shape them until they properly fit in place.

After seven years of construction, in 960 BC, the Temple was completed, and it stood in that spot for nearly four hundred years. The entire story of the construction of the Temple is found in broad sections of 1 Kings chapters 5–8 and 2 Chronicles chapters 1–7.

Model of the First Temple

Solomon's Disobedience

Solomon's kingdom was unmatched in its great beauty and influence, and the wisdom he had received from the Lord was legendary. However, even after the king was warned by God Himself, Solomon apparently couldn't resist the opportunities his powerful position presented to his lustful heart. We only have to think of celebrities of our time to understand how sexual lust ruins lives if not governed by the Holy Spirit.

So the king, despite his beginnings as a man who loved the Lord and who was blessed by God with wisdom, great wealth, and power, soon pulled away from God's instructions. He collected like trophies seven hundred wives and three hundred concubines, or female slave mistresses, from every people and culture with whom he came into contact—often receiving the new wives as part of diplomatic relations with other nations. This practice was expressly forbidden by God, who had stated that neither the people of Israel nor their king were to intermarry with other peoples. This was as terrible in God's view as the sexual impurity that came with having many wives and mistresses.

Does this prohibition against interracial marriage mean God is racist? Of course not. He is "no respecter of persons" (Acts 10:34). But, the prohibition wasn't centered on skin color; it was centered on faith. Solomon's intermarriages were often with women who believed in pagan gods. For example, one of the pagan gods worshipped by a number of Solomon's wives was Molech, the god to whom worshippers sacrificed babies in a stomach-turning ritual that involved placing the live infant into the outstretched, heated-to-scalding hands of the metal statue. Marriage to women like these was a slap in the face to the Lord, who declared Israel to be His wife. Solomon and the people had become like harlots in God's eyes; they had committed adultery.

The Bible says King Solomon was warned that such women would turn his heart from the true God. They certainly did. As a matter of fact, the king went so far as to build places of worship for these pagan women in areas surrounding Jerusalem.

Sin Exacts Price

God's people would pay a very high price for their sins. Jeremiah had prophesied the results of the people's unfaithfulness. He foretold the seventy years captivity of the children of Israel, the destruction of the Temple, and the fate of those who would destroy it:

> And it shall come to pass, when seventy years are accomplished, that I will punish the king of Babylon, and that nation, saith the LORD, for their iniquity, and the land of the Chaldeans, and will make it perpetual desolations.
>
> And I will bring upon that land all my words which I have

pronounced against it, even all that is written in this book, which Jeremiah hath prophesied against all the nations.
(Jeremiah 25:12–13)

God was angry because Solomon had turned his back on Him. However, Solomon finally came back to the Lord. Many scholars believe the book of Ecclesiastes to be the king's account of his foolish, wasted life away from God. The Lord, for David's sake, let Solomon live out his years as king with the Temple undisturbed. But Solomon's heirs, the future kings of Israel, would again be plagued by war. King Nebuchadnezzar of Babylon destroyed Solomon's magnificent Temple when in 586 BC the captain of his hosts, Nebuzaradan, ordered his invading forces to completely burn the Temple and all the houses of the most prominent men of Jerusalem. The magnificent Temple was destroyed and the people were driven out of the land of promise.

The kingdom was eventually divided into the northern kingdom of Israel and the southern kingdom of Judah. Twenty kings all total, some quite evil, a few quite good, ruled during this era. At one point, the Egyptians invaded and took many of Israel captive. All the while, the Temple continued to decline in beauty and glory until, just as Jeremiah prophesied, God's judgment on Babylon came to pass.

The Persians conquered that nation and, following Israel's seventy-year Babylonian prison sentence, allowed the children of Israel to return to the land. While many returned, some stayed in Babylon. Those who returned did so with the intention of rebuilding the Temple and the walls around Jerusalem. The return at that time is an amazing testimony to fulfilled prophecy. Although we haven't the space to devote to that story here, it is well worth the time and effort to delve into the matter to see how precisely this prophetic timeline was accomplished.

The Second Temple's foundation was laid in 535 BC and, after a number of delays, it was finally completed on March 12, 515 BC. That Temple sat in the middle of much turmoil. The Greeks defeated the

Persians. Then the Romans defeated and replaced the Greeks' control over the area. Herod the Great ruled in Israel, under Roman control, from about 47 BC to 4 BC. During his reign, around 20 BC, he launched a vast renovation of the structure, which involved enlarging the Temple as well as building courts and walls. The work continued beyond Herod's death to the year AD 63.

As discussed in an earlier chapter, Jesus, just before He was crucified, had prophesied the destruction of this Second Temple. His prophecy would come true thirty-something years later when Jewish revolts in the region surrounding Jerusalem brought attacks by Roman General Titus in AD 70. His forces besieged the city and the Temple Mount.

Titus actually wanted the Temple left undamaged. The Romans didn't wish to make the Jewish people angry, because they had their hands full fighting the revolutionaries in the area. Also, Titus argued that the Temple was a sort of treasure or jewel for the Roman Empire. Leaving it untouched would be best for Rome. But the Roman soldiers were used to having their way in any battle they fought. "To the victor goes the spoils" was their belief. Besides, the soldiers were resisted violently by rebels using the Temple as a fortress. This greatly angered the Romans and, despite the powerful general's orders not to harm the building that had stood in service for about 584 years, the troops were crazed. As discussed earlier in the book, they knew the holy house was covered in many places with silver, gold, and precious stones, and they set the building on fire so the precious metals adorning the walls, cracks, and crevices would melt and be more easily gathered. They would have their spoils of battle in a very big way! The Roman forces then took the place apart stone by stone to get at any precious metals or gems that might be found in the rubble, fulfilling with breathtakingly specific detail Jesus' prophecy to His disciples that "there shall not be left here one stone upon another, that shall not be thrown down" (Matthew 24:2). Later, upon the order of Caesar, the Temple Mount was plowed, salted, and smoothed flat.

Secular History Perspective

Jewish-Roman historian Flavius Josephus wrote the following eyewitness account of the events leading up to and during the destruction of the Second Temple in his history titled: "The Jewish War":

> In the morning Titus commanded that the fires should be put out and a road made to the gates to allow entry of his troops. His generals then came together to discuss what should be done with the temple. Some wanted to destroy it, because it would give the Jews a reason for uprising. Others argued that if the Jews would clear out of the temple it should be allowed to stand, but if they use it as a fortress, it should be destroyed. Titus then gave the command that no matter what happened, the temple should be spared, because it would always be an ornament to the empire. Three of his chief generals agreed, and the meeting was disbanded....
>
> Titus then went into Antonia, intending the next morning to attack and overwhelm the temple with his entire force. But on that day—the tenth of Lous [August 30, AD 70], the same day on which Solomon's temple had been destroyed by the king of Babylon, the structure was doomed. The rebels again attacked the Romans after Titus retreated, and a battle took place between the Temple guards and the Roman troops who were trying to put out the flames in the inner court. The Romans scattered the Jews and pursued them into the sanctuary. At that same time, a soldier recklessly grabbed a torch....
>
> He hurled the firestick through the doors of gold on the north side which allowed entry to chambers around the sanctuary. On seeing the flames, a cry went up from the Jews, and caring nothing for their lives, they rushed forward to put out the fire.
>
> A messenger rushed to the tent of Titus to inform him of the fire. Immediately, Titus ran to the temple to put out the flames.

But because of the battle that raged on, the soldiers either could not or would not hear his commands, or obey the waving of his hand. The wrath of his troops could not be stopped, and at the doorway many soldiers were trampled by their own forces. There among the burning ruins they fell, sharing the same fate as their enemies.

Pretending not to hear the commands of their general, and filled with hatred, the soldiers rushed on, hurling their torches into the temple. The helpless rebels made no attempt at defense. Fleeing for their lives, with bloodshed all around, many civilians were caught in the battle. Even the steps of the altar were stained with the blood of the dead.

When Caesar could not hold back his troops, he and his generals entered the temple and viewed for the last time the Most Holy Place. Since the fire had not yet reached the inside, but was still feeding on the outside chambers, Titus made one last effort to save it. Ordering a centurion to club anyone if they disobeyed his commands, He rushed forward and pleaded with his soldiers to put out the flames.

But because of their hatred of the Jews and the hope of plunder, the soldiers disregarded the orders of their general. Seeing that all the surroundings were made of gold, they assumed that the interior was filled with great treasure. And when Titus ran out to hold back his troops, one of those who had entered with him thrust a torch into the hinges of the temple gate, and a flame shot up inside. Caesar and his generals withdrew, and thus, against his wishes, the sanctuary was burned....

The city and the temple was then leveled to the ground by the command of Caesar. Only the highest towers and part of the western wall remained to show all mankind how the Romans overpowered such a strong fortress.[70]

Nasser's Nastiness

Most of the Jews eventually were put out of the land of promise following the Temple destruction, and they remain without a comparable place of worship to this day. Ancient hatreds followed them and they were never at rest, no matter where they resided. Yet the Jews again entered the land in significant numbers, and their enemies' rage soon caused hostilities to burst forth.

A modern Egyptian pharaoh's heart became harder and harder while he watched Israel's prosperity grow in the region now called Palestine. Gamal Abdel Nasser, who grabbed power in 1954, declared himself leader of the Muslim cause shortly after taking over in Egypt. He worked to get the British peacekeeping forces removed from the Suez Canal zone. This done, he put into motion his devilish plan to destroy all the Jews in the region.

With the British gone, Soviet ships soon brought weapons of war to the Arab forces through the Suez Canal on a regular basis. The Soviets thereby gained an increasingly strong foothold in the Middle East. At the same time, Nasser refused to let Israel use the canal to ship and receive shipments necessary to their national life. He commanded the respect and fear of all Arab nations in the area in 1956.

The Egyptian president was leader of the Arab League, whose member nations included Egypt, Jordan, Syria, Iraq, Lebanon, and Saudi Arabia, as well as less significant Arab states. The league vowed to push the new Jewish state into the Mediterranean Sea. Despite Israel having won tremendous—some say miraculous—victories to gain independence in 1948, now the small nation's hard-won freedom hung in the balance, and a monstrous fight was shaping up.

The Nasser-led Arab league put its forces in place, intent on totally wiping Israel off the land. Israel's people wanted only peace after all the war they had fought so recently. But they took a collective deep breath and gathered their weapons yet again. They fought with great bravery against forces more than six times their numbers.

Before long, Britain and France joined the battle in the Israeli cause. Israel did much more than defend its land; it took through battle huge portions of its aggressor enemies' territory. Only the United Nations stepping in and bringing about a peace of sorts kept the Arab league from losing much, much more land to the Israeli forces.

It was just as Zechariah had prophesied:

In that day will I make the governors of Judah like an hearth of fire among the wood, and like a torch of fire in a sheaf; and they shall devour all the people round about, on the right hand and on the left: and Jerusalem shall be inhabited again in her own place, even in Jerusalem. (12:6)

The leaders of the Jews were like burning torches lighting fires in the Arab League straw! Although Zechariah's prophecy undoubtedly is for the Tribulation period, the fighting foreshadowed things to come in the cauldron known as the Middle East.

Also like the Zechariah 12 foretelling, soon Jerusalem would again be firmly if not safely inhabited by the children of Israel. The Temple storm continued to build.

Rome Fulfills Temple Mount Prophecy

If the Roman Caesar had ordered the Temple Mount cleared off, plowed, and salted thinking it would make the site undesirable to future people who might again begin fighting over it, he was mistaken. No piece of real estate in the world is as desired as the Temple Mount.

Rome didn't know it, but it had fulfilled prophecy: "Therefore shall Zion for your sake be plowed as a field, and Jerusalem shall become heaps, and the mountain of the house as the high places of the forest" (Micah 3:12). Just as Micah said, Zion had been "plowed" and Jerusalem is now built upon many "heaps" of former city structures.

The Arab League, controlled by Muslim radicals, was bent on keeping the Jews from claiming any part of Mount Moriah. Certainly, in Nasser's mind, there would never be a Jewish Temple built there.

The Al-Aqsa Mosque, most often called the "Dome of the Rock," was built on the Temple Mount in AD 687. The golden-domed building, the most recognizable landmark in Jerusalem, is the major obstacle standing in the way of the Jews building the Third Temple, which is prophesied to be on top of Mount Moriah during the Tribulation period. (See chapter 15 for more on the Third Temple.)

Arabs' All-Out Assault

Nasser again stirred the Arab enemies of Israel to action in 1967. The Egyptian president and his fellow Israel-haters announced in Cairo, Egypt, that the Strait of Hormuz, which controlled access to the Gulf of Aqaba, would be closed to Israeli shipping. If action against this wasn't taken, Israel's ability to move into the Red Sea by water would be stopped. The nation's lifeblood of imported supplies would be slowed to a trickle.

Nasser told the United Nations secretary-general that he was kicking UN peacekeeping forces out of Egyptian territory. When Egyptian military forces rumbled into the Sinai Peninsula, which had formerly been a zone to buffer between Israel and Egypt, Israel's Air Force went on alert status.

Egypt began shelling Israeli border towns on June 6, 1967. Israel's Air Force struck back violently. Israeli planes took out targets with precision strikes in Egypt, Jordan, and Syria. Israeli jet fighters completely dominated the air, downing hundreds of Egyptian, Jordanian, and Syrian planes. Israeli victories were greater in scope than Israeli victories in the 1948 and 1956 wars combined, according to some military experts.

Enemy troops fled under the Israeli onslaught. The casualties of battle were light on both sides, many historians believe, because the Arab League forces did not stand and fight.

General Moshe Dayan declared victory on behalf of Israel in the lightning-like Six Day War of 1967. The city of Jerusalem was now in the hands of the Israeli government, concluding a string of events that seem to be a small preview of His mighty work to come on behalf of His chosen people described in Zechariah 12:

> The LORD also shall save the tents of Judah first, that the glory of the house of David and the glory of the inhabitants of Jerusalem do not magnify themselves against Judah.
>
> In that day shall the LORD defend the inhabitants of Jerusalem; and he that is feeble among them at that day shall be as David; and the house of David shall be as God, as the angel of the LORD before them. (Zechariah 12:7–8)

Dayan's Dumbfounding Deed

Israel totally defeated its enemies, despite the fact that the enemy nations' populations added up to 63 million people as compared to Israel's 3 million. Even so, the Israeli leaders, as usual, still didn't get it.

God gave Israel the victory, but General Dayan, truly a great military hero, turned around and did a thing that flabbergasts most people who think they understand what the Bible says about Jerusalem, the Temple, and the Jewish people. He gave the Temple Mount, which Israel had just won back after so many centuries, to the enemy Islamic leadership.

The prophet Micah, who said the following, must have rolled his eyes in heaven:

> Thus saith the LORD concerning the prophets that make my people err, that bite with their teeth, and cry, Peace; and he that putteth not into their mouths, they even prepare war against him....

Hear this, I pray you, ye heads of the house of Jacob, and princes of the house of Israel, that abhor judgment, and pervert all equity.

They build up Zion with blood, and Jerusalem with iniquity. (Micah 3:5; 9–10)

The heads of God's chosen nation again had listened to the world's voices rather than to the Lord God of Israel. All the world had done for the Jewish people since the time of the first Egyptian bondage and even before that was to try to do away with them. In spite of the historical record of the bloody trail left by the red dragon's tail as he trampled generation after generation of the house of Israel, Dayan seemed totally blind rather than having a patch over only one eye when he gave control of that site back to the Arab Palestine Islamists. The normally very wise Jewish leader and the Israeli government should have known better.

With destroyed Soviet war machinery littering the desert battle zones, Soviet Prime Minister Alexei Kosygin had the audacity to demand in the United Nations that Israel pay for Egyptian losses. He insisted that Israel be roundly condemned for "aggression" against the Arab League nations. Although neither of Kosygin's stipulations was carried out, United Nations and world media pressures built to the point that Dayan returned the Temple Mount, the most important piece of real estate on earth, in the name of so-called peace. As we know, there is still no peace in the Middle East.

World diplomats and the world media had watched as the evidence of Adolf Hitler's satanic evil was revealed after World War II. It was the latest of atrocities committed against God's chosen people. Jewish victims' flesh was literally flayed from their bones to make lampshades and other things. Their leg bones were used to make table legs. Their bodies were burned and crushed to bits and pieces in the crematoriums of Europe.

The internationalist diplomats and media still don't seem to see as unreasonable the great pressures placed upon the Jewish people and the nation Israel—nor do the leaders of Israel seem to realize that land and other concessions can never bring true peace. Micah's words on behalf of the God of Israel still have not gotten through to many in that nation:

> And I said, Hear, I pray you, O heads of Jacob, and ye princes of the house of Israel; Is it not for you to know judgment?
>
> Who hate the good, and love the evil; who pluck off their skin from off them, and their flesh from off their bones;
>
> Who also eat the flesh of my people, and flay their skin from off them; and they break their bones, and chop them in pieces, as for the pot, and as flesh within the caldron. (Micah 3:1–3)

Israel Isolated

Astonishingly, Israel was looked at as the aggressor against the Arab League, rather than the other way around. This is the view of most of the world's geopolitical observers today. The internationalist powers that be, for the most part, continue to isolate that small country in terms of meddling in an independent state's sovereignty.

For example, the UN continues to stick its diplomatic nose in all of Israel's business. Additionally, whenever missiles fly from Gaza or from points north, the current American president, in concert with the international community hand-wringers, pressures Israel to take it without retaliation against the actual aggressors. From Israel's dealings with its Palestinian citizens to its election process and its choice of weapons development and deployment (putting into service), the "international community"—in effect, the UN—tries to influence every aspect of Israel's business. At the same time, the UN often looks the other way when nations like Somalia and China commit human-rights violations. The organization talks big, but lets Islamist dictators violate practically every known human right.

The United Nations, along with the European Union, has for a number of years sought to put a peacekeeping force in the Israeli-governed areas of dispute. The UN and EU would, in that case, violate the sovereignty of the nation. They want to control Jerusalem, not merely the problems between the Israeli military and the radical Palestinian militarists. Look for that intervention in things to do with Jerusalem to ratchet up in the not-too-distant future. Such a scenario could be the forerunner of the prophecy involving the peace covenant found in Daniel 9:26 and 27.

It seems as if the words of Micah 2 are aimed right at the world's diplomatic community:

> Woe to them that devise iniquity, and work evil upon their beds! when the morning is light, they practise it, because it is in the power of their hand.
> And they covet fields, and take them by violence; and houses, and take them away: so they oppress a man and his house, even a man and his heritage. (Micah 2:1–2)

It's as if they stay awake at night devising ways to give Israel's enemies advantages so they can get more land for a peace the diplomats know the terrorists will never honor.

But the God of heaven has given the land to His chosen people. Jerusalem is the apple of God's eye, and He pronounces a curse on those who devise to take or keep that land from them. The Lord still intends to honor His promises to Abraham and his descendants.

Sharon's Shocker

God draws the Jewish people as a nation to the Temple Mount like a powerful magnet attracts iron, and He directs their attention to Zion, where Israel's Messiah will one day sit upon the throne of King David. Although back in the land in unbelief at present, the Jewish people obviously instinctively sense that this one holy site holds their destiny.

As recounted earlier, Ariel Sharon, Israel's former prime minister who lay in a coma since suffering a stroke in 2006, shocked the Middle East peace process when, before he became prime minister, he went to the top of the Temple Mount on September 28, 2000. Sharon, the last of the old leadership of Israel, a former defense minister, and former Israeli Defense Forces (IDF) major general, made the trip to protest then Prime Minister Ehud Barak's action concerning the Temple Mount.

Remember, Barak had turned over the Jewish holy site to Palestinian Liberation Organization (PLO) Chairman Yasser Arafat after first instructing Israeli foreign minister, Shlomo Ben-Ami, to plead with Arafat to honor Jewish rights to worship at the Temple Mount traditional worship sites. Arafat, of course, had no intention of honoring such a request, according to most pro-Israeli observers.

Sharon's march to the top of the Temple Mount with an armed guard for protection set off Arab Islamic fundamentalist radicals' anger. The radical Arab Islamics whipped many thousands of Palestinians into a frenzy of rioting, which brought quick and firm armed responses by Israeli police and military.

Terrorist Troublemakers

Terrorist troublemakers finally got what they wanted and needed to stir many people against the Jewish state. Most of the deadly terrorist groups within radical Islam, such as Apah, Hamas, Islamic Jihad, Hezbollah, etc., no doubt did all they could to make the fires of rioting as hot as possible.

The words of Psalms 7 speak for themselves:

God judgeth the righteous, and God is angry with the wicked every day.

If he turn not, he will whet his sword; he hath bent his bow, and made it ready.

He hath also prepared for him the instruments of death; he ordaineth his arrows against the persecutors.

Behold, he travaileth with iniquity, and hath conceived mischief, and brought forth falsehood.

He made a pit, and digged it, and is fallen into the ditch which he made.

His mischief shall return upon his own head, and his violent dealing shall come down upon his own pate. (11–16)

These are God's words of warning to those who conceive and carry out persecution of the innocent. Such evil will eventually come down on their own heads. And, the Israeli police and military, though showing great restraint in using deadly force, proved themselves willing and able to see that the most violent troublemakers among the rioters receive the response they earned. News cameras, however, focused almost exclusively on the few children who, tragically, were struck by gunfire. The Israeli troops, of course, got the blame, regardless of the facts.

Ariel Ascends

Ariel Sharon not only ascended Mount Moriah to stand in a place the Islamic authorities forbade Jews to stand; he ascended to be prime minister of Israel. Then, when he was in his seventies, Sharon had seen the lies and false promises of Arafat and his terroristic brothers over the years. He would not be duped, as had been his predecessor, the former Prime Minister Barak. The people of Israel, for the most part, seemed to know that; his election to the nation's top office proved it.

The God of Israel long ago promised His chosen people that crying and lamenting over being cast away from Temple worship would get them nowhere. They must change their ways and call upon the Lord of their protection and salvation—then they will be allowed to build and worship in the Temple.

These things will happen. But it will be a painful journey back to their blessed Temple Mount. It will take the Great Tribulation spoken of by Jeremiah the prophet and the Lord Jesus Christ to convince them as a people to turn to their Messiah in repentance.

CHAPTER 12

MIDDLE EAST MADNESS

THE DEVASTATING ATTACKS that brought down the massive towers of the World Trade Center are forever burned into our thoughts. Those horrific assaults are only the tip of the iceberg. Hatred runs deep within the world today. Sometimes it seems like the whole planet has gone mad.

Anger comes at us from every direction. Have you driven in your town lately? Do you get honked at or shouted at if you don't move quite fast enough away from a stop sign or light turned green? Have you had any wild-eyed motorists cut in front of you or do something just as aggressive?

It seems that a new level of such outrage behind the wheel was ushered into our time during the oil crisis of the 1970s. Remember the short tempers in the very long gasoline filling station lines? Of course, many will not remember that unpleasantness. They were either too young or weren't even born yet.

There is a madness today, an insanity of sorts. It is Middle Eastern in its origin as surely as were the causes of those long gas station lines of several decades ago. Terrorism at the heart of that bloody madness threatens to involve the whole world in war.

A news report from some time ago frames in horrific reality the terrors the people of Israel face daily:

Israel called off its self-declared policy of restraint on Saturday, just hours after a suicide bomber killed 18 young people in the bloodiest terror attack the nation has seen in five years.

All but one of those killed and many of the wounded were recent immigrants from the former Soviet Union.

The Israeli Cabinet said after a seven-hour emergency session—an extremely rare occurrence on the Jewish Sabbath—that it held Palestinian leader Yasser Arafat directly responsible for Friday night's blast and other terror attacks....

Asked about the truce, Transport Minister Ephraim Sneh told The Associated Press that "there is no cease-fire because we are under attack."

The explosion, heard for miles around the city, went off around 11 p.m. Friday in front of the Pacha nightclub in a former aquarium building that faces a promenade lined with restaurants, bars, hotels and office towers.

"I was about to enter (the disco), suddenly I looked in the direction of the blast, I saw people thrown backward," said Dudi Nachum, 21. "I saw parts of a brain, things I have never seen before. It was terrible."

Bodies covered by white and black tarps lay on the ground in front of the entrance to the nightclub. One of the victims appeared to be a girl in her early teens, wearing a red top, her arms and legs sticking out, platform shoes on her feet.

Hospital officials said 17 Israelis were killed, including two sisters, ages 16 and 18. Of the wounded, 15 remained in critical or serious condition Saturday....

The explosive contained ball bearings, nails and screws that caused particularly severe injuries when they flew out in all directions.

About a dozen cars parked in front of the club were heavily damaged by the blast, their windows shattered and pieces of flesh and blood splattered on them....

On Saturday morning, crowds of angry Israelis gathered outside the Defense Ministry in Tel Aviv, where the Cabinet was meeting, and at the gates of a mosque across the street from the disco. Demonstrators chanted "Death to the Arabs" and demanded that Sharon order harsh retaliation. Several people threw stones at Muslim worshippers emerging from the mosque.

Since fighting erupted last September, 484 people have been killed on the Palestinian side—including Friday's attacker—and 104 on the Israeli side.

Friday's blast was the deadliest since a series of suicide bombings by Islamic militants in the spring of 1996.

There were conflicting reports about who was responsible for the attack. The Qatar-based Al Jazeera satellite station said a group calling itself the Palestinian Hezbollah claimed responsibility. Abu Dhabi TV said the assailant apparently was a member of the militant Islamic Jihad group from the West Bank town of El Bireh.[71]

The Region's Raging Resentments

Things haven't changed much since the time King David penned the words, "Shew thy marvellous lovingkindness, O thou that savest by thy right hand them which put their trust in thee from those that rise up against them" (Psalms 17:7). Enemies surround the shepherd boy's once and future throne. They are passionately determined to do away with Israel and everything to do with it.

Again, to be fair, many Arabs—some who are Israeli citizens—

harbor no such hatreds. As a matter of fact, there are a growing number of Arab Christians and other Christians who are not Jews in the region now called Palestine. They are true children of the living God and wish only to live in peace. Jerusalem and all of the area of Palestine is the only home they have known. But Israel's enemies surround that small nation and number in the millions. Their rage has made itself known in several major wars.

Envy Escalates

Following the Arab League defeat in 1956, Israel was pressured, through UN influence, to give back much of the land it had won in battle. Gamal Abdel Nasser, despite having been soundly beaten in that conflict, nonetheless claimed the victory.

In the Middle Eastern culture, even overwhelming defeat can be viewed as an overwhelming victory by the aggressors. Nasser declared himself winner. Therefore, in the minds of millions of angry, resentful Arabs who hated Israel, Nasser became a hero of almost mythical proportion.

Israel still possessed much of the land it took from its enemies. The Arab League members were furious and more determined than ever to avenge their losses. Nasser again began preaching jihad against the Jewish state. Arab factions fanned smoldering sparks of resentments and envy into full-fledged flames of war. Even the very young of the Arab radicals got caught up in the frenzy. The Arabs opened the Suez Canal again to Soviet ships, bringing them a tremendous number of weapons for the war soon to come.

The words of David's psalm must have echoed within the fears of the religious Jews and Christians who knew the dangers:

Keep me as the apple of the eye, hide me under the shadow of thy wings, From the wicked that oppress me, from my deadly enemies, who compass me about....deliver my soul from the wicked, which is thy sword. (Psalms 17:8–9; 13b)

Israel did indeed need the protective wings of the Lord at that crucial moment in the nation's troubled history.

Beatings, Brutality, and Bombs

Middle East madness continued to grow in violence, despite a sort of peace between 1970 and 1973. Police and military on all sides sometimes looked the other way when vicious beatings took place in disputed areas where races and religions mingled. Terrorists crawled from their holes to cause death and damage whenever they could. Bombings and shootings as well as incidents involving stone-throwing grew, particularly in parts of Jerusalem. Religious differences, the most ancient of all hatreds, became an ever-growing problem that was getting harder to control. The Temple Mount, as always, was the chief spot of resentment and rage.

Resentment among the Islamic factions grew into demonstrations, then into violent confrontation with Israeli military forces in Jerusalem and surrounding areas. As discussed earlier, the Islamic authorities were given the Temple Mount by Moshe Dayan and the Israeli government following Israel's victory over the Arab League forces in the 1967 Six Day War. Still, great anger grew over the fact that Israel now claimed Jerusalem to be under that nation's control. Racial strife increased daily between Arabs and Jews. Rioting broke out in Jerusalem and the surrounding areas. Terrorism was a more serious problem. Threat of death and injury sometimes caused Israeli troops to react with deadly force, and the conflict grew worse.

Religious Jews, too, became increasingly restless, desiring to worship freely around the Temple Mount. This caused resistance everywhere and every time such worship was attempted. The rumble of war was on the horizon!

Arab League Lightning

The world had gotten another preview of how Israel's protector-God will ultimately deal with those who want to destroy that nation when Moshe Dayan gave back the Temple Mount. But Israel annexed the old city of Jerusalem, the part that is most ancient (some of it was there in Christ's time), bringing howls of protest by nations around the world. The pushback came not only from the Arab countries, but from Europe, Russia, and, sadly, the United States as well. Jews were again in control of the city.

Now, the 1949 ceasefire lines that had divided the areas controlled by Jordan from those controlled by Israel were erased. New lines replaced the old ones. Judaea and Samaria, Gaza, and the Sinai Peninsula were now controlled by the Jewish state. This new arrangement freed Israel's northern villages from exposure to Syrian shelling, something they had endured for nineteen years. Also, shipping to and from Israel could proceed safely through the Straits of Tehran.

United Nations Resolution 242 called for acknowledgment of the sovereignty, territorial integrity, and political independence of each state in the region. All nations were to have the right to live peacefully within diplomatically recognized and secure borders. They were all to be free from threats by their neighbors. Arab radical militants had other ideas.

The Khartoum Conference in August 1967 produced angry declarations. The Arabs vowed there would be no peace with Israel, nor would there be any negotiations with or recognition of the Jewish state. Egypt began to provoke Israel with armed actions along the banks of the Suez Canal in 1968. Fighting increased.

Small-arms clashes were followed by duels between heavy artillery and fighting between Israeli and Palestinian guerillas. There were mounting casualties on both sides until a UN-arranged ceasefire in 1970.

Diplomatic Deceivers

Once again, the powers that be in the UN and the world's diplomatic community made promises they couldn't keep. The Israeli government was given assurances that the UN peacekeepers would act as a buffer between Israel and enemy Arab aggressors.

Israel again gave in to the international pressure, once more agreeing to allow UN forces to serve as a buffer. But Arab rage continued to burn because of the displacement of millions of Arab people, who either left the war zones because of danger or were forced to leave by the Israelis or others. In truth, however, it was the actions of the Arab leadership that caused the displacement; those leaders had inflicted two decades of hate-filled conflict upon Israel. They had no one to blame but themselves for the refugee problems.

The Arab world grew angrier and angrier against their ancient—and at the same time modern—enemy. Despite the fact that it was the Arabs threatening war, the nations of the world looked at Israel as the stumbling block to peace in the Middle East.

Israeli military leaders had to be alert to the collective Arab force, which faked one military thrust after another. These war games, the Israeli generals knew, were not games at all, but preparation for yet another sudden strike. Although there was a lack of all-out war during the years 1970 to 1973, Israel could enjoy little feeling of peace.

Stunning 1973 Strike

Like the word of God says in Hosea 4:1, the Lord does seem to have "a controversy with the inhabitants of the land," even today. It seems that war is made for the land, and the land is made for war.

Again, as we've explored earlier, when Egyptian and Syrian forces suddenly attacked on October 6, 1973—Yom Kippur, also known as the Day of Atonement and Israel's holiest day of the year—the Arab forces, led by Egypt's President Anwar Sadat, struck in a two-pronged attack on Israel. Egyptian military forces invaded from the east across the Suez Canal, pushing back the Israeli defenders. At the same time, Syrian forces, with the help of Iraq, Jordan, Libya, and smaller Arab nation military forces, attacked from the north. The Israelis were taken off guard by the swiftness of the assaults. It took several days to fully get their forces together and on the offensive. Bloodshed once again plagued the land of promise.

Another Israeli Victory

Israel met the aggressors head on, caused them to turn and retreat, then pursued them into their own territory. Israeli forces advanced to within twenty miles of the Syrian capital of Damascus. They also crossed the Suez Canal and advanced well within Egyptian territory. Israel accomplished complete victory within three weeks and again captured huge chunks of its enemy's land.

Costs in lives were much heavier in the 1973 war than in the 1967 conflict, however. Both sides suffered more death and injuries because the Arab forces fought more fiercely rather than choosing to retreat.

Two years of negotiations between Israel, Egypt, and Syria brought the return of much of the captured lands. Great pressure from the UN was applied in the process, mostly upon Israel. Israel nonetheless kept the Golan Heights for defensive purposes.

Sheiks Punish U.S.

Although the Arab world had no nuclear bombs, it dropped something almost as powerful: an oil embargo. This allowed the Arabs to get even with those who supported Israel in the best way they knew how. They cut off oil supplies to the United States as well as other nations to a lesser extent.

The oil sheiks, particularly those among the royal family of Saudi

Arabia, let the U.S., supposedly their good friend, know their opinion of our standing by their number-one enemy, Israel. Saudi oil sheiks led OPEC in the embargo. By 1974, the price of oil had risen to a level four times greater than the pre-1973 Mideast war price of oil. The idea was to punish America and most of Europe for supplying Israel with arms and other goods, and for their diplomatic support of that country as well. The Arab nations' method of punishment was very effective indeed.

The tremendous rise in prices, along with the embargo, had a terrible influence on prices worldwide throughout the rest of the 1970s. The latter part of that decade saw greatly inflated prices on practically every consumer product sold to people in the United States. But nowhere in the world were more troubles created than at gasoline service stations in America.

Oil Crisis Craziness

Oil prices went from about three dollars per barrel in 1972 to about twelve dollars per barrel by March 1974. These prices seem puny by today's standards, but the results of the increase during that era were profound. Energy prices paid by consumers went higher and higher. Purchasing by consumers and investments in business ventures slowed dramatically. Worldwide recession was the outcome. This meant that less money was in circulation. Companies didn't sell as much; people lost their jobs. It was a vicious cycle the world, and particularly America, couldn't stop. Still, prices of goods of practically every kind went higher and higher. This was inflation, meaning that costs were much higher than normal.

One of the worst effects of the oil crisis of 1973–1974 was that it brought out the ugly side of America's people in many cases. This side of America included both buyers and sellers. The term "price gouging" came into the language to describe what happened when companies raised prices unnecessarily. Buyers, on the other hand, became angry and, in many cases, unruly because of the rise in prices. More than that, they often turned violent because of the inconvenience to their lifestyles.

Having to wait in the long lines created by gasoline shortages drove many wild. If you think people are rude today when it comes to their cars, trucks, and other vehicles, it was pretty bad back then, too. Horror stories emerged from the gas crisis of 1973–1974. Many who didn't want to wait to get their ration of gasoline tried to pay others to get their ration and move ahead in the lines. Curse fights and fistfights broke out often. Deliberate ramming of vehicles into other vehicles, out of anger and frustration, happened more than once. Knifings and shootings were not unheard of in those long lines.

Prophecy students of those times could easily look at 2 Timothy 3 and declare that the last days had definitely arrived: "Men shall be… incontinent, fierce." Otherwise calm, rational people sometimes turned into gangster-like thugs in those awful lines, particularly in the big cities.

Make no mistake: The Middle East oil sheiks still have tremendous power. The madness from that region continues to threaten major problems in the highly mobile, industrial nations of the world. In my thinking on what future situations might develop, with the multi-trillion-dollar deficits continuing to build in America and the other nations, economic enslavement, shaped by oil's influences, presents a threat of profound proportions.

Despite the alternate fuel sources such as solar, nuclear, and others being developed, petroleum still is said to be the fuel of necessity for the foreseeable future. As we've seen in previous chapters, that region holds the majority of most cheaply accessible oil reserves. At the same time, radical environmentalists' ludicrous assertions that the planet is being destroyed by fossil fuel carbon emissions control the thinking of national and global politicians. That minority influence prevents new drilling and new techniques for extracting oil that would greatly decrease the need for such intensive interactions with Mideast oil suppliers. Again, it is the Middle East oil madness that will no doubt bring all nations into conflict at Armageddon.

Prime Minister Befriends Foe

Well, maybe "befriends" isn't exactly the right word at this point. However, the two Middle Eastern leaders did achieve a friendship of sorts before the matters were concluded. Even with the hatreds against his nation, Israeli Prime Minister Menachem Begin called for a comprehensive peace negotiation with the Arab leaders. Egypt's President Anwar Sadat, himself once a fierce fighter as a general in Egypt's army, courageously answered the call to the peace table.

Sadat Softens

Begin first extended an invitation to Sadat to visit Israel—even though Sadat had been the top leader against Israel in the 1973 Yom Kippur War. The Egyptian president graciously accepted, coming to Jerusalem in January 1977 to address the Israeli Knessett, that nation's legislature. The visit went well and the new era of peace between the two nations began. The American government was invited to act as a go-between for the process, and the Carter administration eagerly said, "Yes."

Egyptian President Anwar Sadat and Israeli Prime Minister Menachem Begin forged a peace agreement on March 26, 1979, in Washington, D.C., with U.S. President Jimmy Carter looking on. Source: Library of Congress

The Israeli prime minister and the Egyptian president were successful in negotiating a peace treaty between their nations. Thirty years of constant war between Egypt and Israel came to an end when the two leaders signed the peace documents on March 26, 1979, in Washington, D.C. With U.S. President Jimmy Carter standing between Begin and Sadat in the White House Rose Garden, the peace that had been agreed to while at Camp David on September 8, 1978, was affirmed by the two leaders shaking hands.

Though Egypt and Israel haven't gone to war since that time, Arab hatreds in other Arab nations have grown. Sadat, whom I believe truly wanted peace for both nations, paid a high price for his bravery. He was assassinated by an angry Islamic militant terrorist on October 6, 1981.

Interestingly, many prophecy scholars don't find Egypt mentioned in the predicted attack against Israel in Ezekiel chapters 38 and 39. However, it is clear that the clouds of war still rumble atop Moriah!

Barak's Bizarre Bargaining

An unfaithful wife seems one of the most tragic of situations that involve human relationships (an unfaithful husband, likewise). Israel is, in God's all-seeing view, His wife. He has married that nation through His covenants with her. He refers to Israel in many places in the Bible as being like an unfaithful wife. The nation has more often than not pulled away from his loving kindness and has worshipped false gods.

Always, the Lord disciplines those who are His own. Israel has, therefore, gone into bondage after being put out of the Promised Land on a number of occasions. God says about the matter of Israel's unfaithfulness: "And I said unto her, Thou shalt abide for me many days; thou shalt not play the harlot, and thou shalt not be for another man: so will I also be for thee" (Hosea 3:3).

God disciplines those He loves, but He never kicks them out of His family. Israel has always returned to Him, seeking His help in getting out of one bad situation or another. The other nations and their gods have been like adulterous Israel's lovers. God has therefore given the nation over to them. Those nations and their material goods have constantly abused Israel and treated her like a harlot.

When, in 1999, Israel Prime Minister Ehud Barak offered Yasser Arafat an unbelievably large portion of Israel's tiny territory in exchange for peace, God's holy eyes must have filled with tears of rejection. The Lord had seen Israel through many battles: the 1948 war of independence; the 1956 war against Arab enemies; the 1967 Six Day War; the 1973 Yom Kippur War…God had given Israel victory after victory. Yet Barak, with the agreement of many of his fellow Israelis, timidly offered a terrorist enemy land that God Himself had given Israel.

Barak even offered Arafat full control of Mount Moriah, the Temple Mount! All of the things this leader offered to give away for the hope of a peace that will never be realized were not his to give. The land and the Temple Mount are God's alone. The world's international community called it a courageous thing to do. Those who knew better called it foolishness at best and insanity at worst.

Deadly, Deceptive Enemy

At the time, American President Bill Clinton reportedly sent his political campaign team to help Ehud Barak take Israel from Prime Minister Benjamin Netanyahu. Barak's victory wasn't a surprise. The people of Israel were taken in by the claims of the internationalist media and others who made Israel's government mostly responsible for the lack of progress in the peace process.

Of course, it wasn't true. Israel's enemies, starting with the PLO and its chairman, Arafat, never had intentions of agreeing to the Israeli state.

It was true that Netanyahu was an obstacle. He refused to give in to the PLO, the other terrorist organizations, and to the internationalist media and diplomatic community. He stood firm, while playing the PLO game better than the PLO played it. He "agreed to agree" to talk things over, but never gave in to the deadly demands of giving away vital land for peace.

The voters of Israel did what their enemies couldn't do. They cleared the path for negotiating away their birthright, the land given the Jews by the Lord God. In a wishy-washy display of deluded disregard for his nation, Ehud Barak—who had been critical of the Oslo Accords that had been aimed at robbing Israel of its defensively strategic territory (mainly, the Golan Heights)—as the new prime minister decided to give in to his newfound friends. Those friends, Arafat and the internationalists, praised him as a great leader in the cause of peace.

Arafat's Phony Friendliness

Barak was aware of the treacherous nature of PLO chairman Yasser Arafat. As an Israeli soldier, Barak had seen the brutal Arafat's murderous activities up close. During the Lebanon war, Barak served as the second in command of an armored corps made up of about one thousand tanks. He fought bravely and enthusiastically with the courageous Israel Defense Forces troops whose job it was to remove Arafat and his ten thousand terrorists from Beirut.

It is all the more amazing, therefore, that upon becoming Israel's prime minister, Barak fell for Arafat's posed smiles for news cameras and phony hints at peace. Even the assassinated leader Yitzhak Rabin, when he was prime minister, would never have considered using the Temple Mount as a bargaining chip. Both Rabin and Barak called the ultra-liberal Labor Party their political home. Both men, though considered brave warriors during their military service, were, astonishingly, willing to give away land for peace.

But Barak's concessions went further than Rabin's, whose widow, Leah Rabin, said on her deathbed, "Yitzhak would turn in his grave if he were to see the concessions Ehud is making in Jerusalem."[72] Even United Nations officials and America's liberal network news anchors seemed surprised when Barak offered 90 percent of what Arafat and the Palestinian Authority demanded in return for peace. They were surprised, not because the equally liberal-minded Barak offered the many concessions, but that Arafat turned down the offer.

The bottom line for today is that there is only one way to satisfy the Israeli haters in Palestine: Israel must cease to be a nation!

Sharon's Staunch Stand

The LORD hath also a controversy with Judah, and will punish Jacob according to his ways; according to his doings will he recompense him.

He took his brother by the heel in the womb, and by his strength he had power with God:

Yea, he had power over the angel, and prevailed: he wept, and made supplication unto him: he found him in Bethel, and there he spake with us;

Even the LORD God of hosts; the Lord is his memorial. Therefore turn thou to thy God: keep mercy and judgment and wait on thy God continually....

And I that am the LORD thy God from the land of Egypt will yet make thee to dwell in tabernacles, as in the days of the solemn feast. (Hosea 12:2–6; 9)

Jacob continued to pay for his trickery against his brother and his father Isaac for the rest of his life. Even with his heart changed toward God and his name changed to Israel, his treacherous dealings with others continually came back to haunt him.

Laban, Jacob's uncle, tricked the younger man by giving Jacob his daughter Leah for a wife instead of his daughter Rachel—this, after Jacob (now Israel) had worked for Laban for seven years for the opportunity to marry Rachel. Laban then said Jacob could have Rachel if he would work yet another seven years. Jacob's own sons tricked him by selling their brother Joseph into slavery; the boys told their father Jacob that an animal had apparently killed him.

Jacob's chickens had come home to roost, as the southern saying goes. The Bible says it the correct way. "Your sins will find you out" (Numbers 32:23). Or, as God's Word also says, "Whatsoever a man soweth, that shall he also reap" (Galatians 6:7). Our sins may be forgiven by God's matchless grace, but the consequences of our earlier sins still usually come home to us. God doesn't guarantee to suspend His natural laws in this life.

Israel continues to suffer from Jacob's sins, in a sense. The tribes of Israel, fathered by Jacob's sons, have throughout their history gone far away from their God. They are back in the land in unbelief today. That is, most Jews are more worldly than religious. Certainly more are secular than they are godly.

God has always dealt with His people when they strayed from Him, as we've looked at in depth. He continues to deal with them today. Their amazing, puzzling troubles in the land of promise today relate directly to their unbelief. But the Lord has planted in their hearts their need for Him. This deep longing for the God of their fathers is what brought Ariel Sharon to the Temple Mount on September 28, 2000. The Likud party leader, who would soon replace Barak as prime minister, probably didn't consider that he went atop Moriah as the beginning of the journey back to God for his people. But that was the effect. Again, it will be a long, hard return. But, Sharon, I believe, took the first steps in that direction.

Sharon going to the Temple Mount with a heavily armed guard was a political more than a religious move in the leader's view, no doubt. He was showing Barak, the Israeli people, the Palestinian Islamic radicals, and the world that the Temple Mount would never be given away in a land-for-peace deal. He was telling the world that this was the very heart and soul of the land God gave the Jew.

Barak himself said during a visit to Egyptian President Hosni Mubarek, "By his [Sharon's] visit to the Temple Mount, Sharon challenged my policy, as he had the right to do." Why Barak had a policy to give away the Temple Mount to Arafat is beyond figuring out. But, Barak, by his own words, implied that the Jews have a right to the Temple Mount.

Ariel Sharon stood staunchly atop Mount Moriah, thereby declaring Israel will never give up the holiest of its sites. Again, it was the first step in Israel's return to the God of its fathers.

Jacob repented. He had wrestled with the angel of the Lord at Bethel, hanging on with all his might until God blessed him. If the people of Israel will but turn their attention to God, He has promised to "yet make [them] to dwell in tabernacles, as in the days of the solemn feast" (Hosea 12:9).

Palestinian Powder Keg

Even though Yasser Arafat rejected the unbelievably comprehensive land and political giveaways that included the Temple Mount in return for a mere hope of peace, the Palestinian Islamic fanatics went berserk when Sharon went to the top of Moriah.

The Islamic radicals used the visit to stir up Islamic Palestinians. It was reported that two hundred thousand to three hundred thousand people demonstrated following Sharon's action. From the demonstrations came acts of violence against people and property within Jerusalem and outlying areas.

Ariel Sharon seemed to have changed his mind. Before he was elected to Israel's highest office, he was totally against two states, Israel and the proposed new Palestinian nation. As prime minister, he sometimes talked of the possibility of giving approval to a separate state.

It was obvious to most who truly understood Sharon's mind during the time of that situation and circumstance in the region that he played the same sort of sly political games former and future Prime Minister Benjamin Netanyahu plays today. Netanyahu is a master of that game to the very moment of the writing of this sentence.

Sharon, like Netanyahu, agrees to talk about the matter of Palestinian statehood. Their true thoughts, however, have been far from wanting dual statehood for the same proximity to become a reality. Most believe that granting statehood to Palestinians would mean the death of Israel. At the very least, such a state right up against Israel would bring, many believe, a legitimate government that would harbor terrorists. Israeli forces would have to go against the U.S. authority and all alliances that the Palestinian state would make in order to retaliate against the increased attacks that would surely come. Much more importantly, such an action would be a slap in the face of the God of Israel.

Israel must come to realize that its only reliance is on the Lord. With millions upon millions of enemies surrounding the tiny sliver of land that is present-day Israel, that nation needs friends.

The international community certainly hasn't proven to be Israel's friend. Almost to the last nation among the world's diplomatic community, all want Israel to give away what little land it has to pacify Israel's warlike neighbors.

But Israel has one Friend, if they will but turn to Him. What a powerful friend He is! He says to Israel today as He said so long ago: "But in me is thine help. I will be thy king: where is any other that may save thee in all thy cities?" (Hosea 13:9b–10a).

Alas, however, Bible prophecy seems to indicate that some form of division of this most significant area of God's Promised Land to the Jews will be divided. The result will be disastrous for the whole world. As a matter of fact, God Himself will bring all peoples into the battlefield of Armageddon because of the division:

> I will also gather all nations, and will bring them down into
> the valley of Jehoshaphat, and will plead with them there for
> my people and *for* my heritage Israel, whom they have scattered
> among the nations, and parted my land. (Joel 3:2)

My good friend David Allen Lewis, an excellent Bible prophecy scholar, who was for many years an astute observer of the nation Israel before his death, said the following:

> At the end of the Tribulation, all Gentile nations will come against Jerusalem to make war against God's chosen people (Zech. 12–14). This will be the final provocation of divine anger. Our Lord, Messiah Himself, will lead heaven's hosts for the final conflict of this age. The Battle of Armageddon shall be fought and won by the Son of God. Only Judah [Israel] is seen as standing on God's side against Antichrist and his band of incorrigible rebels (Zech. 14:14). All Israel shall be saved (Rom. 11:26–27), and God will remove iniquity from the land in a single day (Zech. 3:9).[73]

Intifada Ignites!

Madness in the Middle East is the match that is lighting the fuse to Armageddon. God must be growing tired of the mindless bloodshed and insane anger that seems to be increasing daily in that region. The Lord's words in Jeremiah 7: 19–20 speak to the Palestinian-Israeli conflict today—indeed to the Arab Spring and every other movement of explosive violence in the whole of the Middle East:

> Do they provoke me to anger? saith the Lord: do they not provoke themselves to the confusion of their own faces?
>
> Therefore thus saith the Lord God; Behold, mine anger and my fury shall be poured out upon this place, upon man, and upon beast, and upon the trees of the field, and upon the fruit of the ground; and it shall burn, and shall not be quenched. (Jeremiah 7:19–20)

The Lord is speaking today as surely as He spoke to the people who lived so long ago. He is changeless—the same yesterday, today, and forever. There comes a point in His timing when the sin that grieves Him so must be judged. That judgment will ultimately occur during the last seven years of human history, particularly the last three and a half years of that period. (Read of those judgments in the book of Revelation, chapters 6 through 18.)

"Intifada"—the word invented by militant Arab Islamic radicals to mean "a shaking"—is the word for that Armageddon fuse, in my view. It was a large Palestinian uprising that began December 8, 1987, in the Israeli-occupied territories of Palestine. The radical leaders who pushed intifada claimed that the uprising was to protest bad treatment of Arab and other non-Jewish people in the area. Israeli observers claimed intifada as nothing less than an excuse to promote violence against Israel.

Unrest began following the 1967 Six Day War, in which Israel defeated the Arab League aggressors. Israel's crackdown on violence was taken by many Palestinians as excessive use of force. The intifada has grown from that resentment until today, when the movement, which has now morphed into jihad that infects all of Islam, threatens to spark all-out war against Israel.

Intifada grew into a gigantic swell of protest following Ariel Sharon's visit to the Temple Mount. Indeed, there is a shaking in that land at present. It is a supernatural earthquake that could bring the world to the brink of war. Almighty God doesn't cause the murders and horrors of terrorism and war. However, He, in His desire to bring people and nations to repentance, sometimes uses the evil produced by sin to bring judgment. Madness in the Middle East today might lead to that coming seven years of terror, which will be the wrath of the Lord on a generation that will not turn from its wicked ways.

God will at some point bring the righteous fire of judgment in the land of promise in order to bring Israel to its senses and cause His people to recognize that He alone is its salvation. He will also judge the whole world for the sin from which it will not repent.

CHAPTER 13

AGITATION, APPEASEMENT, AND ASSASSINATIONS

STRANGE THINGS CONTINUE to happen in the Middle East. Anger and hatred bubble to the surface of the Palestinian pot. Outsiders—namely the United Nations, the European Union (EU), and even the U.S.—try to smooth over the Arab radicals' temper tantrums with talk of peace. These internationalist powers almost always insist that Israel give in to one degree or another to Palestinian Liberation Organization (PLO) demands.

When Israel caves to the pressures, the enemies become more violent, demanding more and more concessions. When calmer thinking comes to the peace process and national leaders from both sides step up and try to establish at least a civilized tone for working out differences, those leaders are assassinated—not by their enemies, but by those who are supposed to be on their side. This is proof that Satan, the author of confusion, not God, the Author of true peace, is at the center of the false peace process taking place today in the Middle East.

Temple Mount Troubles Grow

When you were a child, did you ever play "king of the hill"? That's like what is being played out in the Middle East today. But it is not child's play; it's a deadly game with worldwide consequences.

War and peace, life and death hang in the balance of this contest for control of the Temple Mount. As we've seen, much blood has been shed in modern times over the Temple Mount feud. Things aren't getting better, but worse, because neither the Islamics nor the Jews will follow what the true God said about the matter. All sides are determined to do what Psalms 2:1–3 says:

Why do the heathen rage, and the people imagine a vain thing? The kings of the earth set themselves, and the rulers take counsel together, against the Lord, and against his anointed, saying, Let us break their bands asunder, and cast away their cords from us.

The United Nations, the European Union, the United States, the Palestinian Authority, Israel, and everybody else are all determined to do what is right in their own eyes. This has always been fallen man's fatal flaw. From the people before the Flood of Noah's time, to Nimrod and the tower of Babel, to Israel's decision not to take the land from the inhabitants at the time God directed it to do so, to Ehud Barak offering the Temple Mount to Arafat for the sake of peace—everybody has wanted to do it his or her own way, not God's way. The result is that rather than things getting better and better, as the evolutionists tell us, things are getting worse and worse, as the Bible says: "But evil men and seducers shall wax worse and worse, deceiving, and being deceived" (2 Timothy 3:13). The Temple Mount in Jerusalem will continue to draw violence until Christ returns at the end of Armageddon.

War Workers

Looking at the issues of war and peace surrounding Jerusalem and Palestine in recent years, we notice an absence of all-out war. Some would call this a positive sign of improvement over the war woes of previous decades.

While there has been an absence of all-out war, however, no true observer of the Mideast situation can honestly proclaim that the region has had real peace. The fact is, the attempts to control the violence since the last major conflict—the Persian Gulf War—and the War on Terrorism following the World Trade Center and Pentagon attacks of September 11, 2001 have acted like a pressure-cooker lid for the region. The Middle East is indeed a *cauldron*. Unfortunately, the false peace makers (the international community, including the U.S.) have been able to do nothing to do away with the causes of the trouble building between Israel and its aggressive Arab-Islamic radical neighbors. That's because the problems are supernatural at their roots; they are satanic.

Threats of all-out war surrounding and involving Israel have been in the headlines for years. Most recently we think of Syria and the possibilities of war being ignited by the battle to oust Bashar Al Assad as the country's dictator/president. Consider the tremendous dangers building within the Israeli/Iranian confrontation over Iran's nuclear weapons program.

Added to this are the boiling anxieties and turmoil initiated when the Muslim Brotherhood, under the false promises of the Arab Spring eruptions, ousted Hosni Mubarak from Egyptian leadership. All the while, the many enemies surrounding the Jewish state remain resolute about erasing Israel from the map. As a matter of fact, maps used by many of the Arab nations have no references outlining or even mentioning Israel.

A time will come, the Bible says, when those who work to agitate for war will cause God's anger to bring judgment: "God is jealous, and the Lord revengeth; the Lord revengeth, and is furious; the Lord will take vengeance on his adversaries, and he reserveth wrath for his enemies" (Nahum 1:2). He will take vengeance on those who come against His people, to whom He gave the land of promise—which includes the Temple Mount.

Stormy Islamics

The storm of rage has been building since Israel no longer seems willing to give away land and other concessions with nothing given by Palestinian adversaries in return. There seems little Israel's Palestinian enemies can now achieve by continuing with a negotiating process for a peace they don't want anyway.

Up until the year 2000, Arafat and company had reason to come to the peace table and at least pretend an interest in peace. A steady stream of concessions flowed to them with little effort on their part. They finally got an Israeli-free territory, being allowed to have a Palestinian armed police force of more than thirty thousand.

Things changed once this was achieved. Arafat refused Barak's seemingly insane offer of the Temple Mount and many other concessions. If Arafat had accepted Barak's offer, many observers believe the PLO chairman would have been assassinated by his own people, as was Anwar Sadat following his peace treaty with Menachem Begin.

Most observers believed, also, that once the PLO and the Islamic radicals got all they could at the peace table, the hardball issues would have to be addressed—issues like border determinations, water rights, bringing Palestinian refugees back to disputed territories, the ultimate status of Samaria and Judea, and, of course, the sovereignty over Jerusalem.

Sovereignty over Jerusalem includes control of the Temple Mount and the authority to make arrangements for access to it. Corridors for pilgrims to the holy sites must be maintained. These corridors must be arranged so as not to cross opposition territory. For Israel's foes in the region to accept a final settlement would mean the Islamic radicals would have no further claims. This they will never agree to accept.

The so-called Middle East peace process between Israel and the Muslim forces of the nations surrounding the tiny Jewish state has been ongoing for decades. These are Arab nations, and all contain fiery Islamist fanaticism that openly declares that Israel must be destroyed. John Loeffler, an observer/commentator of that peace process, frames, in an all-encompassing thought, the seeming hopelessness of the situation:

> Everyone also realized that once the peace process played out, the Arabs would have no further incentive to remain at the negotiating table and behave themselves, leaving a new round of war(s) as the only remaining option. The act of accepting a final agreement would force the Arabs to relinquish any future claims on the Israeli state, its people, and the very existence of Israel itself. It would be final; the events begun in 1947–48 would be over. In the world's eyes, the Arabs would lose all "legitimacy" for further struggle.[74]

Israeli Retaliations

No matter how vicious the attacks by the terrorists against the people of Israel, when that nation responds with force, the world news organizations and world community declare the response to be overreaction.

There are almost always sympathetic voices for the Palestinian aggressors who throw stones and Molotov cocktails, and even for those who fire with heavy-caliber weapons upon Israeli forces. It is amazing to watch as a bully attacks someone who is trying to live in peace, then hear an entirely different report on what you are witnessing. Instead of reporting that the fighting has been started by the Palestinian troublemakers, the world news reports invariably imply that Israeli forces brutalize their victims with overwhelming military power.

For example, on Sunday, May 30, 2010, a fleet of six flotillas set sail from Cyprus for the Gaza strip, carrying pro-Palestinian activists and humanitarian aid to the area. Included in that fleet was the Mavi Mara, a Turkish cruise liner chartered by IHH, a group that, in addition to performing humanitarian efforts, also supports radical Islamic terrorist networks, including Hamas.[75] Israel and the Israeli navy gave numerous warnings to the fleet prior to setting sail, as well as during the journey. They also offered an alternative plan for the fleet to dock at Ashod, where cargo could be inspected and then transferred by land. The fleet defied these warnings and instead attempted to break the Israeli naval blockade.

The next day, the Israel Defense Force (IDF) decided to board the flotillas and force them to redirect to Ashod. Five were boarded without incident; however, when IDF soldiers attempted to board the Mavi Mara, they were met with violent attacks by Palestinian activists wielding clubs, knives, and a gun—with all of the activity supported by video evidence. IDF soldiers returned fire, killing nine activists. Seven IDF soldiers were also wounded.[76]

The incident was characterized in nearly every major news network as a brutal attack on humanitarian aid workers by Israeli forces, provoking international condemnation. In September 2011, the United Nations published a report of its findings about the incident. The report exonerated Israel, but not without characterizing the incident as "excessive and unreasonable."[77] Again, nearly every major news headline emphasized the description "excessive and unreasonable" rather than highlighting the exoneration.

Israel is not without fault, of course. The Israeli military has no doubt been brutal at times in use of force. But, only in cases of defensive-oriented, preemptive action has Israel struck at its neighbors first.

Israel might be back in the land of promise in unbelief, but it seems to take the Lord at His word in the matter of self-defense. Considering the history of the nation's hostile neighbors, heeding God's advice has been very wise indeed!

New World Order Builders

The prophet Nahum's words more and more seem written to describe our time:

> The good man is perished out of the earth: and there is none upright among men: they all lie in wait for blood; they hunt every man his brother with a net.
>
> That they may do evil with both hands earnestly. (Micah 7:2–3a)

It does appear from events in our nation and around the world that there aren't many good people left. The brutality people inflict upon each other is widespread and extremely troubling. This is one of the excuses those who want to build a new world order use to justify their desire to control all people. The one-world builders say they have answers to all the violence and brutality.

If everyone could become equal in every way, then jealousies, envies, hatreds, and all the other factors that cause trouble would be eliminated. In this way, mankind would again achieve a degree of goodness that has been lost, they apparently believe. Fighting at every level, robberies, murders, and all the rest would be eliminated in their perfect world order. Everyone would have the same status in life, thus everybody would be content.

Of course, the one-world-order builders would have a higher position than the rest of us, as they govern their better world. This means they would not be subject to the same limitations as we worker bees. They would have the Rolls Royces and the private jets, etc.

This proposition is preposterous! God's Word says: "And Jesus said unto him, Why callest thou me good? none is good, save one, that is, God" (Luke 18:19). Until Christ changes a person from within, that person's sin nature remains unchanged. People never can be transformed by mankind's institutions and social architecture. Still, the one-worlders dream and plan and plot, determined to bring us to a time like it was at the tower of Babel (see Genesis 11).

"Global governance" is a term put into our language by the new-world-order crowd meaning that it is not one world government they seek, but authority over all national governments. They want to operate, at least at first, like the U.S. government. A "federal" system of government is what they want at first. The global governance would have top priority over any decision, law, or regulation of any nation. There would be a judicial or legal system that could override any nation's court.

The one-worlders want a controlling authority over every aspect of life, including economic, judicial, social, technological, ecological, and military matters. No doubt, they want to control religion also. And they especially want to appease the most vicious elements of those who hate Israel. Despite agitations by Hamas, Hezbollah, Islamic Jihad, and other terrorist groups stirring the Palestinian people to violence, the UN and the would-be, one-world controllers demand that Israel not retaliate. The—supposedly—most intelligent, best-informed globalist leaders make these demands, yet it is plain to most everyone else that the radical Islamics have no interest in reasoning together. They can be appeased only if Israel is driven into the Mediterranean Sea.

Nonetheless, Jerusalem and the Temple Mount are seen as the trigger to nuclear Armageddon. The fanatics must be appeased at all costs. Unfortunately, President Barack Obama has proved to be caught up in the appeasement as of this writing.

Peace Perpetrators

The globalists want peace at any price—that is, as long as it doesn't cut into their perks or benefits. The one-world architects are like the people in high authority described in the book of Micah:

> The prince asketh, and the judge asketh for a reward; and the great man, he uttereth his mischievous desire: so they wrap it up.

The best of them is as a brier: the most upright is sharper than a thorn hedge. (Micah 7:3b–4a)

Everyone will have to make sacrifices for the cause of world peace—everyone, that is, except them. Israel is under terrific pressure to yield to the demands of the international community. The internationalists want peace at all costs in the Middle East so that the oil will continue to flow freely to the Western industrialized governments, which fund their big plans.

Undoubtedly, some within the globalist movement want genuine peace—for genuinely compassionate reasons. But the movement itself is geared toward achieving power by stepping on the backs, heads, and bodies of anyone who gets in their way.

The UN and other one-world architects exert pressure on Israel to yield to the demands of the international community for the cause of world peace. Source: Aotearoa

The ultimate globalist will be Antichrist. The Bible says "by peace [he will] destroy many" (Daniel 8:25). The world's last dictator will gather to himself all the power he can in order to enforce global peace. But, it will not be true peace; it will be the ultimate war on individual freedoms—and it will result in the greatest world war in history: Armageddon.

Energy Villains

Technology has forged ahead dramatically in most every field except one. The world still depends upon petroleum to produce the fuel that runs industry and transportation.

Have you wondered why, despite all the progress in other areas, we still have the internal combustion engine that burns fossil fuels at a tremendous rate? Why has a practical solar-battery-powered engine not been produced? Or why don't we have a safe, efficient, nuclear-powered car that runs every bit as well as the internal combustion motor?

The "green energy," liberal-minded environmentalists have managed to siphon billions of dollars of U.S. taxpayer funding into their useless machinery. The Obama administration has channeled funding into these totally failed efforts, only to turn around and channel more funds into more failed green energy debacles. It's as if an insanity has set in at the highest governmental levels. These "public servants" spend our hard-earned greenbacks, but produce no-yield, green-energy alternatives.

There is no answer that I or others have been able to determine except this: The powers that be have so much invested in the internal combustion engine that they are not willing to abandon it or even phase it out.

The money powers also have great economic interests tied up in oil around the world. Weaning people from the gas guzzlers would be cutting the money powers' economic throats.

There are answers beyond that, however—supernatural ones. Satan, the prince of the power of the air, this earthly realm, knew from the beginning that the shortage of fossil fuels would eventually bring the showdown in the Middle East. The serpent still has his cunning ways. He appeals to the minds of men, tempting them with the world's riches the Lord Jesus Christ refused on the Mount of Temptation.

The top money powers of the world will not cut into their profits and develop new fuels and engines to power the industrialized world. That is, they will not do so until the petroleum reserves are so low that they must do so in order to continue their profitable ways. By the time the reserves are that low, however, it might be too late. Every petroleum interest will be looking for the same, dwindling source. Because of the great reserves from the time after the Fall in the Garden of Eden, the place of that dwindling source will be the Middle East.

God will gather these money powers to Armageddon. It is likely He will use their greed and the oil fields of the Middle East to bring them together for the feast He is going to provide for the scavenging birds and beasts to enjoy. Bringing them to the valley of Megiddo will not be an act of cruelty on God's part; it will be His righteous judgment on a wicked people like those described in Micah 6:10–12:

> Are there yet the treasures of wickedness in the house of the wicked, and the scant measure that is abominable?
>
> Shall I count them pure with the wicked balances, and with the bag of deceitful weights?
>
> For the rich men thereof are full of violence, and the inhabitants thereof have spoken lies, and their tongue is deceitful in their mouth.

The globalists will have worked their lies and appeasing ways to the harm of God's chosen people, Israel. Vengeance is the Lord's! (See Romans 12:19.)

American Apathy

With the tremendous upheavals taking place around the world, America's people as a whole seemed not to notice at all—that is, not until September 11, 2001. That was indeed a 911 call to us all. When those gleaming, towering buildings collapsed and the huge Pentagon complex was struck a devastating blow, our attention instantaneously turned to the reality all around us. Suddenly, our luxurious, unmatched way of life was threatened.

Our richly blessed culture exceeds that of any that has ever existed. Do you have trouble believing that? Did Alexander the Great have a TV set? Did Cleopatra have central heat and air? Did Julius Caesar have a microwave oven, a refrigerator, or a laptop? Considering even just the technological blessings of this generation of Americans, ours is the most blessed ever.

So…what's the point?

The point is that the very blessings we enjoy today make American people the most pampered. History has shown that pampered people are headed down a one-way path to decline and fall. Historian Edward Gibbons in his *Decline and Fall of the Roman Empire* recounts precisely the point that ease of life brings about the death of a culture.

The Romans, from the time of Christ's birth until the empire ceased to be in the AD 400s, went deeper and deeper into self-serving pleasures. Their leisure time greatly increased, and they filled it with every form of entertainment their wicked minds could imagine. Such has been the fate of every culture that achieved leisurely contentment.

Even the hard-working men and women of America can come home and throw their feet up on their recliners' footrests and get lost in nightly TV entertainment of every sort. (My apologies to the wonderful mothers of America, whose work never seems to allow such leisure.)

So, again, what's the point? Such leisure is a mighty tool in Satan's hand. We are examining here the *cauldron* of war and peace. Appease-ment of the American people comes in the form of tremendous blocks of leisure time. Apathy, or the "who cares?" attitude, is the result of self-absorbed living.

Americans today are appeased, as far as attitudes about issues of war and peace are concerned. We choose leaders who promise to make our lives of leisure better. Voters simply don't care about the other issues very much. They often choose leaders whose characters and activities are very bad indeed. Character, as we've been told time and time again, just doesn't matter. But, God's Word says otherwise. Leaders with upside-down thinking can lead a people down the path to decline and fall. Hitler is one such leader who comes to mind.

The point is, then: America's apathy has led to choosing bad leaders in the past. Other nations at other times have chosen leaders of terribly flawed character. The results have been, in many cases, that those nations turned against God's chosen people, the Jews, to one degree or the other. No matter how haughty, high-minded, or technologically sophisticated a nation becomes, God says He will bring such a people down.

It is reasonable to wonder: Has the Lord, because of the way Israel is being treated internationally and because of the anti-God attitude prevalent today, begun to deal in judgment with America and the more financially privileged nations of the world?

Financial crisis exploded in 2008 with the collapse of Lehman Brothers and the banking problems that followed. Since that time, America has seen its national debt climb into the trillions of dollars, some believing that we are as of this writing headed toward more than $140 trillion in debt. This means that there is no hope for America to survive as the nation we have known it to be, if the figure is correct. As a matter of fact, the entire world of finance will have to be completely changed at some point to reconstruct any semblance of economic sanity.

Such apathy and disregard for godly direction one day, perhaps soon, will lead to America and the rest of the world turning to the ultimate Jew-hater, Antichrist. He will seek to get rid of everyone who dares to oppose his devilish plans to make all people worship him as God. Antichrist's regime will be a completely dominating economic order. (Read 2 Thessalonians 2 and Revelation 13.)

Shots Stop Sadat

Perhaps it is good at this point to again emphasize the violent reactions to things that transpire within the Muslim world, and especially within the

Middle Eastern cauldron. In particular, the death of Anwar Sadat translates directly to the current time, with regard to the turmoil erupting in Egypt.

If you can't beat 'em, join 'em. This was apparently the outlook of Egyptian President Anwar El Sadat following Israel's 1973 victory over Egypt and Syria. Sadat had fought fiercely against Israel as an officer in Egypt's army in earlier wars. He became president of Egypt following Gamel Abdul Nasser's death. He shortly thereafter led the Yom Kippur war strike in 1973.

Many who watched the Egyptian president reach out to Israel in 1977 feared at the time that it was just another Arab trick to look good in the eyes of the United Nations and the international community. Looking at Sadat's peace overture now, however, his action must be seen as heartfelt and genuine.

The process of making friends of ancient enemies didn't come easily. Even so, the weeks between 1978 when the peace agreements were signed and October 6, 1981, were filled with goodwill between Anwar Sadat's Egypt and Menachem Begin's Israel.

Tragically, a hail of bullets ended Sadat's participation in an effort that some believe could have resulted in a much wider peace for the Middle East. What Sadat's enemies in the many wars he courageously fought could not do, a group of cowardly assassins accomplished.

God's words through the prophet, Obadiah, echoed down through the centuries:

"All the men of thy confederacy have brought thee even to the border: the men that were at peace with thee have deceived thee, and prevailed against thee" (Obadiah 1:7). It was Sadat's Islamic militant brothers who betrayed him in the name of Allah.

Fearsome Foes

Anwar Sadat and all of his Arab league brothers were wrong in their hatred of Israel. The wars they started were begun in total opposition to the true God. However, Sadat and his fellow warriors fought mightily, believing it was a righteous cause for which they made war.

Menachem Begin, himself a soldier and one of Israel's war heroes, fought for his nation's survival with fierceness as terrible as Sadat's. God's chosen people, though back in the land of promise in unbelief in the Lord God, had in their hearts a supernatural ferocity in battle. The wars they won against overwhelming enemy forces proved that fact in every battle.

It wasn't that Israeli soldiers were better equipped, better trained, or braver than Sadat and his fellow fighters. God won the victories as He had won them for Israel in days long past. How else can we explain victories over forces six-to-one greater in numbers?

Look again at the several chapters just previous to this one to review the wars modern Israel has fought against her enemies. Sadat's change of heart was astonishing to everyone. Even his wife reported her surprise at what came next.

The Egyptian president seemed to look deeply within his heart and mind to try to understand why Israel was apparently invincible. Although it has never been reported anywhere I have found, I'm convinced that he came to believe that God was on the side of Israel. Perhaps he saw himself and his armies in Scriptures such as the following from the book of Psalms:

The wicked plotteth against the just, and gnasheth upon him with his teeth.

The Lord shall laugh at him: for he seeth that his day is coming.

The wicked have drawn out the sword, and have bent their bow, to cast down the poor and needy, and to slay such as be of upright conversation.

Their sword shall enter into their own heart, and their bows shall be broken. (Psalms 37:12–15)

Weary Warriors

Following his 1973 Yom Kippur War defeat, during a time of relative peace, Sadat said, "As long as there is an Israeli soldier on my land, I am not ready to contact anyone in Israel at all."[78]

His announcement, therefore, caught even his wife, Jihan, by surprise. Her husband told CBS television news anchor Walter Cronkite, on November 14, 1977, that he was prepared to go to Jerusalem to talk peace with Israel if asked. In what has been described as the diplomatic sensation of the century, Israeli Prime Minister Begin sent Sadat a formal invitation on behalf of the Israeli government.

The Egyptian leader was hailed by the internationalists as a peace-maker for his initiative—and deservedly so! But the earlier U.S. diplomatic efforts in the peace process were also seen as key to bringing the two enemies together for trying to establish stability in the region. The "shuttle diplomacy"—diplomatic trips back and forth between Washington, D.C., and the Middle East—of Secretary of State Henry Kissinger under both the Nixon and Ford administrations moved the peace process forward. That helped reestablish the U.S. as the major influence in the Middle East, which had been coming more and more under Soviet influence.

War worries were again building when Sadat flew to Jerusalem at Israel's invitation. The buildup to another outburst of fighting was following the same old pattern of decades of hostilities between Israel and its neighbors. Sadat's action for peace almost singlehandedly defused the latest round in the cycle of war in the Middle East.

Never in modern Middle Eastern history had Arab leaders officially sat down at the negotiating table with their enemy, Israel. Those leaders even refused to stay in the same hotels when "unofficial" meetings took place. Anwar Sadat changed all that. He came to Jerusalem to speak to Israel's Knesset. In doing so, he made enemies who would come back to haunt him.

Earlier, Israel's Prime Minister Yitzhak Rabin and American President Jimmy Carter parted in their views of the way to help settle things in the Middle East. Sadat used the split to begin talking to Carter.

Egypt was in trouble. Its economy was so bad that most people lived below poverty levels. The government could no longer afford to spend money on military hardware. Increasing riots convinced the Egyptian leader that he must turn his efforts from acquiring more war machinery to developing the nation's economy.

Sadat sought and got a $1.54-billion economic aid package from combined donors including the U.S., Saudi Arabia, and other oil-rich Arab countries. Sadat moved closer to America and Carter when the American president proposed the possibility of a separate Palestinian homeland in lands occupied by Israel.

The militant Menachem Begin's surprise election in May 1976 was feared by some to become a major stumbling block to peace. But Sadat, when learning of Begin's election, said: "It does not matter who governs Israel. There are no doves in Israel, only hawks."[79]

The Egyptian president was more concerned about the inroads the Soviet Union had made in the region. He was suspicious of Moscow, believing the Kremlin was helping stir up the riots in Cairo. He thought—rightfully so—that the Soviets wanted to overthrow the moderate regimes in the Middle East, such as his.

Begin had been considered by many within his own country to be an aging has-been. They thought of him as an old, right-wing warrior in Israel's fight for independence. He was all of that, but he was much more, too, and it was most likely his weariness of war that made him reach to take the hand of another weary warrior, the hand of his enemy, Anwar Sadat.

These fierce foes could not find peace of heart through constant fighting. Perhaps they could do so by choosing a path of meekness like that recommended in Zephaniah 2:3: "Seek ye the Lord, all ye meek of the earth, which have wrought his judgment; seek righteousness, seek meekness: it may be ye shall be hid in the day of the Lord's anger."

Handshake Stops Heartbeat

Man-made attempts at making peace can be noble gestures. Most elements of the peace between Sadat's Egypt and Begin's Israel continue in place to this day, in spite of obvious efforts by those within Egypt, such as members of the Arab Brotherhood, to break all bonds formed by Begin and Sadat. Satan still stalks up and down the sands of the Middle East, and man-made peace is doomed to failure. He wants Israel destroyed and will stand for nothing less.

Lucifer's henchmen are everywhere among the nations, because all who are not God's children are the devil's children; Jesus Himself said so (see 1 John 3:10 and John 8:42–44). With things looking better for Mideast peace, Satan had his people ready to disrupt things.

To the Islamic fanatics, the White House Rose Garden handshake between Sadat and the hated Israeli, Begin, was blasphemy. In the terrorists' minds, the Egyptian president was as good as dead.

While Sadat sat with others of his government and military reviewing a military parade, several fanatic Islamic gunmen jumped from one of the parade vehicles. They rushed the reviewing stands, their automatic weapons pointing toward Sadat. In what some called his last show of great courage, the Egyptian president, dressed in his military uniform, chose to stand and confront his attackers rather than scramble to protect himself. A number of bullets struck him, and he later died.

Sadat's death greatly affected his former enemy, as prophecy scholar Dr. Jack Van Impe said on his television program: "We [Van Impe and his wife, Rexella] went to the home of Menachem Begin to interview him for our program…and suddenly he rushed out and said, 'I'm so sorry, folks, but Anwar Sadat of Egypt has been shot, and I have to go to see what happened to my friend.'"[80]

It is ironic that Anwar Sadat had been much safer in the Knesset and with his new friend, Begin, than with his family and friends back home in Egypt. But Satan tears apart families and friends with his lying, false doctrines, and hate-filled ideologies.

Wrath Rips Rabin

Assassination remains one of murderous mankind's favorite ways to carry out political aims. This remains true no matter where around the world we look. The U.S., which we think of as the most civilized place in the world, is among the guiltiest in this regard. We have had four presidents removed by assassination and a number of others assaulted by assassination attempts.

Fanatics and radicals capable of murdering for political removal from office are found everywhere, including among God's chosen people. Political assassination cuts across every persuasion and ideology.

The counterpart to Sadat's assassins struck Israeli Prime Minister Yitzhak Rabin on November 4, 1995. Just as Anwar Sadat had been assassinated because he shook hands with Menachem Begin, so Rabin was murdered because he shook hands with Yasser Arafat. Middle East peace efforts bring out the war in man's heart, it seems. And the greatest wrath apparently is found within one's own house rather than the camp of the enemy.

Sadat, in 1977, landed in Jerusalem and was met by his bitter enemies. He stood at attention with Begin. First, the Egyptian national anthem was played, then the Israeli. Sadat then walked along the receiving line and shook hands with Israel's fiercest one-time generals, Moshe Dayan, and Ariel Sharon. He also shook hands with former prime ministers Golda Meir and Yitzhak Rabin.

The scene was strange, these enemies greeting solemnly, yet with genuine hopes that Sadat's visit would eventually produce peace in the Middle East. No one could know at that promising moment that two of those leaders would be cut down by assassins' bullets…that politics on both sides would produce the poison of ultra-fanatic militant action that went far beyond true patriotism.

Like Sadat, Rabin had been a top military and civilian leader. Both men were considered military heroes who fought viciously against their nations' enemies. Yet both would come to be hated among certain people within their own circle of patriots. They became hated because, in the view of those who despised them, they became too willing to compromise with their enemies.

In reality, the deep-seated angers of those who hated Sadat and Rabin were more religious in nature than political. The assassins in both cases seemed to harbor the ancient racial and religious grudges that continue to separate the Arabs from the Jews.

Rose Garden Roulette

Leaders or people who leave God out of their plans are playing Russian roulette. Trusting in the enemy to do the right thing is a gamble that is indeed foolish to undertake.

Rabin did such a thing, in the view of some, when he met in the White House Rose Garden with Arafat. To meet with and try to compromise with a man who has vowed to wipe every Jew from the Middle East, in the minds of many of Israel's defenders, placed the nation in great danger.

Rabin's dealings with the treacherous Arafat, whose record of terrorism the Israeli knew well, was as if he was a man who would not hear advice to proceed with caution. That he was really so naïve as to think he could trust Arafat is doubtful. That his strange dealings with Arafat were due to pressure from the appeasement-minded politicians within his liberal Labor Party is the more likely reason for his astonishing land-for-peace offers.

Rabin's actions during the negotiations and the Rose Garden handshakes with Arafat and President Bill Clinton on September 13, 1993, were eerily like the words from Psalms 38: "But I, as a deaf man, heard not; and I was as a dumb man that openeth not his mouth. Thus I was as a man that heareth not, and in whose mouth are no reproofs" (13–14).

The first part of that scriptural text is even more eerie. It seems almost to foreshadow Rabin's fate: "They also that seek after my life lay snares for me: and they that seek my hurt speak mischievous things, and imagine deceits all the day long" (Psalms 38:12).

Rabin Assassinated

The people of Israel seem confused about their leadership, according to their voting history. They have swung wildly in their elections in recent times. They have gone from the liberal/moderate Rabin to the conservative Benjamin Netanyahu, to the liberal Ehud Barak, to the ultra-conservative Ariel Sharon, and, eventually, as of this writing, back to Netanyahu.

It is as if the following passage from the book of Psalms describes present-day dissatisfaction, confusion, and shame over the picture of their nation presented to the world:

> Thou makest us a reproach to our neighbours, a scorn and a derision to them that are round about us.
>
> Thou makest us a byword among the heathen, a shaking of the head among the people.
>
> My confusion is continually before me, and the shame of my face hath covered me, For the voice of him that reproacheth and blasphemeth; by reason of the enemy and avenger. (44:13–16)

But the problems causing dissatisfaction, confusion, and shame felt by Israelis come from a much more sinister source than actions by any of their recent prime ministers. As emphasized throughout this book, Israel today is under malicious attack by the ultimate doer of evil. Satan is the one who puts a negative spin on Israel's relationships with her hostile neighbors. Rabin's assassination is one incident in Lucifer's ongoing assault on God's chosen nation. The murder is but one more strange piece of the puzzle involved in the issues within the cauldron of Mideast war and peace.

A number of things led to Israel and the PLO deciding to try again at peace talks. The circumstances greatly changed the PLO position and its leadership became convinced that it was time to talk. By 1992, several things had happened to change the complexion of the Middle East:

- The Soviet Union had just collapsed. And, because the USSR had been the chief supplier of weaponry and a big contributor to many Arab nations, money-wise, funding to fight wars dried up.
- The PLO had backed Saddam Hussein and Iraq in the 1991 Gulf War. This nearly bankrupted the organization.
- The most moderate-to-liberal Israeli government to that point in history was elected in 1992. This opened the door, so PLO leaders thought, to the possibility of winning concessions through talk, for the time being, rather than through fighting.

Newly elected Prime Minister Yitzhak Rabin saw the possibility that some headway might be made as far as trying to bring peace to the region was concerned. He had made a campaign promise that he would make an honorable agreement with the PLO that would stop the fighting and terrorism.

Secret negotiations took place between Israel and the PLO. The Oslo Accords, also known as Declaration of Principles, was signed August 23, 1993. The agreement surprised even the diplomatic world because things had been negotiated under such secrecy.

The meetings took place mostly in Oslo, Norway. The agreement was called a partnership of interdependence: If one side failed to uphold its part of the bargain, the agreement was automatically cancelled. The concessions on both sides were supposed to be so significant that neither Israel nor the PLO would want to betray the trust of the other.

The issues involved were indeed important. The PLO agreed to postpone demands for Palestinian sovereignty (a Palestinian state within current Israeli territory). Also, the PLO agreed to put off for the time being the demand that Jerusalem be divided, and that it be declared its capital. These issues were to be resolved within five years under the Oslo Accords.

Meanwhile, Israel would, during the five-year period, begin withdrawing from Jericho and the Gaza Strip. This meant, in the PLO thinking, that they would sometime after five years have self-rule over those areas.

Further negotiations would give Palestinians a pathway toward eventual statehood. Meanwhile, Israel was to treat the Palestinians as equal partners in the interdependent accords, rather than as inferiors.

PLO Chairman Arafat assured Rabin and the Israeli government that he would keep a lid on the terrorists among his people. Each side agreed to recognize the other as legitimate peoples in the land.

When Rabin and Arafat signed the document in the White House Rose Garden in 1993 with President Clinton looking on, there were subdued smiles and handshakes, but not everyone was pleased. Ancient and modern hatreds would insert themselves again.

Despite the withdrawal from some of the disputed territories, as stipulated in the Oslo Accords, acts of terrorism by Palestinian fanatics continued. Arafat, whether he truly wished to do so or not, was powerless to stop them.

A young Israeli college student, who later told the world that God told him to do it, shot Yitzhak Rabin several times on Saturday night, November 4, 1995, while the prime minister attended a peace rally at Tel Aviv. Rabin died a short time later at a Tel Aviv hospital.

The ongoing search for peace in the Middle East, it seems, continues to be a deadly quest.

CHAPTER 14

POWERFUL PRESSURES FOR PEACE

EVERYONE IS LOOKING for peace today. That is, we all want the inner calm and satisfaction that removes all unpleasantness and fear from our lives.

Some believe the peace they seek can be found in riches—money can solve all their problems. Some think fame that makes them look great in the eyes of the world will bring peace that satisfies in the deepest part of their souls. Many believe that romance with just the right person will reward their loneliness with inner satisfaction, happiness, and wonderful peace.

But if we examine the lives of the rich, we often find discontentment, disappointment, and emptiness. When we look at the famous, we can many times see the same terrible things. Romance, as often as not, can soon fade into anger, resentment, and separation. In America, for example, the divorce rate is now well over 50 percent.

Can't there be riches with contentment? Can't a person have fame and at the same time joy in life? Cannot people have both romance *and* happiness for life?

Yes! Absolutely!

True peace, you see, is found in the soul that has at its heart the complete satisfaction given by Jesus Christ. As we've said many times in these pages, Jesus is the Prince of Peace! A person receives the peace that only Jesus can give by doing what God's Word says: "For whosoever shall call upon the name of the Lord shall be saved" (Romans 10:13). He alone gives "the peace of God, which passeth all understanding" (Philippians 4:7).

Nations are made up of people, human beings who want peace, but cannot find it. Wars and rumors of wars are the result of the absence of peace in this world. The answer nations seek for the peace they can't find can be found only in one person: Jesus!

The issues of Mideast war and peace are wrapped up in who makes war and who tries to enforce peace. Let's look at the overall view of where our generation stands today in the matter of the peace process. Also, let's consider what it all means in regard to what the Bible says about God's prophetic timeline.

Daniel's Prophecy

God's Word warns our generation about the last-days attempts to enforce peace—peace that doesn't include Jesus Christ. Daniel the prophet, a man very close to God's heart, was chosen to deliver the prophetic message to those alive during his own time, and to our generation. It is recorded in Daniel 2:1–45:

> And in the second year of the reign of Nebuchadnezzar, Nebuchadnezzar dreamed dreams, wherewith his spirit was troubled, and his sleep went from him.
>
> Then the king commanded to summon the magicians, and the astrologers, and the sorcerers, and the Chaldeans, for to show the king his dreams. So they came and stood before the king.
>
> And the king said unto them, I have dreamed a dream, and my spirit was troubled to know the dream.

Then spoke the Chaldeans to the king in Aramaic, O king, live forever: tell thy servants the dream, and we will show the interpretation.

The king answered and said to the Chaldeans, The thing is gone from me: if ye will not make known unto me the dream, with the interpretation of it, ye shall be cut in pieces, and your houses shall be made a refuse heap.

But if ye show the dream, and its interpretation, ye shall receive from me gifts and rewards and great honor; therefore, show me the dream, and the interpretation of it.

They answered again and said, Let the king tell his servants the dream, and we will show the interpretation of it.

The king answered and said, I know of certainty that ye would gain the time, because ye see the thing is gone from me.

But if ye will not make known unto me the dream, there is but one decree for you; for ye have prepared lying and corrupt words to speak before me, till the time is changed; therefore tell me the dream, and I shall know that ye can show me its interpretation.

The Chaldeans answered before the king, and said, There is not a man upon the earth that can reveal the king's matter; therefore, there is no king, lord, nor ruler, that asked such things of any magician, or astrologer, or Chaldean.

And it is a rare thing that the king requireth, and there is no other that can reveal it before the king, except the gods, whose dwelling is not with flesh.

For this cause the king was angry and very furious, and commanded to destroy all the wise men of Babylon.

And the decree went forth that the wise men should be slain; and they sought Daniel and his fellows to be slain.

Then Daniel answered with counsel and wisdom to Arioch the captain of the king's guard, which was gone forth to slay the wise men of Babylon.

He answered and said to Arioch, the king's captain, Why is the decree so hasty from the king? Then Arioch made the thing known to Daniel.

Then Daniel went in, and desired of the king that he would give him time, and that he would shew the king the interpretation.

Then Daniel went to his house, and made the thing known to Hananiah, Mishael, and Azariah, his companions;

That they would desire mercies of the God of heaven concerning this secret; that Daniel and his fellows should not perish with the rest of the wise men of Babylon.

Then was the secret revealed unto Daniel in a night vision. Then Daniel blessed the God of heaven.

Daniel answered and said, Blessed be the name of God forever and ever: for wisdom and might are his,

And he changeth the times and the seasons: he removeth kings, and setteth up kings: he giveth wisdom unto the wise, and knowledge to those who know understanding;

He revealeth the deep and secret things: he knoweth what is in the darkness, and the light dwelleth with him.

I thank thee, and praise thee, O thou God of my fathers, who hast given me wisdom and might, and hast made known unto me now what we desired of thee: for thou hast now made known unto us the king's matter.

Therefore Daniel went in unto Arioch, whom the king had ordained to destroy the wise men of Babylon: he went and said thus unto him; Destroy not the wise men of Babylon: bring me in before the king, and I will reveal unto the king the interpretation.

Then Arioch brought in Daniel before the king in haste and said thus unto him, I have found a man of the captives of Judah, that will make known unto the king the interpretation.

The king answered and said to Daniel, whose name was Belteshazzar, Art thou able to make known unto me the dream which I have seen, and the interpretation of it?

Daniel answered in the presence of the king, and said, The secret which the king hath demanded cannot the wise men, the astrologers, the magicians, the soothsayers, reveal unto the king;

But there is a God in heaven who revealeth secrets, and maketh known to the king, Nebuchadnezzar, what shall be in the latter days. Thy dream, and the visions of thy head upon thy bed, are these:

As for thee, O king, thy thoughts came into thy mind upon thy bed, what should come to pass hereafter; and he that revealeth secrets maketh known to thee what shall come to pass.

But as for me, this secret is not revealed to me for any wisdom that I have more than any living, but for their sakes that shall make known the interpretation to the king, and that thou mightest know the thoughts of thy heart.

Thou, O king, sawest, and behold a great image. This great image, whose brightness was excellent, stood before thee; and the form thereof was terrible.

This image's head was of fine gold, its breast and its arms of silver, its belly and its thighs of bronze,

Its legs of iron, its feet part of iron and part of clay.

Thou sawest until a stone was cut out without hands, which smote the image upon its feet that were of iron and clay, and broke them to pieces.

Then were the iron, the clay, the bronze, the silver, and the gold, broken to pieces together, and became like the chaff of the summer threshingfloors; and the wind carried them away, that no place was found for them; and the stone that smote the image became a great mountain, and filled the whole earth.

This is the dream; and we will tell its interpretation before the king.

Thou, O king, art a king of kings: for the God of heaven hath given thee a kingdom, power, and strength, and glory.

And wherever the children of men dwell, the beasts of the field and the fowls of the heaven hath he given into thine hand, and hath made thee ruler over them all. Thou art this head of gold.

And after thee shall arise another kingdom inferior to thee, and another third kingdom of bronze, which shall bear rule over all the earth.

And the fourth kingdom shall be strong as iron: forasmuch as iron breaketh in pieces and subdueth all things; and as iron that breaketh all these, shall it break in pieces and bruise.

And whereas thou sawest the feet and toes, part of potters' clay, and part of iron, the kingdom shall be divided; but there shall be in it of the strength of the iron, forasmuch as thou sawest the iron mixed with miry clay.

And as the toes of the feet were part of iron, and part of clay, so the kingdom shall be partly strong and partly broken.

And whereas thou sawest iron mixed with miry clay, they shall mingle themselves with the seed of men; but they shall not adhere one to another, even as iron is not mixed with clay.

And in the days of these kings shall the God of heaven set up a kingdom, which shall never be destroyed; and the kingdom shall not be left to other people, but it shall break in pieces and consume all these kingdoms, and it shall stand forever.

Forasmuch as thou sawest that the stone was cut out of the mountain without hands, and that it brake in pieces the iron, the bronze, the clay, the silver, and the gold; the great God hath made known to the king what shall come to pass hereafter: and the dream is certain, and its interpretation is sure.

Daniel Delivers on Dream

To understand where we are today, so far as the powerful pressures for peace are concerned, we will first look at what the Bible says about world government. Daniel—greatly beloved by God, no doubt because he loved Him with all his heart and sought to obey Him in all situations—was given a look into the future of human government. The prophecies God gave him are extremely relevant to our time. Daniel was a Hebrew living in Babylon. The nation of Israel had been taken to Babylon because of the disobedience of Israel's people over many years.

Nebuchadnezzar was, by God's own words, the greatest of all earthly kings. What he said was unquestioned. Heads were lopped off or other undesirable things happened if people went against this king's wishes in any way. Captives from other countries were usually put in areas of work in Babylon, according to where the masters wanted them. Yet Daniel, a captive foreigner, was a man Nebuchadnezzar came to hold in high regard. He was considered one of the king's wise men or fortunetellers, although he never dealt with things that were occult. When King Nebuchadnezzar was troubled by a nightmare, a supernatural one, and his other fortunetellers couldn't even tell the king what his dream was, much less tell him the interpretation of the dream, he got mad. He told his military men to kill the whole bunch.

Daniel told a guard that his God could not only tell the king his dream, but interpret it as well. Nebuchadnezzar decided to give him a chance.

Daniel and his three friends, Shadrack, Meshack, and Abednigo, prayed about the matter all night. God answered, giving Daniel both the dream and the interpretation. Nebuchadnezzar was so amazed by the results that he fell on his face before Daniel. (By so doing, the king was worshipping God, not Daniel. We can know this because Daniel did not correct the king, telling him not to worship himself, that is, Daniel.)

The dream was a prophecy of four world kingdoms. These were

identified through the king's vision of a gigantic statue of a man made of four different metals, each less valuable than the previous. This most likely indicates that each succeeding kingdom was less powerful—in other words, each kingdom that came on the world scene had less influence and authority over the world than the one that was before.

The head of the great statue was gold, representing Nebuchadnezzar and the Babylonian kingdom. The chest and arms were silver, indicating Medo-Persia, the empire that history tells us followed Babylon as a world empire. The statue's belly and thighs were bronze; they represented Greece, which history proves was Alexander the Great's world empire. It followed, historically, the Medo-Persian Empire.

The legs and feet were iron, with the feet and toes a mixture of iron and clay. This was the great Roman Empire that took over world domination from Alexander's empire. The Roman Empire split into two divisions, one with its capital at Rome and the other capital at Constantinople.

The strangest parts of this great statue were the feet and, particularly, the toes of part iron and part clay. This indicated that the very end of this fourth world government would have weaknesses. The government, it was shown through the toes, would not be one solid institution, but one made up of ten separate though single governmental authorities.

Prophetic scholars and students who hold God's prophetic Word as literal rather than merely symbolic believe the ten toes of the metallic monster to represent the very end of human history, just before Christ's return to earth. Most believe our generation is in the era of the ten-toes governmental system.

The European Union is considered by many as the nucleus of this developing world government. I agree. However, it's my view that the ten toes represent ten major regions around the world when Antichrist comes fully into power. The prophet Daniel was given a vision of end-times prophecy, the stage-setting for which I believe our own generation is witnessing.

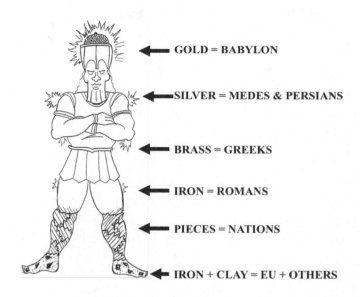

GOLD = BABYLON

SILVER = MEDES & PERSIANS

BRASS = GREEKS

IRON = ROMANS

PIECES = NATIONS

IRON + CLAY = EU + OTHERS

An illustration of the strange beast statue in Nebuchadnezzar's dream depicts the significance of the metallic imagery. Credit: Karen Melton

The Almighty Allows the Prophet a Peek

If the imagery and wording of Daniel's interpretation of Nebuchadnezzar's dream seems wild, the symbology used in describing Daniel's own dream of what it all means in terms of human government yet to come in the world is even more stupendous…even nightmarish. But one thing is for sure: Daniel and everyone who has read it since have had a vivid picture in their brains of something astounding predicted for the world! Here is the passage describing the vision God gave the prophet concerning the end times:

> In the first year of Belshazzar king of Babylon Daniel had a dream and visions of his head upon his bed: then he wrote the dream, and told the sum of the matters.
>
> Daniel spake and said, I saw in my vision by night, and, behold, the four winds of the heaven strove upon the great sea.

And four great beasts came up from the sea, diverse one from another.

The first was like a lion, and had eagle's wings: I beheld till the wings thereof were plucked, and it was lifted up from the earth, and made stand upon the feet as a man, and a man's heart was given to it.

And behold another beast, a second, like to a bear, and it raised up itself on one side, and it had three ribs in the mouth of it between the teeth of it: and they said thus unto it, Arise, devour much flesh.

After this I beheld, and lo another, like a leopard, which had upon the back of it four wings of a fowl; the beast had also four heads; and dominion was given to it.

After this I saw in the night visions, and behold a fourth beast, dreadful and terrible, and strong exceedingly; and it had great iron teeth: it devoured and brake in pieces, and stamped the residue with the feet of it: and it was diverse from all the beasts that were before it; and it had ten horns.

I considered the horns, and, behold, there came up among them another little horn, before whom there were three of the first horns plucked up by the roots: and, behold, in this horn were eyes like the eyes of man, and a mouth speaking great things. (Daniel 7:1–8)

Daniel's dream is all about the future course of human government, and it gets to the heart of what we're looking at in this book. The movement toward man-made peace we see today is tremendous. However, I believe it is but a foreshadowing of the powerful pressures through a phony peace process we will see developing in the near future.

Antichrist himself will one day come in proclaiming to be a maker of peace, as represented by the first horseman of the apocalypse, who gallops onto the world stage riding a white horse (read Revelation 6: 2). This great leader will promise peace, safety, and plenty for everyone. But, it will be total war, not blessed peace, that will eventually result from this leader's rule over the earth!

In Daniel's vision, prophetic words on human government are wrapped in an awesome scene of stormy turbulence. There is a dramatic absence of peace in that scene Daniel described when he was getting on in years, during the time of King Belshazzar, grandson of Nebuchadnezzar.

Daniel told of violent winds that came from every direction, whipping up furious waves on the "great sea"—most likely, the Mediterranean. At the same time, many students and scholars in prophecy believe the term "great sea" symbolizes the many peoples of the earth. The winds of troubles Daniel saw, in other words, greatly stirred the masses (or "sea") of people all over the then-known world.

The violent dream-vision stirred the old prophet, too! He was greatly troubled at the fearful beasts he saw. Four weird-looking, animal-like beasts arose out of the storm-driven waves. The first was like a lion, but it had wings. The wings were plucked from it and it seemed to transform into a man. The second beast that looked like a bear raised up partly, apparently ripping flesh and bone from the thing it was eating. This bear was instructed to eat a lot more.

The third beast came out of the sea. It was like a leopard, but had four wings like a bird. This strange animal had four heads, and it was given tremendous power and ruling authority.

Now these three beasts were an astonishing sight for Daniel to try to understand. But the next monster of the nightmarish vision was truly flabbergasting. The fourth beast was unlike anything ever beheld by Daniel before, "dreadful and terrible" as it arose out of the violently heaving sea. Its strength was awesome, and it had huge, iron teeth. It not only tore its victims apart and ate them, but it stomped them and trampled their remains.

This beast was totally different from the other three supernatural animals that came before. This one had ten horns. While Daniel carefully studied and wondered about the ten horns, amazingly, another "little horn" came up among the ten. As the little horn arose, three of the larger ten horns were ripped from the monster's head. Daniel then saw that the little horn had eyes—the eyes of a man. The little horn also had a mouth, and it was speaking tremendously important things.

Daniel was no doubt exhausted by these awesome things he had witnessed. Try to imagine this is your own nightmare! But in this case, the vision is more real than things you see when fully awake. That's how it was for the old prophet. Although the creatures were symbols, they were representing something even more terrible. This wasn't merely a nightmare; it was supernatural reality. Daniel, terribly upset that he couldn't understand what it all meant, saw another being standing nearby—an angel, no doubt—and Daniel "asked him the truth of all this" (Daniel 7:16).

Beast-Vision Overview

The being told Daniel the interpretation and, somehow, made him understand at a deep level what he was witnessing:

> So he told me, and made me know the interpretation of the things.
>
> These great beasts, which are four, are four kings, which shall arise out of the earth.
>
> But the saints of the most High shall take the kingdom, and possess the kingdom for ever, even for ever and ever.
> (Daniel 7:16b–18)

So, the vision was about four kings who would have great kingdoms of world-wide scope; they basically would control the entire known world at the time of their rule. The being didn't stop with that revelation; he quickly added that the saints of the Most High would take the world kingdoms from these kings and then would possess the earth forever.

This short overview of what Daniel was seeing covered some tremendous truths from God's prophetic Word. Although the being didn't spell it out in detail, we know that Daniel, himself, was part of the first beast-vision. The lion with the wings was the great kingdom of Babylon.

Think back to Daniel 2, in which Daniel interpreted Nebuchadnezzar's reign as the head of gold atop the gigantic, metallic statue. Remember that Daniel prophesied four kingdoms. In the prophecy of Daniel 7, we see the same order of world kingdoms: The lion with the wings corresponds to the Babylonian kingdom (head of gold). The bear chewing on flesh and bones corresponds to Medo-Persia (chest and arms of silver). The leopard with four wings and four heads corresponds to the belly and thighs of brass or bronze (Alexander the Great's Grecian empire). The fourth beast of Daniel 7 corresponds to the legs, feet, and toes (last kingdom). That final world governmental system is a continuation of the Roman Empire. It never was defeated and destroyed; it just faded away or melted into the various governmental systems of the world, including our own.

God's microscope of prophetic vision draws Daniel and us even closer to the truth of the last world kingdom. We get a look at the little horn that grows to leadership and domination over the ten kings of history's last governmental order.

The little horn is a man! He comes to full power by overcoming and getting rid of three leaders who stand in his way. Additionally, we're shown the destructive, all-consuming nature and power of this last kingdom. It is truly a wild, vicious beast that represents a composite of all three of the previous world systems. The last human system of world government will include bits and pieces of all previous human, governmental, one-world orders. It will be man's final attempt to take control from Almighty God.

But just like in the case of the huge man-statue when the toes are smashed to pieces and the wind blows the powder away, so the fourth beast's power and authority are taken away. The book of Revelation gives further details about this final world kingdom and its fate.

John—the disciple who, like Daniel, God's Word describes as "much beloved"—was later given a spectacular vision of, apparently, the same strange beast Daniel saw:

> And I stood upon the sand of the sea, and saw a beast rise up out of the sea, having seven heads and ten horns, and upon his horns ten crowns, and upon his heads the name of blasphemy.
>
> And the beast which I saw was like unto a leopard, and his feet were as the feet of a bear, and his mouth as the mouth of a lion: and the dragon gave him his power, and his seat, and great authority.
>
> And I saw one of his heads as it were wounded to death; and his deadly wound was healed: and all the world wondered after the beast. (Revelation 13:1–3)

John went on in his great vision of the Revelation to describe the same final world government Daniel portrayed, but with less symbolic narrative:

> And the ten horns which thou sawest are ten kings, which have received no kingdom as yet; but receive power as kings one hour with the beast.
>
> These have one mind, and shall give their power and strength unto the beast.
>
> These shall make war with the Lamb, and the Lamb shall overcome them: for he is Lord of lords, and King of kings: and they that are with him are called, and chosen, and faithful. (Revelation 17:12–14)

Fourth Beast Foretold

Then I would know the truth of the fourth beast, which was diverse from all the others, exceeding dreadful, whose teeth were of iron, and his nails of brass; which devoured, brake in pieces, and stamped the residue with his feet;

And of the ten horns that were in his head, and of the other which came up, and before whom three fell; even of that horn that had eyes, and a mouth that spake very great things, whose look was more stout than his fellows....

Thus he said, The fourth beast shall be the fourth kingdom upon earth, which shall be diverse from all kingdoms, and shall devour the whole earth, and shall tread it down, and break it in pieces.

And the ten horns out of this kingdom are ten kings that shall arise: and another shall rise after them; and he shall be diverse from the first, and he shall subdue three kings.

And he shall speak great words against the most High, and shall wear out the saints of the most High, and think to change times and laws: and they shall be given into his hand until a time and times and the dividing of time. (Daniel 7:19–20, 23–25)

Daniel was transfixed by the fourth beast, which took peace from the whole earth by waging all-out war and completely destroying anything in its path. What was the truth about this thing that had ten horns, this beast that had a little horn that grew to take authority over the other horns? What did it mean, the violent way in which three of the horns were ripped out by their roots? The old prophet questioned the being about all of these troubling matters, and he got answers.

The fourth kingdom, Daniel was told, will take absolute authority and power over the whole world. It will destroy everything it touches; there will be nothing good about it.

The being told Daniel that the ten horns are the ten ruling kings over this great, worldwide kingdom. The little horn that will arise among the ten will be far stronger in power and determination than any of the ten kings.

The eleventh king will do away with the competition. He will get rid of three kings who oppose him. Once he takes total control of this final world government, this dictator will curse the true God of heaven, mounting an all-out assault against those who belong to God and treating them even worse than Adolf Hitler treated the Jews in the Holocaust.

Antichrist will declare himself to be God. He will, through terror and satanic power, try to make all people on earth worship him. God will allow him to continue in his insane rage for three and one-half years.

Time of the Signs

Daniel was given answers to the questions that so troubled him. But he wanted to know when all these dream-vision things would come to pass. He wanted to know the end of the whole matter. There seemed no resolution to the violence. The beast with the ten horns appeared to be getting stronger and stronger. Would there ever be peace, or would the whole world be destroyed by this raging machine of war?

The being responded:

But thou, O Daniel, shut up the words, and seal the book, even to the time of the end: many shall run to and fro, and knowledge shall be increased....

And I heard, but I understood not: then said I, O my Lord, what shall be the end of these things?

And he said, Go thy way, Daniel: for the words are closed up and sealed till the time of the end.

Many shall be purified, and made white, and tested; but the wicked shall do wickedly: and none of the wicked shall understand; but the wise shall understand. (Daniel 12:4; 8–10)

The statement about the words being "closed up and sealed till the time of the end" clearly leaves the probability open that at some point near the end of this fourth beast's war-making, the book of the prophecy would be opened to full understanding.

The words "many shall run to and fro, and knowledge shall be increased" give a broad, general overview of the conditions that will mark the time when these prophecies will be clearly understood.

These statements are of great prophetic importance. There is a tremendous amount of relevance to our time wrapped up in this brief prophetic declaration. The words didn't help the old prophet's feelings, however. Just when he so desperately wanted to see this terrible war-making and destruction brought to its conclusion so that peace could come, the angel shut off the supernatural television set.

However, through his final words, "Many shall be purified, and made white, and tested," the being encouraged Daniel to stop worrying. These things would be in the future, beyond the prophet's lifetime. God would purify many through salvation. Many would become saints and be given the white robes of righteousness before the things in the vision played out. Many of God's chosen (those who believe God for salvation) will be tried or persecuted because of their faith in the Lord God before human history concludes.

The angel-being's words that "the wicked shall do wickedly: and none of the wicked shall understand; but the wise shall understand," told the old prophet that the wicked would continue to do wicked things until God's prophetic plan is completed.

Who are the wicked? These are all who don't have a personal relationship with God. They do not know him as their Lord and Heavenly Father. But the wise—children of God who have accepted Jesus Christ as Lord and Savior—will understand all of these end-time matters at the close of human history when the prophecies' fulfillments come into view.

Luke 21:28 tells the generation about these end-time things: "And when these things begin to come to pass, then look up, and lift up your heads; for your redemption draweth nigh." At the very center of "these things" prophesied to come to pass is the thing all mankind longs for. Peace!

False Prince of Peace

Daniel was given prophetic insights about the end of the age (Church Age) in chapters previous to chapter 12. The prophet obviously wasn't allowed to put it altogether in his own mind because the prophesied matters were still far in the future. Answers to the mystery of all these issues, however, are coming more and more into focus with every day that passes in our time.

Nothing is more apparent than the fact that we are living in the middle of the prophesied end-time peace process. But it is a false peace process that will end up being a covenant or agreement made with death and hell, according to what the Bible says.

Daniel prophesies that "a king of fierce countenance" (8:23) will come on the world scene at the end of the last of the four kingdoms predicted in Daniel chapters 2 and 7. By that time, people will have come to be very wicked indeed. The fierce king, Antichrist, will understand what he must say in order to get this wicked generation to follow him. His great words will hypnotize the masses, and he will be a thousand times more powerful in his attractiveness than Hitler. The Scripture says his "power shall be mighty, but not by his own power" (8:24)—in other words, his great abilities will not be human gifts, but will be given by Satan.

This satanically driven man will "destroy wonderfully" (8:24), meaning that his destruction will be both deceptive and complete. In other words, the people will believe he is a wonderful person interested only in their own good. He will promise plenty for everyone. He will promise, especially, the one thing they want most of all: peace.

The Bible says that this dictator "will cause craft [deceit] to prosper in his hand" (8:25). This is taken two different ways by various prophecy students. Either Antichrist will do this in the sense of deceit or craftiness, or he will do it in the sense of industry, meaning he will produce great prosperity, etc. I personally believe this could be a double reference, wherein both interpretations might be correct.

Antichrist will not be seen as Antichrist at this point. He will be, simply, the greatest man who ever lived in the view of most of the world's inhabitants. He will agree totally with that assessment of himself: "He shall magnify himself in his heart" (8:25).

But the thing that will mark this satanically inspired man is his dealing with the peace process. He will be the opposite of the Prince of Peace, Jesus Christ. He will be the false prince of false peace. Daniel 8:25 prophesies that he will, through peace, "destroy many." The Bible says further, "For when they shall say, Peace and safety; then sudden destruction cometh upon them, as travail upon a woman with child; and they shall not escape" (1 Thessalonians 5:3).

A question we can ask ourselves to see where we most likely stand on God's prophetic timeline is this: "Do we hear a cry for peace and safety today?" And another: "Do we see a peace process today involving God's chosen nation, Israel?" We will soon learn that these issues are crucial to understanding prophecy as it relates to the cauldron that bubbles with the issues of Mideast war and peace.

The great prophecy scholar Dave Breese framed in powerfully descriptive terms the coming to ultimate power of the beast of Revelation chapter 13:

> One can easily envision such a leader presenting himself on international television as "the man with the plan." One could almost hear him say: "Dear friends of earth, brothers and sisters. Let me extend a great call to sanity. We are now presented with the possibility of nuclear holocaust, but such a thing does not have to come to pass. Why should millions die when it could be otherwise? Let us meet together under the great cause of world peace, and let us plan our tomorrows as civilized men. Yes, I have a plan whereby we can move beyond the threat of war into a millennium of peace, and yes, a new age of prosperity."

With these and many other words, a beguiling voice could easily attract the attention, the loyalty, and the cooperation of the nations of the world.[81]

Nuclear Nightmares

For, behold, the day cometh, that shall burn as an oven; and all the proud, yea, and all that do wickedly, shall be stubble: and the day that cometh shall burn them up, saith the LORD of hosts, that it shall leave them neither root nor branch. (Malachi 4:1)

Two developments in the mid-twentieth century took place almost at the same time that cannot be mere coincidence. Until the middle of 1945, man's war-making ability was great. Millions had been killed in some fifteen thousand wars. But that early morning, when the night sky lit up brighter than any day that has ever been, man's ability to make war changed forever.

The first atomic explosion brought mankind to the brink of self-destruction. As a matter of fact, the scientists weren't at all certain that when the bomb ignited on that early morning at Alamogordo, New Mexico, the atmosphere itself wouldn't continue to explode in a chain reaction that could not be stopped. True to man's fallen nature and his tendency to destroy everything he touches, the scientists were willing to take the risk.

At the same time of the first atomic test, the horrific facts about Hitler's murder of 6 million Jews were revealed before the eyes of the world. So great was the reaction that even the elite leaders who wanted to achieve one-world government through the infant United Nations organization couldn't stop the sympathy for the Jews from producing the rebirth of Israel.

These two monumental events—the birth of the atomic bomb in 1945 and the rebirth of God's chosen nation three years later—set the stage for one of the most dramatic prophecies in the Bible regarding end-time matters.

Filling Up a Cup of Trembling

Again we come to the prophet Zechariah's forewarning about Jerusalem and the Middle East region, which God says He will make a "cup of trembling" for the whole world:

> Behold, I will make Jerusalem a cup of trembling unto all the people round about, when they shall be in the siege both against Judah and against Jerusalem.
>
> And in that day will I make Jerusalem a burdensome stone for all people: all that burden themselves with it shall be cut in pieces, though all the people of the earth be gathered together against it....
>
> And it shall come to pass in that day, that I will seek to destroy all the nations that come against Jerusalem. (Zechariah 12:1–3, 9)

The cup—or, cauldron, as our book's title would have it—is filled with an interesting mixture indeed! It is a mixture of ancient hatreds, nuclear weaponry, and Mideast oil. The Lord didn't fill up this cup of deadly ingredients; fallen mankind did. God simply says He will use man's own sinful mixture to bring this world system to a conclusion so that His Messiah, Jesus Christ, can restore order on this dying, decaying planet.

The cleansing scheduled to take place will see pillars of fire mixed with the blood of the rebels opposed to God. The Bible describes in a number of places warfare that might be nuclear in nature, such as the scene described in Joel 2:2–3, which predicts that on "a day of darkness and gloominess, a day of clouds and of thick darkness...a fire devoureth before them; and behind them a flame burneth."

Even the remaking of the earth at the end of the Millennium seems to be thermonuclear. But, this is not surprising. Science has told us for many years about the nature of the atom, which is held together in some way no one really can explain. The electron, neutron, proton, etc., revolve and stick to each other in some mysterious way. Yet, at the same time, the atom gives off great heat and energy.

Jesus, of course, ultimately holds all matter together (see Colossians 1:17). It is Jesus, not the false peace makers who want to rule the world, who will take the burning fuse from the nuclear nightmare and bring real world peace: "The way of peace they know not; and there is no judgment in their goings: they have made them crooked paths: whosoever goeth therein shall not know peace" (Isaiah 59:8).

Satan's Signature

Satan's first attempt to establish world government was stopped. God personally came to earth and stopped it! The Genesis 11 account of the tower builders of Babel on the plains of Shinar is the story of humanism, mankind's philosophy about who should be in charge on planet earth. That philosophy puts forward the declaration that man can take care of himself and the planet without any help or interference from God. Actually, humanism declares, according to its champions like German philosopher Friedrich Nietzsche that God is dead.

Today there is a movement back to the attitude of the tower builders. Satan's fingerprints are all over present-day attempts to kick the Creator off the planet. We see this attitude in our own nation's recent history.

Prayer and Bible reading in public schools were stopped by Supreme Court decisions in 1963. In 1973, the Supreme Court's decision in the abortion case, Roe versus Wade, began the killing of more than 52 million babies in their mothers' wombs at last estimated account.

Since those decisions, the U.S. has endured a rise in deadly violence in public schools. Life, in the view of many young people, seems to have been cheapened to the point that murder rather than schoolyard scuffles are taking place with more regularity in school hallways and classrooms. Humanism is increasingly ingrained in the thinking of our school children. The philosophy is "do what is right in your own eyes," echoing the warning in Proverbs, "The way of a fool is right in his own eyes" (Proverbs 12:15).

The ultimate humanist does what is right in his own eyes; he becomes a law unto himself. Satan's world dictator, Antichrist, will be that ultimate humanist.

The global power brokers are gathering to play God. They think they can force peace upon the rest of us. These internationalist governmental leaders and politicians intend to put an end to war so their New World Order can bring heaven to earth.

The true Christ, of course, is always left out of their plans. The whole world will one day, however, accept a false Christ who promises that elusive thing called peace. Satan will at last have achieved putting his Antichrist in place as absolute ruler of this fallen world. He will bring not peace, but man's worst war ever. When the Lord lifts His mighty hand of restraint from the earth, all peace will disappear. God will give the humanists enough rope, and they will hang themselves.

The Dotted Line...

Daniel was given a staggering prophecy for the end of the age:

> And after threescore and two weeks shall Messiah be cut off, but not for himself: and the people of the prince that shall come shall destroy the city and the sanctuary; and the end thereof shall be with a flood, and unto the end of the war desolations are determined.
>
> And he shall confirm the covenant with many for one week: and in the midst of the week he shall cause the sacrifice and the oblation to cease, and for the overspreading of abominations he

shall make it desolate, even until the consummation, and that determined shall be poured upon the desolate. (Daniel 9:26–27)

The prophecy indicates a peace process presided over by the devil himself. The satanically possessed human called Antichrist will force the peace that will destroy many. Daniel, above, prophesied that after the Messiah lays down his life in sacrifice, the Temple and Jerusalem will be destroyed. The people of the prince who will come will be the destroying force.

Who are these people?

There is a growing swell of insistence that the beast of Revelation 13—Antichrist—will be a Muslim and that the religion of Islam will be the one ruling at the time of Antichrist's reign. While I understand all of the arguments, I must continue to respectfully disagree with the conclusions reached in this proposed scenario. It is more than obvious that Scripture tells and history proves that the Romans are the people out of which this "prince" of darkness will come.

Antichrist will emerge from the revived Roman Empire. Wars will continue until the seven years of Tribulation reaches its conclusion. Daniel's 9:27 prophecy stipulates that from the time the Temple and Jerusalem are destroyed until the end of human history, there will be no true peace.

The prince to come will make and sign a covenant of security or peace for one week—that is, seven years. After three and a half years of the treaty, however, he will break the agreement, beginning what Jesus called the Great Tribulation and what Jeremiah 30:7 refers to as a time of great trouble, the likes of which no one has ever seen before or will ever see again. This is also called the Apocalypse.

The first part of these awesome prophecies has been fulfilled, as we've already seen when, in AD 70, General Titus attacked the rebels in Jerusalem and his troops completely destroyed the Temple as Jesus had predicted. Many prophecies, however, are yet to be fulfilled. Growing global talk of peace proves that tremendous pressure is building. Not only Mideast war and peace are at issue, but world peace is at stake.

One day Satan, himself, in the human form of the greatest world leader ever seen, will step forward to sign on the dotted line. The peace arrangement will supposedly promise peace between Israel and her enemies. But the Bible says it will be a covenant made with death and hell (Isaiah 28:15, 18).

Antichrist, the first beast of Revelation 13, will, three and a half years later, sit in a rebuilt Jewish Temple on Mount Moriah and declare himself to be God. Let's look at what is presently being done in preparation for building that Tribulation Temple.

CHAPTER 15

THIRD TEMPLE TENSIONS

PSALMS 10 SEEMS to anticipate the present-day tensions in Jerusalem:

Why standest thou afar off, O LORD? why hidest thou thyself in times of trouble?

The wicked in his pride doth persecute the poor: let them be taken in the devices that they have imagined.

For the wicked boasteth of his heart's desire, and blesseth the covetous, whom the LORD abhorreth.

The wicked, through the pride of his countenance, will not seek after God: God is not in all his thoughts.

His ways are always grievous; thy judgments are far above out of his sight: as for all his enemies, he puffeth at them.

He hath said in his heart, I shall not be moved: for I shall never be in adversity.

His mouth is full of cursing and deceit and fraud: under his tongue is mischief and vanity.

He sitteth in the lurking places of the villages: in the secret places doth he murder the innocent: his eyes are privily set against the poor.

He lieth in wait secretly as a lion in his den: he lieth in wait to catch the poor: he doth catch the poor, when he draweth him into his net.

He croucheth, and humbleth himself, that the poor may fall by his strong ones. (1–10)

Palestinian Liberation Organization (PLO) police, supposedly in charge of policing terrorist activities in Jerusalem trouble spots such as the Temple Mount, often have acted like terrorists themselves. They look the other way when Palestinian rioters, stirred up by PLO leaders like Arafat and his successors, throw stones and Molotov cocktails, and even fire guns at Israeli policemen and Israeli military troops.

Far from calming the crisis situations that arise daily in that region, the Palestinian police behave more like armed thugs when their own people haven't joined in the riots or demonstrations of hatred for the Jews in the area. Frequently, innocent Palestinian people have had their homes burned or destroyed by bombs and have family members murdered by PLO officials.

These acts are rarely reported by news media. Instead, Israeli police and military are falsely pointed to as the guilty parties. This is not to say that the Israelis haven't done their share of evil. Hatreds often cut both ways. However, news accounts from Jerusalem almost certainly go only one way: in favor of the PLO.

The terrorists of the area, as the psalmist describes, have ungodly, murderous ways. Tensions around the Temple Mount will indeed lead to World War III and Armageddon. The tensions, as stated often throughout our book, are supernatural in their origin. And they are intensifying with talk—and actions—concerning the construction of a Third Temple.

Cornerstone Crusaders

The Jews, whenever they have been put out of the land of promise, have wanted above all else to return to Jerusalem and worship at the Temple. When there was no Temple, they wanted to build one. For two thousand years, the religious Jews have prayed five times a day for a return to worship in a rebuilt Temple. Passover every year brings the reverently whispered words, "Next year in Jerusalem."

Many Jewish people mean these words only in a ritual sense. They don't really think it is possible to build a Temple on or near where the Muslim Dome of the Rock now sits. After all, even though the area is under Israeli sovereignty, the Mount itself—called by Muslims Haram al-Sharif—is controlled by the Islamic Waqf, a joint Palestinian-Jordanian religious body.

The third most holy site in Islam (after Masjid al-Haram in Mecca and Al-Masjid an-Nabawi in Medina, Saudi Arabia), the Al-Aqsa Mosque and the golden-crowned Dome of the Rock overlooking the city attract crowds of Muslim worshipers, with Jews only having access for four and a half hours per day under Waqf regulations that, among other things, prohibit Jews from praying, kneeling, bowing, prostrating, dancing, singing, and/or ripping clothes. However, there is growing demand gathering political support for this status quo on the Temple Mount to be changed: The outcry is for Jews to be allowed to pray upon their ancient site of worship (a fact that Muslims dispute; they say no Temple existed there before).

To accomplish this—and in spite of many Goliath-like obstacles— there are Jews who are not only interested in rebuilding a Third Temple, but who are absolutely determined to see it done...and in their lifetime! Probably the most notable movement toward this end in recent times is the Temple Mount Faithful, founded by Israeli Gershon Salomon. The Temple Mount Faithful tried to place a cornerstone on the Temple Mount site in 1990, causing a tremendous riot in which seventeen people were killed. Salomon hasn't been allowed to visit the place since that time. Under his leadership, the Temple Mount Faithful conducts a symbolic cornerstone laying each October to remind the people of Israel that God has commissioned the Jewish people to build His house.

These people still intend to lay a cornerstone on Moriah someday. They believe the Temple will be built upon and around that foundation.

The very thought of such an action drives the fundamentalist Muslim radicals wild. They will stop the laying of a cornerstone for the Third Jewish Temple at all costs. That is what most worries the international politicians who have taken it upon themselves to make sure World War III doesn't break out beginning at Mount Moriah.

Weapons of Worship

Adding to the mix of Middle East worries are the activities carried on by the Temple Institute. Located near the Western Wall Plaza with a clear view of both the Western Wall and the Mount, the Institute is "dedicated to every aspect of the Biblical commandment to build the Holy Temple of G-d on Mount Moriah in Jerusalem."[82]

"Our goal is to fulfill the commandment of 'They shall make a Temple for me and I will dwell among them,'" says Rabbi Chaim Richman, international director for the organization that, reportedly, has had blueprints for the Third Temple completed for quite some time.

Holding that religious law on the matter is too unclear, rabbis have generally taken the position that rebuilding the Temple shouldn't be undertaken until the Messiah comes. However, Richman and the Institute take a different position, stating that there are no Jewish legal barriers against rebuilding a Temple. The only obstacles that exist are political ones, they say.

Since its establishment in 1987, the Institute's primary goal has been to make preparations for worship in the Temple once it has been rebuilt. Under the guidance of twenty scholars who study Temple law full time, much of that preparation centers on carefully restoring and crafting the sacred instruments of worship "from the original source materials, such as gold, copper, silver and wood." The instruments, the Institute emphasizes, "are authentic, accurate vessels, not merely replicas or models," and are all "fit and ready for use in the service of the Holy Temple." Reports have it that more than half of the required items have already been made, and cases at the Institute's headquarters display forty such objects, including the following:

- Silver trumpets to be blown by priests
- A wooden lyre
- Pans with lengthy handles—one for collecting blood from small animal offerings and another for large sacrifices such as the Passover lamb
- Vestments with azure weaves, gold thread, and a breastplate with twelve precious stones to be worn by deputy priests and the high priest (It reportedly took eleven years and more than $100,000 to complete the outfits for worship.)
- A massive, twelve-spigot sink with electric faucets, modern technology Richman says will be permitted in the Temple
- A golden, two-hundred-pound, seven-branch menorah

Further, the Temple Institute has recreated the rituals and ceremonies that duplicate as nearly as possible the methods of worship used in the First and Second Temples, and it has been training young men to serve as the rabbis who will perform the services of offerings and sacrifices.

Another component essential for Temple worship is a pure red heifer, which must be sacrificed by burning it to ashes. The ashes are then to be added to water and the water used to wash parts of the Temple and the implements of worship in a cleansing ritual stipulated by God in preparation for worship. Anyone who has been around a dead person, whether in a hospital room, a funeral home, or even a graveyard, must be ritually cleansed with this mixture before they can enter the holy site.

There is not yet a red heifer of three years old, as required. Those responsible for the quest to find one thought they had succeeded in 1994. But the heifer, named Melody, born to a black-and-white Holstein mother, was found to have several white hairs in her tail. Reportedly, there are a number of red cows in Israel now that might eventually produce such a heifer.

The menorah planned for use in the Third Temple has already been crafted. Source: A & D

Rabbi Richman's passion—obvious from the following excerpt—reflects the strong sense of longing for a return to Temple worship atop earth's most holy spot:

All of our outreach here at the Temple Institute is about deepening our feeling of connection—not our feeling of loss, not our feeling of mourning—but our joy with the possibility of our generation being the generation that is leading to the rebuilding of the temple," said Rabbi Chaim Richman, head of the Temple Institute International department in an interview with *Israel National News*.

The Temple Institute website says its short-term goal is to "rekindle the flame" of the temple in people's hearts, and its long-term goal is to rebuild the temple in "our time."

"We consider the rebuilding of the holy temple to be one of the positive commandments. Unfortunately because of the whole long diaspora experience, a lot of ideas crept into our sub-consciousness, and even our consciousness, and there are those that say that the temple is going to come down from heaven, there are those that say that only Mashiach (the Messiah) can build the temple, there are those that say, 'well, the whole idea is just not relevant at all,'" Richman said.

"Our position is really just that our lives are like, on hold. The Jewish people are just a skeleton of what they could be. The whole world is really, totally muted and just completely drained of its vibrancy because we don't have the holy temple. And so what we're really trying to emphasize during these days is to rekindle the anticipation and the beauty and the longing for having that closer relationship…when the divine presence returns to the world."[83]

Chaim: "Lost Ark" Isn't Lost

The reason God directed construction of a Temple in the first place (as we looked at in chapter 11) was to provide His people with a way to meet with Him, a place where, through a detailed system of highly symbolic guidelines, they could worship Him, make offerings to Him, and receive His mercy and forgiveness. The sacred Ark of the Covenant was the very essence of that system. For a glimpse at the supernatural significance of the chest-like vessel, we need only read the description of its placement in the First Temple that was completed by Solomon:

Then Solomon assembled the elders of Israel, and all the heads of the tribes, the leaders of the fathers of the children of Israel, before King Solomon in Jerusalem, that they might bring up the ark of the covenant of the Lord out of the city of David, which is Zion....

And the priests brought in the ark of the covenant of the Lord unto its place, into the inner sanctuary of the house, to the most holy place, even under the wings of the cherubim....

And...when the priests were come out of the holy place, that the cloud filled the house of the Lord,

So that the priests could not stand to minister because of the cloud; for the glory of the Lord had filled the house of the Lord. (1 Kings 8:1, 6, 10, and 11)

While theories about where that original chest-like vessel is located now have abounded, biblical scholars throughout history have generally agreed that it must have been destroyed along with the Temple by the Babylonians in 587 BC—and there is no biblical record of a new one having been built for the Second Temple. However, Jewish tradition holds that the Ark of the Covenant is not lost, but is actually hidden:

Tradition records that even as King Solomon built the First Temple, he already knew, through Divine inspiration, that eventually it would be destroyed. Thus Solomon, the wisest of all men, oversaw the construction of a vast system of labyrinths, mazes, chambers and corridors underneath the Temple Mount complex. He commanded that a special place be built in the bowels of the earth, where the sacred vessels of the Temple could be hidden in case of approaching danger. Midrashic tradition teaches that King Josiah of Israel, who lived about forty years before the destruction of the First Temple, commanded the Levites to hide the Ark, together with the original menorah and several other items, in this secret hiding place which Solomon had prepared.

This location is recorded in our sources, and today, there are those who know exactly where this chamber is. And we know that the ark is still there, undisturbed, and waiting for the day when it will be revealed. [84]

That's definitely an intriguing theory—but are there those who really believe this? Absolutely. One journalist's recent interview with Rabbi Richman indicates that of all the obstacles standing in the way of the rebuilding of the Third Temple, having an Ark—*the Ark*—to place in the Holy of Holies is not even a remote concern:

> Rabbi Chaim Richman shows me into a darkened room, strokes his beard and pulls out his smartphone. He has a specially designed app that works the lights. The room illuminates. He taps the screen again, and a heavy curtain slides open. There, resplendent in brilliant gold—and rather smaller than I expected—lies the Ark of the Covenant.
>
> "This isn't the real lost ark," he says. "The real one is hidden about a kilometre from here, in underground chambers created during the time of Solomon." I look at him askance. "It's true," he says. "Jews have an unbroken chain of recorded information, passed down from generation to generation, which indicates its exact location. There is a big fascination with finding the lost ark, but nobody asked a Jew. We have known where it is for thousands of years. It could be reached if we excavated Temple Mount, but that area is controlled by Muslims."[85]

Many folks in addition to those affiliated with the Temple Mount Faithful and the Temple Institute are just as devoted to a Third Temple being built—and are involved in political pressures to do just that. They engage in political lobbying and try to persuade the Jewish community to visit the Temple site at every opportunity.

Some who carefully observe efforts surrounding the project see hope for a peaceful way of accomplishing its construction. One analysis of why that is so states, in part, the following:

Although the prospects of peace are always tantalizing, the likelihood that peace talks will raise unrealistic hopes and stir long-held tension is a real and present danger.

The proposed Two State Solution is an imposition on Israel's 65-year peace process, and does not necessarily address the sensitivities of the people and regimes required to actually make and maintain peace. Besides settlements, recognition of Israel, Gaza and other significant issues, the heart and soul of the conflict is reflected in the microcosm of Jerusalem's Temple Mount....

The prospects of sharing the Rock are difficult because the traditional location associated with the Jewish Temple Holy of Holies is also the Dome of the Rock—a Muslim shrine built in 691 CE....

No amount of coercion can stem the tides of Jewish or Muslim demands for exclusive access to, and possession of, the Temple Mount....

But there is an authentic and ancient proposition...offering hope that a Jewish Temple on Mount Moriah can be realized in peace. If religious authorities agree that the new excavation at the recently discovered site in Jerusalem's City of David is the penultimate location for the Third Temple's altar, then according to Orthodox Jewish law, a sea-change will have occurred. This site, if true, could shift perspective, tradition, and reality. The emergence of a peaceful solution from the epicenter of conflict is a characteristic of Jewish thinking and could be persuasive.[86]

Most prophecy watchers who take a literal view of the prophetic Scriptures believe it will take the supernatural, satanic powers of Antichrist to clear the way for the rebuilding to begin. Under current circumstances, any effort to remove the Dome of the Rock and the al-Aqsa Mosque would mean that the more than 1-billion-strong Muslim world would launch World War III. At this point, talk of a Third Temple must remain just talk.

Strangely, it must be noted, seemingly right on cue, there comes a most perplexing proposal from a most unexpected source. A Muslim pundit, no less, interjects his opinion that the Islamist world should also promote the idea of a Third Temple on Moriah.

Freedom of worship is an essential issue. The Temple Mount, where the First and Second Temples stood, is the holiest place to the people of Israel. However, it is no less holy to both Muslims and Christians. Since this is a location that God has announced to be a "house of prayer for all nations," it should be a place of festivity for all believers. As all who call on the God of Abraham are brothers, Jews and Christians should be able to offer prayers there in dignity and peace along with Muslims. To cast believers out from such a place, to prevent worship there, is a heinous and, quite frankly, cruel policy, which is an offense not only to men, but to Islam. God Himself condemns anyone who forbids worship:

> *"And who is more unjust than he who forbids that in places for the worship of God, God's name should be celebrated?— whose zeal is (in fact) to ruin them? It was not fitting that such should themselves enter them except in fear. For them there is nothing but disgrace in this world, and in the world to come, an exceeding torment." (Koran 2:214)*

Likewise, the Tanakh declares the will of God to make this unique spot a common sanctuary where all people learn to coexist and pray together:

> *"For then will I turn clear language to the Nations, that they may all call upon the name of God, to serve Him shoulder to shoulder." (Zephaniah 3:9)*

Anywhere one prays to the One and Only Almighty God is a house of prayer. Therefore, it is an atrocious thing to forbid anyone from praying at the Temple Mount. The longings of Bnei Israel to pray in that place can never be an offense to a Muslim. On the contrary, it is very pleasant to see Jewish people praying at the Temple Mount. Indeed, all the faithful people should be able to pray there.[87]

Again, Daniel 9:26–27 is the place in the Bible that holds the key to understanding that a Temple must stand on Mount Moriah before Christ's Second Coming. There will first come, however, a tremendous end-of-the-age supernatural storm. Its center of power will hover over the Temple Mount in Jerusalem.

End-Time Turbulence

Many readers remember the shuttle missions of U.S. secretaries of states as they were shown getting on the big jets that were headed for the Holy Land. Henry Kissinger, James Baker, Warren Christopher, and others within the State Department tried to move the peace process forward between Israel and its enemy neighbors.

The latest diplomatic effort as of this writing is by Secretary of State John Kerry, sent by President Barack Obama to try to bring the Israeli government and Palestinian Authority together in resuming the peace process. To do nothing, it is feared by many within the international community, will cause the animosities and anger to grow to full-blown war. Such world diplomatic distress is predicted in the Bible.

The whole Middle East was rocked by the Arab Spring movement, which is only briefly mentioned earlier in the book. The movement, a shake-up begun by supposed Arab factions who wanted to bring democracy to the people who had lived under dictatorships for so long, is said to have started on December 17, 2010, with Mohamed Bouazizi's self-immolation in Tunisia. He was a merchant forbidden to conduct business and committed suicide to protest the regime's tyranny.

Tunisian President Zine El Abidine Ben Ali, Egyptian President Hosni Mubarak, Libyan President Moammar Gadhafi, Yemeni President Ali Abdullah Saleh, and later, newly installed Egyptian President Mohammed Morsi were ousted as a result of the Arab Spring, with Gadhafi killed when his government was overthrown by foreign military intervention. Syrian President (dictator) Bashar Al-Assad's regime as of this writing continues to be under assault by so-called rebels who are thought to be part of the Arab Spring movement.

No matter how "democratic" the Arab Spring is said to be, the movement was hijacked—infiltrated and greatly influenced all along—by the Muslim Brotherhood. The ultimate aim of that organization is the same as that of Egyptian President Gamal Abdul Nasser when he instigated attacks on Israel in 1956 and 1967. The purpose is also the same as that stated by the former Iranian President Mahmoud Ahmadinejad: Completely remove Israel from the Middle East.

Focus has been turned to other matters for a time. The peace talks seem to be taken off the table of diplomatic discussion and filed away. The Roadmap to Peace was given to Great Britain's former Prime Minister Tony Blair to try to interject into the issues that make Jerusalem a most likely place to spawn World War III.

Then came the Arab Spring; the Muslim Brotherhood; the murders of our diplomats at Benghazi; domestic U.S. scandals like that involving the IRS using pressure on certain Americans like Tea Party members and other conservative groups to influence a presidential election; and the National Security Agency spying on U.S. citizens against the Fourth Amendment of the Constitution. The Roadmap to Peace seemed to disappear, and Jerusalem and the Temple Mount seemed to fade in importance.

But, the prophet Daniel said there would be a "covenant" of peace that "the prince that shall come" will sign at some future point (read Daniel 9:26–27). So, just as always happens, Israel, Jerusalem, and Mount Moriah again took center stage when Kerry again started up the shuttle diplomacy as part of the peace process. All cameras and microphones again were directed at that ancient point of world contention.

More than a hundred Palestinian terrorist prisoners were released by the Israeli government as a goodwill gesture in restarting the peace process. Political pressures on the Netanyahu government by its powerful U.S. ally were responsible for the release for the most part.

Meanwhile, Iran, aided by Russia and China, continues to build its nuclear program. New missile defenses provided by those nations add to the difficulty of a future preemptive strike by the Israelis. The turbulence builds!

Tribulation Temple

The Lord has declared that His Son sitting on the throne in Jerusalem is as good as done:

Yet have I set my king upon my holy hill of Zion. I will declare the decree: the LORD hath said unto me, Thou art my Son; this day have I begotten thee. Ask of me, and I shall give thee the heathen for thine inheritance, and the uttermost parts of the earth for thy possession. (Psalms 2:6–8)

A Third Temple will be built, God says. However, with all the plans in place, the terrible fact remains that it will be a Temple not of great joy, but of great sorrow, for the Jewish people. As a matter of fact, the Third Temple will be the Tribulation Temple—the Temple during the time of Jacob's trouble (Jeremiah 30:7), which Jesus said will be the most horrendous time in human history (Matthew 24:21). This is where the Antichrist will take center stage.

When the Antichrist enters the rebuilt Jewish Temple in Jerusalem exactly three and one-half years into the seven-year treaty [the peace covenant Antichrist will confirm, according to Daniel 9], he will stop the daily sacrifice and defile the temple after which he will be assassinated by a wound to the head and resurrected by satanic power. At that time, he will be indwelled by Satan. The false prophet will declare the Antichrist to be God on earth. The Antichrist will demand that everyone worship him as God at which time the false prophet will institute the Mark of the Beast.[88]

Thankfully, this most terrible time in the planet's history will pass. A glorious future is promised to all who love the Lord in spirit and in truth. Jesus, the Jewish Messiah and the Savior of the world, will one day Himself build a Temple—the Fourth Temple—that will be His headquarters throughout His millennial reign. King David will also rule there at the side of Jesus for a thousand years. Jesus will reign as King of all Kings; David, in his resurrected body, will reign as king over all of Israel. Thus, his is called the "Throne of David."

It will be a time of joy and great glory beyond any mankind has known, when Jesus builds that Temple:

And speak unto him, saying, Thus speaketh the LORD of hosts, saying, Behold the man whose name is The BRANCH; and he shall grow up out of his place, and he shall build the temple of the LORD:

Even he shall build the temple of the LORD; and he shall bear the glory, and shall sit and rule upon his throne; and he shall be a priest upon his throne: and the counsel of peace shall be between them both. (Zechariah 6:12–13)

CHAPTER 16

EARTH'S FINAL FURY

WAR-LIKE CONVULSIONS IN the Middle East are like earth tremors forewarning of prophesied explosive end-time events to come.

In the movie *The Devil at 4 O'Clock* starring Frank Sinatra, prisoners on a volcanic island hear the rumbles of the boiling mountain. They feel occasional earthquakes. The rumbling warnings and the quaking become more and more frequent. Finally, the governing authority orders all to leave the island, because there is going to be an eruption.

Throughout the film, a series of lesser, then greater, rumblings and shakings signals impending doom. Sometimes all is still and quiet, but the sense is that this is the calm before the storm and the prisoners and others on the island are never really at peace.

Finally, most of the island's people get away in a ship. They get far out to sea, then it happens! The volcano erupts, and the whole island goes up in one tremendous explosion.

Not only the Middle East, but the whole world, is experiencing rumblings and shakings today like never before. It is like that volcanic island: Sometimes things seem to become quiet, but, it is just the calm before the great end-time storm prophesied throughout the Bible.

Christians, like the shipload of people who escaped the island's explosion in the movie, will be taken from this earth before God's wrath falls. This is called the Rapture. All who have accepted Jesus Christ as Savior and Lord will be taken home to heaven with Jesus when He comes to call them to meet Him above the planet.

There's a whole lot of shaking going on! Let's try to put God's earthquake detector, the prophetic Word, to the task of finding how near this generation might be to earth's final fury.

Signs of the Times

But as the days of Noah were, so shall also the coming of the Son of man be.

For as in the days that were before the flood they were eating and drinking, marrying and giving in marriage, until the day that Noe entered into the ark,

And knew not until the flood came, and took them all away; so shall also the coming of the Son of man be. (Matthew 24:37–39)

End-Time Sign 1: Society and Economy

Unlike in the movie, *The Devil at 4 O'clock*, people of this volcanic cauldron called planet earth have been lulled to sleep. They have trouble feeling all but the most violent rumblings and shakings.

Jesus, in the Olivet Discourse, said it was like that just before the Flood of Noah's day. He said it would again be that way just before He returns to this sinful planet.

People are going about their daily lives, apparently not even recognizing the signs of the end all around them. But the deluge of end-time events will take them into a holocaust of judgment, just as surely as the Flood swept all of sinful mankind away to their deaths.

The sad fact is this: Christians today are as lulled to sleep as those who don't know Jesus as Savior and Lord. Too many are asleep in the pews!

"And that, knowing the time, that now it is high time to awake out of sleep; for now is our salvation nearer than when we believed," the Bible says (Romans 13:11). It is time to awaken and to awaken others: Island earth is about to explode!

The apostle Paul wrote that the last days would be a dangerous time. He then listed the characteristics of people who would live at the end, just before Christ's return to earth:

> This know also, that in the last days perilous times shall come.
>
> For men shall be lovers of their own selves, covetous, boasters, proud, blasphemers, disobedient to parents, unthankful, unholy,
>
> Without natural affection, trucebreakers, false accusers, incontinent, fierce, despisers of those that are good,
>
> Traitors, heady, highminded, lovers of pleasures more than lovers of God;
>
> Having a form of godliness, but denying the power thereof: from such turn away. (2 Timothy 3:1–5)

Lovers of Their Own Selves

Is ours a generation of self lovers? Have you ever surfed the cable channels on your TV? On any given early morning or late night, you will find products and services to make you personally prettier, bigger, smaller, faster, calmer, richer—better! Everything is to build your self-esteem. The infomercial promoters certainly believe we are a self-absorbed generation; their profits prove it.

Covetous

Does money have a place of affection in our society? Even the question must be asked with tongue in cheek. Many today are obsessed with striking it rich. When we consider the banks and the usury (interest) they charge, we know that many have already struck it rich. The credit card industry has enslaved us to the point that national consumer debt is at financial-crisis level.

And, what about the government reaching deeper and deeper into the taxpayers' pockets? Yet the nation is barely able to pay interest on the multi-trillion dollar social programs and pork-barrel projects the politicians have used to, in effect, purchase votes.

But, it is the individual lust for riches that takes the place of trust in God that most fits Paul's term "lovers of money." America is full of people who have the love of money, which, the Bible warns, is "the root of all evil" (1 Timothy 6:10).

Boastful and Proud

Do we see arrogance in our society today? Arrogance is pride that refuses to submit to higher authority. Politicians, once they are in office, often seem above the law. In many cases, they seem to consider themselves above having to answer to those who elected them. They want to "rule" rather than "serve."

We pick on the politician too much, maybe. What about us, individually—do we want things our own way? Do we insist on doing what is right in our own eyes?

Blasphemers

No characteristic of these end times is more offensive, in my view, than this one: blasphemy against the name of the Lord Jesus Christ. Not only can we hear His holy name being used in heated moments as an outright expression of anger, but in general conversation as a point of frustration. It is as if the Savior of the world is so frivolous as to be a mere name that equates to the most unpleasant things in life we must endure.

His name—the name that is above every other name—is used by film scriptwriters, it seems, at every opportunity in today's movies. It seems that they have a certain number of times to use His name in a blasphemous way within the ninety or so minutes of the film's running time.

More and more, the use of Jesus' name and that of God the Father are heard being used blasphemously even on network television. As this generation moves farther from godliness, our thinking and language turn to rage against the one who loves us most of all, and who, alone, offers hope of safety in this condemned world.

Disobedient to Parents

Are our children more disobedient today? Yes. There can be no other answer for the news accounts that are just too many and too frequent to explain away. Children, teenagers, and even grown-ups exhibit the end-time characteristic of being disobedient to parents. Young people, like others in society today, don't want authorities telling them what they can and cannot do. When parents' authority and young people doing what they want to do collide today, the situations can end in tragedy.

Too often, children leave angry and get into trouble. More and more, we hear of family members killing other family members in a temper rampage. The causes of disobedience to parents are many: parents giving in to their children, parents divorcing, parents having a lack of attention, the pressures of the drug culture, the rebellious effects of a sinful entertainment culture…these and other factors contribute to this last-days symptom.

Unthankful, Unholy

Who gets the praise in today's society? People today are proud of the things they have. They are sometimes grateful to others for what they possess or have attained; however, for the most part, people use the word "thankful" not in the sense of thankfulness to God, but in the sense of being glad and pleased.

To be truly thankful to God, people must be holy. That is, they must be children of God, saved by the shed blood of Christ. Those who haven't been made holy in Christ can't really thank a God they don't believe in.

The vast, unholy masses today don't know, nor do they seek to know, the true God of heaven. They reject the Son of God, who said, "No man cometh unto the Father, but by me" (John 14: 6).

This fallen world views the biblical truth that Jesus is the only way to God as a "narrow-minded" concept that can't and won't be tolerated by an enlightened people of the twenty-first century.

Without Natural Affection

What's wrong with free love? Being "without love" is perhaps the easiest characteristic to spot.

Hollywood's version of love has perverted what true love is all about. The entertainment industry has gotten love and lust mixed up. Sexual activity is at the heart of the confusion.

Since we are just animals, according to evolution, mating is natural. What's the harm in having fun any way, anytime, anywhere? In the 1960s, this philosophy was called "free love." Today it is referred to in its most base sense as "hooking up."

It is disturbing that many Christians enjoy the goings-on in vulgar sitcoms on television. God's people today can't seem to discern what is wrong with sex of every description being implied or displayed before them and their children in their homes.

This is wrong because God says it is wrong! He gave one man to one woman, for life. Love was given by God to mankind. Real love must revolve around the Creator. Sex is a private matter, not a public one.

Also, as some like to say, God didn't make a couple called Adam and Earnest, or Eve and Alice. He made man and woman, called them husband and wife, and intended them to love freely within the bonds of marriage. The many terrible things that come from breaking God's laws in regard to marriage are easy to see in this generation; the break-up of homes, venereal diseases, broken hearts and minds, children in rebellion, and even violence are a few of the outward signs of this term "without natural affection."

Further, nothing is more violent or "unnatural" than murdering a baby. But, in America today, we've made the practice a legal thing under our constitution. Making babies is but an inconvenience that comes from sexual activity. Why not just have birth control after the fact through abortion? It's a woman's right!

Babies should be safest when in their mothers' wombs, but that isn't the case in America today. As previously reported, more than 52 million have been aborted since 1973. By far, abortions have been done for convenience. Birth should be the most wonderful way to show the love between husband and wife. Murder of babies in the womb has become the most unnatural act of all. The Bible says much about babies yet unborn; see, for example, Jeremiah 1:5; Psalms 103:14; and Luke 1:41–44.

Trucebreakers, False Accusers, Incontinent

Truce-breaking (in other words, "unforgiving"), slanderous, and without self-control—could there be three more graphic, yet accurate, terms to describe this generation? Let's look at an American institution as chief example of these three end-time symptoms rolled into one.

Marriage in the U.S. today embodies these as perhaps nothing else. The divorce rate now exceeds that of marriages. That is, there are now more divorces being granted than marriages being performed. Unforgiveness and refusal to commit to make changes for the better can be blamed for many of the breakups.

The person who wrongs the other is not truly sorry for the wrong. Forgiveness either is not given, or is a forgiveness that harbors anger.

But the last-days term "trucebreakers" goes much deeper. There is no greater treaty or agreement than that made between a man and a woman in marriage as far as God is concerned. He likens the union between Christ and the church as a marriage that cannot be broken.

False accusation, or slander, like the other two end-time characteristics, is a trucebreaker in marriage. Usually, harsh, lying words of slander follow a breakup of a marriage. Each slanders the other to gain advantage in the divorce court.

The third term, "incontinent," which simply means "without self-control," is often at the center of the whole problem in a failed marriage. One or the other—maybe both—want everything their own way. They're unable to control their tempers, their emotions, their wanderlust.

And, the term "incontinent" must be looked at a little more closely. Alcoholism, drug use (both overused prescription and illicit), overspending, and all other things that are addictive add to the evidence that we might be in the very last days. Lack of self-control is everywhere. It cuts across gender, race, age, class, and any other demographic that can be named. Ours is a generation that will not—indeed, because of rampant sin, *cannot*—manage self-control.

Fierce

America is one of the most violent places on earth—so much so that many fuzzy-minded people would like to see the Second Amendment right of gun ownership taken away. They don't think long and hard enough to understand that to lessen violence by eliminating potential weapons, every brick, stone, baseball bat, etc., in the country would also have to be outlawed. While we're at it, we would have to cut off everybody's hands as well so people couldn't choke other people.

Violence is in the hearts of mankind. Cain committed the first murder with a rock!

And, the liberal-minded might like to answer this: Since police are already stretched to the limits in fighting crime, who and what would protect us when only the bad guys and the police have the guns?

We certainly don't have to look outside our "civilized" America to find a society that fits the last-days symptom 2 Thessalonians 3 calls "fierce." Just pick up any newspaper and read the front page, or watch your local television news this evening.

Despisers of Those That Are Good

What or who is the "good"—the only good there is? God sees "good" or "righteousness" only in His Beloved Son, Jesus. Anyone who hasn't been washed in the atoning blood of Christ is like a bundle of "filthy rags" in God's holy eyes.

Is it any wonder, then, that the world hates the belief that Jesus Christ is the one and only way to God and heaven? To believe such a thing is narrow-minded, bigoted, and intolerant, the world says.

One famous billionaire said that Christianity is a religion for losers. A famous wrestler-turned-governor said that religion (implying strongly "Christianity") is a crutch for the weak.

Because of public and political pressures, both apologized to a slight extent for their remarks. But their lifestyles seem to reflect a hatred for laws of God that would impose responsibility upon them for the way they conduct their personal lives.

True Christians—those who believe that there is no other way to heaven than absolute belief in Christ's death, burial and resurrection for the cure for sin—are coming under attack more and more. Christian principles are mocked and ridiculed. Christ's name is blasphemed by Hollywood and the entire world.

When prayer was kicked out of America's public schools in 1963, the effects soon became evident. Rebellion of young people grew into greater disobedience, then into rioting, during the "free-love" years and Vietnam. Youthful rage grew and grew until now there are shootings, stabbings, and bombings by children in public schools.

The proof that there is a hatred for the good came when the boys murdered many of their schoolmates at Columbine High School in Colorado. The murderers looked for the students who had been meeting in prayer and Bible reading. They sought out Christian kids to shoot, in particular. Cassie Bernall was shot in the face while she prayed. The one doing the shooting and the others with him hated Christians, according to the reports coming from that tragedy.

The anger against Jesus and all who follow Him is a signal of the end of the age. Satan is stepping up his campaign of hatred while Christ's coming again draws closer.

Traitors, Heady, High-Minded

These symptoms of last-days mankind are in our headlines today. Being a traitor, or acting treacherously, in terms of dealing danger to others for personal gain, was seen in the case of FBI agents who sold secrets to Russia.

Robert Hanssen, considered a trustworthy agent for many years, was convicted for being a traitor and in May of 2002, at the age of 58, was sentenced to life in prison without parole. Under the code name of Ramon Garcia, among others, he sold secret spy investigation information to America's enemies.

This "perilous times" characteristic came again into focus, we remember, when the National Security Agency (NSA) consultant, Edward Snowden, divulged the secretive agency's methods of illegally collecting information on private American citizens, and gathering data surreptitiously on even our closest allies. Some, of course, considered him a hero for outing this violation of the Fourth Amendment. However, the action was greatly damaging to America's relationships around the world. The fact that Snowden fled to Russia, almost certainly providing America's most notable adversary with top-secret information, was a traitorous act.

And, make no mistake: Russia is still an enemy of the U.S., despite the fall of the Soviet Union. The fact that Russia continues to build its nuclear arsenal and threaten those who oppose communist-style oppression proves that nation's true intentions against the U.S. and the West.

The crimes of these men against their nation demonstrate the other two symptoms of end-times man as well. The actions showed a mindset that was rash. That is, they acted out their traitorous crimes regardless of the potential consequences. The fact that they thought they could outsmart those who guard against spies shows a definite conceit.

Lovers of Pleasures More than Lovers of God

Where do we Americans spend most of our time? Ours is a generation of pleasure seekers. No one would argue against the assertion that people in America today spend by far a greater part of their time being entertained than in Bible study, prayer, and church attendance. As we've seen before, our time has been freed by technology to enjoy more and more leisure time. Where is most of our time spent, when we are not working or sleeping?

Having a Form of Godliness, but Denying the Power Thereof

What do we say when asked about our religious affiliation? Many claim that America is a Christian nation. A majority of people say they're Christians, or that they at least belong to one Christian church or another. Only God, who sees into the soul, knows for sure. But the lives of most people today don't reflect Christ in their actions.

Churches are more empty than full on any given Sunday. The exception is on Christmas and Easter. We are a generation that claims Christianity, but denies Christianity's power by refusing to live as Jesus expects His followers to live. This is having a form of godliness, but denying its power. That power is the Lord Jesus Christ. The Bible says that this is a sure sign of the last days.

End-Time Sign 2: Government and Technology

John, a disciple and apostle of Jesus, wrote several books of the Bible, including Revelation. He was given great prophecies of things to come, visions of future events, when he was a very old man stranded on the island of Patmos in the Aegean Sea. Among those visions was a glimpse of the last great earthly government and the man who would rule over the whole world. The final government will be a one-world system as described in the following passage:

> And he causeth all, both small and great, rich and poor, free and bond, to receive a mark in their right hand, or in their foreheads:
>
> And that no man might buy or sell, save he that had the mark, or the name of the beast, or the number of his name.
>
> Here is wisdom. Let him that hath understanding count the number of the beast: for it is the number of a man; and his number is six hundred threescore and six. (Revelation 13:16–18)

Do we see any such thing shaping up in our time? The answer is a definite yes. There are so many movements in the direction of a single government for the whole earth that there isn't space enough here to deal with it all. We'll look only at the most obvious of the many movements.

The initial Millennium Summit held September 26, 2000, brought together the largest group of heads of states in one meeting in history. The summit's purpose was to work toward putting together a plan for "global governance"—another term for one-world government.

The United Nations planned, according to the United Nations Commission on Global Governance in its 1995 report, "Our Global Neighborhood," to ratify a new United Nations charter instituting global governance. For a number of reasons, this action failed. What the globalist planners couldn't get done under official UN approval, they have moved to do through Non-Governmental Organizations (NGOs).

The one-world planners failed to get anywhere near the 150 nations they expected to agree to sign a new UN charter, and are now working fast and furiously to put together as many organizations that share a common desire for a single earthly government as possible. These various though single-minded groups, such as Greenpeace, Green Cross, and others, apparently will act as pressure groups to eventually bring about a one-world government under the United Nations.

Recent developments within the Millennium Summit-type efforts prove the goal of the one-world elitists is still to chain all of us to their neo-Babel agenda. The following excerpt of a report informs further:

> The U.N. Millennium Development Goal has demanded the imposition of international taxes as part of a stated effort of "eradicating extreme poverty, reducing child mortality rates, fighting disease epidemics such as AIDS and developing a global partnership for development."
>
> *Investor's Business Daily* reported the Millennium goal called for a "currency transfer tax," a "tax on the rental value of land and natural resources" and a "royalty on worldwide fossil energy projection—oil, natural gas, coal." It also called for "fees for the commercial use of the oceans, fees for airplane use of the skies, fees for use of the electromagnetic spectrum, fees on foreign exchange transactions, and a tax on the carbon content of fuels."
>
> Indeed, in September 2010, a group of 60 nations, including France, Britain and Japan, proposed at the U.N. summit on the Millennium Development Goals that a tax be introduced on international currency transactions to raise funds for development aid.[89]

Satan's apocalyptic world government is being formed, like it or not. The technology that Antichrist will use to control most everyone on the globe is already here. The computer, combined with the Internet, satellites, fiber optics, and the many Big Brother-like snooping technologies such as Eschalon, Carnivore, and, more recently, Prism, awaits the Revelation 13 beast's guiding hand.

End-Time Sign 3: Geophysical, Astrophysical

"Geophysical" means everything physical that exists on our planet. "Astrophysical" means everything physical that exists in our atmosphere or in space. Jesus gave a very specific warning that at the very end of the age unusual things will be taking place on earth and in the heavens (in the atmosphere and space): "And there shall be signs in the sun, and in the moon, and in the stars; and upon the earth distress of nations, with perplexity; the sea and the waves roaring" (Luke 21:25).

Have we seen anything that unusual in our time? This can be answered both ways, because things taking place today would have absolutely flabbergasted people just prior to the mid-twentieth century and before. But most of these things have become commonplace to people today. So, yes, earlier generations would find these things unusual—and, no, people today, for the most part, don't find them all that unusual.

Nonetheless, looking at technology today, we can see Jesus' words come to life. The computer, television/satellite linkages, cures for deadly diseases and other medical breakthroughs, fantastic conveniences for living in leisure—all of these are almost miraculous compared to earlier centuries.

That takes care of "signs in the earth" the Lord talked about. What about "signs in the heavens"? What would your great, great grandfather have thought about astronaut Neil Armstrong and the others walking on the moon? Some people even today don't believe it. They think it was all staged on a Hollywood set to fool us.

UFO sightings have almost become everyday happenings in our time. Strange things are taking place in the heavens, indeed! While on earth there seems to be a great increase in earthquakes, violent storms, and volcanoes, in the heavens there are lights and objects that move at unbelievable speeds. They appear suddenly and disappear just as suddenly. They turn at angles and move at speeds that no human passenger could survive. Some prophecy scholars believe these strange objects are angelic activities rather than extraterrestrial traffic from other planets. Regardless, they fit Christ's forewarning of signs in the heavens.

End-Time Sign 4: Religion

And Jesus answered and said unto them, Take heed that no man deceive you.

For many shall come in my name, saying, I am Christ; and shall deceive many.…

And then shall many be offended, and shall betray one another, and shall hate one another.

And many false prophets shall rise, and shall deceive many.

And because iniquity shall abound, the love of many shall wax cold. (Matthew 24:4–5; 10–12)

Jesus' warning in these verses that false religion will come in the last days is coming to pass before our eyes today. False teachings by false teachers and false prophecies by false prophets have exploded on the scene. The one-world, end-time church prophesied in Revelation chapter 12 is being formed.

This movement toward a one-world religious system, like the new-world-order geopolitical idea, is based on the call for unity. Everyone must get rid of prejudices. We should all accept the views of others and join together in a wonderful union that will someday turn our world into heaven on earth.

True Christianity is a hindrance that blocks this drive toward unity. Therefore, true Christian beliefs are more and more being put in the category with evil doomsday cults.

The effort to bring about a one-world religious system began in a big way just before the Millennium Summit met in September 2000. It was called the Millennium Summit on Peace of Religious and Spiritual Leaders, and it met August 28–30, 2000, at the United Nations headquarters with the stated purpose of unifying religions around a common idea of peace. The summit advised the UN on spiritual issues, with part of the advice being to recommend condemning any religion that doesn't have all-inclusive doctrines. In other words, every religion must compromise its belief system to include all belief systems.

That meeting focused on how all NGOs can participate in the decision-making process on religious affairs. With the person who contributed $1 billion to the United Nations for peace making the remark that "Christianity is for losers," we must wonder where the message of the Lord Jesus stands with that organization and others who share that philosophy. Jesus said, "I am the way, the truth, and the life: no man cometh unto the Father, but by me" (John 14:6).

Strange Bedfellows Indeed!

Religious transformations that are taking place are amazing. Pope Francis has begun to change the face of Catholicism, and, some say, all of Christendom.

Thomas Horn and Chris Putnam recently wrote *Petrus Romanus*, a book that includes sixteenth-century Irish Bishop Malachy's predictions of all the popes leading up to the final pontiff. Pope Francis is pope number 112 from the time Malachy predicted the list of 112 popes that would reign from his time to the very last pope.

It is fascinating to observe that this pope has made moves contradictory to what Catholic interaction with communistic leaders has been over the past century. While President Vladimir Putin's Russian government claims not to be communist any longer, Putin himself is a powerful leader straight out of the old Soviet KGB.

Pope Francis and Putin's historic meeting on November 25, 2013, is reported in the following:

Pope Francis and Russian President Vladimir Putin met Monday amid high expectations that their visit could mark the beginning of the end of the centuries-old rift between the Roman Catholic and Eastern Orthodox churches. Since becoming pontiff in March, Francis has met with more than a dozen heads of state, but this meeting comes at a unique time.

"What's making (this visit) different this time is who he will meet: a pope, Francis, who for the first time is not from Europe," said Andrea Tornielli, a Vatican expert who writes for the Italian daily *La Stampa*. "And [Francis] being from Argentina, **is not tied to the old idea of Western Christianity, so this could play in [Putin's] favor,**" Tornielli added.[90] (emphasis added)

This pope certainly has proven to prefer moving away from the Catholic Church's views on salvation and homosexuality. He has made statements on a number of occasions that imply he believes the Church (Catholic Church) must begin to have a more open mind, choosing rather to put distance between the Church and the one and only way the Bible presents as the route to God and heaven in the hereafter. The Catholic Church, he indicates, now must accept that there are many ways to God and heaven. He has said the same about homosexuality—that the Catholic Church must be more tolerant and open-minded about homosexuals—presumably meaning so-called gays must be accepted as not violating the heretofore Catholic system's declaration that homosexuality is sin against God.

I in no sense mean to imply that Pope Francis is the pope who will oversee the Catholic Church during its most troubling times in history as St. Malachy's predictions seem to indicate. Nor do I mean to imply that Vladimir Putin is to be the Gog leader of the Ezekiel 38–39 prophesied assault on Israel. But, it is interesting that the pope is taking the Catholic system toward embracing a regime that is run by a leader who was a short time ago a brutal enforcer for what was called an "evil empire" by an American president.

This is taking place at the same time the Iranian Islamist tyrants are cozying up to the same Russian leader, while threatening Israel with nuclear annihilation.

The pope is in a position to influence the direction religion will take over the course of the next few years. He certainly seems to relish his role, as news headlines these days attest.

Revelation 13 foretells that a false prophet will arise, one who will be the ultimate leader of the forming one-world religion. He will give all praise and honor to the political beast, the Antichrist. Then it will not be heaven come down to this world. It will be hell on earth! Everyone will be forced to worship the image of this dictator or be killed.

End-Times Nations Noted

The Bible has much to say about how certain nations will fit within the last-days picture. World situations today involving these particular countries and regions are remarkably similar to the Bible's description of how things will shape up at the end of the age. Let's have a closer look.

Gog, Magog

We've dealt with Russia and its allies most likely being the invasion force predicted by the prophet in Ezekiel 38 (see verses 1–6 and 14–16). It is best here to look a bit into why Russia looks to be this end-time leader-nation that will come against Israel.

It must be repeated, however, that conditions in Russia and the regions north of Israel are ripe for the leader called Gog to get the "evil thought" in his mind. That evil thought will bring all of those prophesied to attack in order to get great "spoil" against the tiny country at some point—perhaps very soon!

Some of the names in the Ezekiel prophecies are quite familiar, such as Ethiopia, Libya, and even Persia, which Iran and parts of Iraq occupy now. Gomer, it is believed, refers to parts of Germany. Togarmah, it is thought, includes much of modern Turkey. Ethiopia in ancient times occupied a far greater land mass than present-day Ethiopia. Libya, too, sat upon a larger land area than the modern Libya. But, these are areas where many developments in our time show potential troubles for Israel.

Other Nations Mentioned

What about America in prophecy? What will happen to the U.S.? These are questions people are always interested in discussing. Although the United States of America isn't mentioned in prophecy specifically by name, some prophecy scholars think it is referenced in the following:

> Sheba, and Dedan, and the merchants of Tarshish, with all the young lions thereof, shall say unto thee, Art thou come to take a spoil? hast thou gathered thy company to take a prey? to carry away silver and gold, to take away cattle and goods, to take a great spoil? (Ezekiel 38:13)

I personally believe America will no longer be a superpower when the time of the Tribulation, or Apocalypse, arrives. I do believe the U.S. could still be around as a nation that has been absorbed into the ten-leader kingdom prophesied in Daniel and Revelation.

In the passage above, there is reason to see America at least indicated as part of a group of symbolized end-time nations. The symbols have a definite relationship to real peoples and places of the past. And, of course, actual regional names are mentioned as well in this passage.

Sheba and Dedan refer to the Arab nations in the Middle East region, such as Saudi, Kuwait, and others. Tarshish, we are told, indicates the region of Europe, including England.

And here's where many think the United States comes into the picture. "All the young lions" seems to refer to the nations that have come out of Europe. England was represented symbolically as a lion in ancient times. America is the most notable offspring, or "young lion," to come specifically from that country.

The reference in this passage seems to represent the whole region of

Europe. This group of nations apparently does nothing to try to stop Russia and its allies from sweeping into the Middle East at this point. They seem only to send a diplomatic note of protest: "Art thou come to take a spoil?" But we know that, according to Ezekiel's prophecies, God Himself will stop the Gog-Magog invaders and will destroy all but one-sixth of those forces.

Revived Roman Empire

Daniel the prophet's visions, as we have seen, told of the strange beast-government that will stomp across the world at the end of the age. This government will be ruled by history's most terrible tyrant, an absolute dictator with a beast-like nature that will make Hitler and Stalin look shy by comparison.

Many prophecy scholars believe he will come out of a revived Roman Empire, a powerful bloc of nations that occupies the same land areas the ancient Roman Empire occupied at the top of its power. It will be centered, at least for a time, in Rome.

This last great earthly kingdom before Christ comes to set up His kingdom is in view today. The European Union is a growing, rising economic group of nations that will soon rival, then surpass, America in power. I didn't say this; God did. We can know that this last great power is Roman in origin because of the prophecy given in Daniel 9:26b–27:

> And the people of the prince that shall come shall destroy the city and the sanctuary; and the end thereof shall be with a flood, and unto the end of the war desolations are determined.
>
> And he shall confirm the covenant with many for one week: and in the midst of the week he shall cause the sacrifice and the oblation to cease, and for the overspreading of abominations he shall make it desolate, even until the consummation, and that determined shall be poured upon the desolate.

"The prince that shall come" refers to Antichrist, the last world ruler, whose people—the Romans—destroyed Jerusalem and the Jewish Temple, just as Daniel prophesied. Again, Antichrist's kingdom, although worldwide in scope and power, will originate in the heart of Europe, which was the center of power for the ancient Roman Empire.

The Antichrist will be backed by the power of the Roman Empire, which will have been revived in every way. "In these very days," notes Dave Breese, "European political leaders, philosophers, and economists...are thinking every moment about a sense of destiny with reference to the future."

Breese continues:

They anticipate and deliberately plan to put together a new power [bloc] that will be second to none across our present world. But they plan largely without including the true God in their ambitions.

How will they do this? It does not strain the imagination to think that there could quickly develop in Europe a composite form of theologically corrupted neo-Christianity plus New Age paganism that could be the initial magnetism to pull Europe together in a program of religious unity. In Europe and across the world, the call for "Christian unity" is coming on very strong. Many denominations—even in America—beset by lack of attendance, financial problems, mediocre leadership, aging buildings, rusting machinery, and spiritual exhaustion, are beginning to think of global religious unity as the answer, producing the dawn of a new age. Look for that call to grow, and especially listen for it to come out of the continent of Europe as the West seeks its soul again.[91]

This revived Roman Empire will bring Israel and her enemies together in an arrangement for peace that God calls "a covenant with death, and with hell" (Isaiah 28:15), because He knows only He can protect Israel in the last days.

The signing of the peace agreement will set in motion the Tribulation or Apocalypse, the last seven years of human history before Christ's Second Coming. War, famine, disease, and death will mark this period, especially the last three and a half years. The many horrendous things prophesied for this era will come upon the world like a flood. The great war called Armageddon will be the final horror, then Jesus will return.

Kings of the East

There has been more war than peace in the Middle East since Adam accepted the forbidden fruit. But all of the conflicts combined will pale in comparison to Armageddon—for one reason, because of the sheer numbers of soldiers prophesied to be involved. Those massive numbers can be seen if we look only at the force called "the kings of the east" mentioned by John in Revelation 16:12 and numbered at 200 million in Revelation 9:16: "And the number of the army of the horsemen were two hundred thousand thousand and I heard the number of them."

Imagine: Two hundred million soldiers will come across the dried-up Euphrates River to do battle in the valley of Megiddo. Amazingly, that is exactly the number we hear so often about the number of troops China could put into action today.

"The kings of the east" prophecy, however, indicates a force that will come out of all of the Orient, not just out of any one nation. There will probably be even more than John heard and reported. He possibly was given a general number rather than a specific one.[92]

Is there any indication in our time that a nation or group of nations in the oriental part of the world might be up to mischief?

The following report, even though from a *U.S. Congressional Report* some years ago, encapsulates the troubling facts about such a force. Those facts have grown even more ominous since that earlier time.

Worldwide, China appears to be progressively positioning itself commercially and militarily along the key naval choke points between the Indian Ocean, the South China Sea; the Straits of Malacca; the central Pacific; the coast of Hawaii; the Caribbean; and now the Panama Canal....

This activity appears to be part of a plan to implement what China refers to as "unrestricted war." The plan theoretically levels the playing field with the vastly superior U.S. military. It calls for strategic positioning of China's military, while employing terrorism, computer sabotage, financial strangulation, drug trafficking, propaganda and other destabilizing schemes to weaken the U.S. and create political upheaval.[93]

Israel

That then the Lord thy God will turn thy captivity, and have compassion upon thee, and will return and gather thee from all the nations, whither the LORD thy God hath scattered thee....

And the LORD thy God will bring thee into the land which thy fathers possessed, and thou shalt possess it. (Deuteronomy 30:3,5a)

We've looked at Israel from most every angle. Put quite simply, Israel is God's prophetic clock! More and more, every news eye and ear turns toward the Middle East for any sight or sound of trouble. That is the one area where everyone in diplomatic circles senses World War III could easily break out.

More specifically, all eyes and ears turn worriedly toward Israel. This, as we have seen, is precisely what has been prophesied for the last days. Jesus and all of the prophets predicted that the Middle East would be the most volatile place on earth at the end of the age.

America's Treachery

Certainly, the Jewish state is at the heart of the rush toward Armageddon. The prophecy by Zechariah—that Jerusalem and Israel will become a burdensome stone and cup of trembling (Zechariah 12:1–3)—made a leap forward in coming into view on the diplomatic front on Sunday, November 24, 2013.

The Obama administration, with Secretary of State John Kerry in the lead, joined with the international community in making an agreement with the Iranian regime that many view as a betrayal of Israel. Just as the sanctions against Iran for pursuing development of a nuclear program to produce atomic weaponry were beginning to make an impact, the U.S., in concert with the world powers that constitute the international community, agreed to lift part of those economic sanctions on Iran for six months. The Islamic republic promised to cooperate with the international nuclear observers and to limit its enrichment of uranium.

The Israeli leadership—which wasn't privy to the behind-the-scenes-dealings—wasn't deceived by the near jubilation displayed by the cabalist diplomats' actions. The Israelis realize that in Islam, it is not only okay to lie in negotiations with enemies, it's preferred. Ends justify means, just as in the Marxist playbook for dealing with adversaries.

The Obama team apparently was not as immune to the venomous deception as Benjamin Netanyahu and his leadership team. The Israeli prime minister said:

What was reached last night in Geneva is not a historic agreement, it is a historic mistake. Today the world became a much more dangerous place because the most dangerous regime in the world made a significant step in obtaining the most dangerous weapons in the world.[94]

Israel's minister of intelligence, Yuval Steinitz, added that the "deal was based on 'Iranian deception and (international) self-delusion.'"[95]

Israel, based upon a long history of dealing with treacherous enemies, is skeptical of Iran's claims that its nuclear program is strictly for peaceful purposes. The Jewish state has threatened a military strike against Iran as a preemptive measure against the acquirement of a nuclear weapon.

Luciferic influence, it is obvious, rules the minds of those globalists who want peace at any price. The deception is becoming overwhelming. Christians, therefore, have no excuse to be surprised by developments in these critical days. This is why it's so crucial for believers to study Bible prophecy, for seminaries to teach the prophetic Word, and for preachers and teachers to follow through in studying the things God has given for these last days.

This is, for those of us who follow Christ, not a day of gloom and doom, but the most exciting time in history.

The destruction of the Twin Towers of the World Trade Center in New York City was indeed a wake-up call. For a time, at least, Americans took notice as we turned our attention to the Middle East and the Israeli/Palestinian conflict.

The explosion of rage with the Arab Spring movement, the tremendous upheaval in Iran, Syria, Egypt, Libya, and many other nations that boil within the Mideast cauldron, give unmistakable evidence of the lateness of the hour in human history. But too many of God's children are asleep in the pews. Far too many ministers are not addressing the end-time issues as put forward by Jesus and the prophets. Christ said in Mark 13:37, "And what I say unto you I say unto all, Watch." Our Lord could return at any moment!

History's Furious Finish

Do you think Antichrist is alive today? This is a question I often get in interviews when promoting a book. Another question is: "Do you think Antichrist might be_____?" Fill in the name of your choice, among today's world figures.

People want these questions answered almost as much as they want to know when the Rapture will happen, or even IF the Rapture will happen. Even secular reporters are asking these questions. As a matter of fact, I sometimes think secular reporters are more interested in prophecy today than are the Christian seminaries, pastors, and people in pews of our churches.

Programs on television channels like Discovery, A&E, and the Learning Channel almost routinely run documentary shows on prophecies. It is true that most of these programs place more emphasis on and belief in the prophecies of false prophets like Nostradamus, Edgar Cayce, and Jeanne Dixon, etc., but, occasionally, these shows will throw in a true prophetic biblical scholar like Hal Lindsey, Chuck Missler, or Tim LaHaye. I myself was a part of *The Nostradamus Effect* series for the History Channel several years ago.

The Bible says that the Rapture of the church will be a surprise to those not looking for Jesus. God's Word tells us also that the Antichrist, referred to as "the man of sin" in 2 Thessalonians 2:3, will not be revealed until there is a great "falling away"—meaning a rebellion or apostasy—first.

The apostasy of the last days is most likely already well underway. The fact that so many Christian schools, preachers, and people in the pews seem not to notice or care about this time of the signs in which we live is a dead giveaway that the Tribulation period and the revealing of Antichrist can't be far off.

The "man with the plan," as Dave Breese called him, indeed could be waiting just off of the world stage. Or, he could be among some of the better known leaders in geopolitical, international affairs today.

I believe, based on the many, many signals of the last days we've been addressing in this chapter, that the one who will be Antichrist is alive today. I hasten to add that I even more firmly believe that if you are a true Christian today, you will not know who this man is—unless, of course, God allows us a look once we're in heaven with Him. We who are Christians during this Church Age are not to look for Antichrist, but for Jesus Christ. Titus 2:13 says we are to be "looking for that blessed hope, and the glorious appearing of the great God and our Savior Jesus Christ." Antichrist will be revealed, you see, in the time of the Tribulation or Apocalypse, the time of God's wrath. Christians of the Church Age are not appointed to wrath (see 1 Thessalonians 5:9).

Armageddon Armies March to Megiddo

The great would-be peacemakers of this world like to use Micah 4:3 in their promises to stop war forever. They have even put it in stone on the United Nations Building in New York: "And they shall beat their swords into plowshares, and their spears into pruninghooks: nation shall not lift up a sword against nation, neither shall they learn war anymore."

But the Bible says that passage is for the Millennium. It will come to pass only after the true peacemaker, Jesus Christ, has come back to rule and reign on this planet. The prophecy in Joel 3 says just the opposite will be true as the end of this age comes to a violent close:

> Proclaim ye this among the Gentiles; Prepare war, wake up the mighty men, let all the men of war draw near; let them come up;
>
> Beat your plowshares into swords and your pruninghooks into spears: let the weak say, I am strong.
>
> Assemble yourselves, and come, all ye heathen, and gather yourselves together round about: thither cause thy mighty ones to come down, O Lord.
>
> Let the heathen be wakened, and come up to the valley of Jehoshaphat: for there will I sit to judge all the heathen round about.
>
> Put ye in the sickle, for the harvest is ripe: come, get you down; for the press is full, the fats overflow; for their wickedness is great.
>
> Multitudes, multitudes in the valley of decision: for the day of the Lord is near in the valley of decision. (9–14)

This prophecy is given for the dark, stormy hours of the Tribulation period and will come to pass as mankind prepares for ultimate warfare at Armageddon, where the Lord God Himself will gather the war-crazed armies. The weapons of Armageddon-like war aren't just now being prepared as the Joel 3 prophecy demands. This has already been done. These implements of great destruction are already prepared and ready to destroy all human flesh! This is one prophecy that has already been fulfilled.

If you don't believe it, just consider the unbelievable power of the hydrogen bomb. The atomic bomb that completely destroyed Hiroshima, Japan, was comparable to about twelve thousand tons of TNT in strength. A one-megaton H-Bomb contains a million tons of TNT!

Russia has tested an H-Bomb that was more than fifty megatons. That's fifty million tons of TNT in one bomb! The power is so horrific that our minds can't grasp the destruction even one of these monster weapons could unleash.

Until recently, America's strategic war plans were based on a concept with the acronym MAD, which stood for Mutually Assured Destruction. Get the picture? If these things are used, no flesh will survive. That's just what Jesus said in His Olivet message: "And except those days should be shortened, there should no flesh be saved: but for the elect's sake those days shall be shortened" (Matthew 24:22). One day, the militaries of the world will begin the prophesied march to Megiddo: "And he gathered them together into a place called in the Hebrew tongue Armageddon" (Revelation 16:16). This rebellious world will prepare for its furious finish.

Fight to the Finish Foiled!

Earth's final fury will be raging on the plains of Esdraelon, in the valley of Jezreel. Armageddon, the long-feared war of all wars, will threaten every living being with extinction. The many armies will be fighting each other with a fierceness the likes of which has never been seen in war before. Antichrist, supernaturally possessed by Satan himself, will look up because of the tremendous brightness that has broken through the boiling, black clouds of pollution, smoke from weaponry, and the judgment of God Almighty. He will see a laser-like shaft of brilliance, then a heavenly army riding on dazzlingly white horses.

The King of Kings and Lord of Lords will lead the way toward the planet's flaming surface. The beast of Revelation 13 will command all the armies at Megiddo to turn their super weapons toward the shimmering hosts that follow their King.

The hate-maddened troops will stop fighting each other and will try to stop the descending multitudes. Then, suddenly, it will be over. Everything will be perfectly quiet and still. Jesus Christ, the Son of God, will instantly settle the issue of Mideast war and peace once and for all.

I believe with all the conviction that is within me that Christ will open His mouth and say three words. Planet earth will be instantly tamed just as was the raging sea of Galilee when Jesus spoke those same words: "Peace, be still."

EARTHLY WAR OR HEAVENLY PEACE?

EVEN AFTER THE devastating attacks on New York and Washington, D.C., by Middle Eastern terrorists, people today are being lulled to sleep, especially in America. The nation and world sit teetering upon the precipice of catastrophe on many levels. The economies of America and nations of the world could literally collapse at any moment. I'm amazed that they haven't done so yet. Only the staying hand of Almighty God has prevented the downfall.

In the U.S., the Constitution is being dismantled one foundational brick at a time by forces that are determined to bring about a one-world, socialistic order. For the most part, Americans are well fed and have plenty of material things like houses, cars, and clothes. Everyday life goes on, and we are fairly comfortable with it. However, a basic transformation of American culture and society has begun, dividing the nation as surely as did the political realities of time just before the outbreak of the Civil War.

On the Brink of Crisis

America moves ever farther away from the solid moorings provided by the founding fathers through the stabilizing pillars of the Constitution. More significantly, the nation's leadership and its citizenry have moved away from the God of heaven. Such rebellion is the poisonous prescription for cultural and societal disaster.

"Change" was the promise of the winning political party's campaign in the 2008 presidential race. This is one promise President Barack Obama has kept 100 percent. The change his administration has brought has been staggering in its direction and scope.

The intervening years since that election have taken America and her people on a downhill run toward socialism more destabilizing than that which has brought Europe to the very cusp of collapse. And, the architects of the blueprint for the promised change haven't let up on the throttle as the nation hurdles toward the economic abyss.

At the heart of the drive to bankrupt America—which, in effect, has already been accomplished—is the president's "affordable healthcare law." That massive grab of the taxpayers' financial security known by all as "Obamacare" has usurped one-sixth of U.S. private industry by starting the collapse of the insurance companies in order to bring about single-payer, government-run insurance that is socialism at its worst.

Despite the so-called roll-out of the program that proved to be an unmitigated disaster, beginning with a nearly $700-million website that went nowhere in helping people sign up for the insurance that was so confusing and inaccessible that it also went nowhere, mainstream media and those wanting the "change" doubled down on efforts to indenture every citizen to government healthcare welfare. It was welfare paid for by the working taxpayers, who proved in poll after poll that they preferred by large majority their health insurance and the health care industry as it was before the president's political party, with a majority in both houses prior to the 2010 elections, steamrolled Obamacare through Congress.

The "change" that has taken place since the Obama administration began its attempt to bring America into a socialistic model has strapped working citizens, their children, grandchildren, and beyond with trillions of dollars of debt that can never be repaid. Many believe this has been done deliberately in order to bring the United States into configuration like and compliance with the New World Order the world's elite financiers and governmental leaders want to construct.

The American political process at the presidential and congressional levels stands starkly in the way, however. Every two, four, and six years, there is the possibility of turnovers in political aims and ideologies. Competing ideas and desires are, by the nature of our Constitution, allowed to disrupt any government voters perceive as going in the wrong direction. That includes the ability to disrupt the New World Order plans to reshape the nation into a world government designed by the global elitists. Thus, we see in this present hour a lawlessness beyond any that could have ever been tolerated by the founding fathers as possibly ripe for disruption by the voters. The founding fathers *did* imagine such governmental tyranny; therefore the safeguards of the Constitution against such tyranny are assured in the founding documents of the nation.

Now we see the reason those safeguards were put there. We also understand why there is the incessant tearing away at that Constitution—the consistent and constant bypassing and ignoring of that all-important document at every turn by this president and the sycophantic media (which, incidentally, is owned and/or controlled for the most part by elitist, globalist-types).

These who want an ever-growing big government to control buying and selling through redistribution of wealth and harsh regulation must somehow do away with constitutional safeguards that protect the rights of the people. The ability of the masses to vote these central-planning, big-government controllers out of office must be eliminated.

There can be sensed a growing dissatisfaction with the anti-constitutional direction into which the nation was swept in the 2008 and 2012 presidential elections. Fear is that the forces, national and international, having made enormous inroads in bringing America the "change" they intended, now sense those gains losing ground. The worry is that these forces, having demonstrated a complete disregard for lawfulness and constitutionality, won't hesitate to do whatever is necessary to prevent losing those gains.

Therefore, it is more than possible, in the thinking of many, that as the midterm and presidential elections approach, if it looks like their socialist ideology will lose at the ballot box, the administration and its political party will do whatever it takes to control the outcome. Illegal voters and voter intimidation have become an increasing part of election fraud. It is suspected that methods much more dangerous to our representative democracy are being planned as the anti-constitutionalists see the possibility of the changes they've begun to slip away.

Specifically, there is suspicion, whether based in truth or paranoia, that those "change" agents, so intent on altering America to fit their socioeconomic reconstruction, will create a crisis of magnitude serious enough to issue an executive order suspending elections. Martial law!

One such crisis, it is thought, might involve creating an economic situation dire enough to suspend welfare payments. This could, some believe, cause civil unrest even worse than what occurred in Greece and other places in Europe when state-provided funding was cut off some months ago. A financial fiasco of even greater dimension and scope might be forthcoming, it is supposed, because of other manipulations by those who are in control of government.

Rumors abound, as anyone who has access to Internet will attest, that Federal Emergency Management Agency (FEMA) is reported to be preparing for civil disasters and/or unrest of some sort.

Be watchful for a crisis of some sort to develop that the media will assist in magnifying, if the political fortunes of those in political power begin losing ground in the polls. All of the internal goings-on in America constitute a pressure cooker almost as incendiary as the cauldron that the Middle East troubles represent.

The Doomsday Clock

When we look at the world situation today through Bible prophecy, it becomes clear that this Earth Age is quickly approaching its end. Even nonreligious experts who watch world conditions see that the end might be near for mankind.

One of the most highly respected of these earth-watcher organizations is made up of the world's top atomic scientists who have a unique way of pointing out where they think we are on history's timeline. Some have, since 1947, been setting an imaginary clock to warn the world how near man might be to atomic destruction. These scientists put out a publication known as *The Bulletin of the Atomic Scientists*. The first issue in June 1947 had on its cover a large clock. The hour hand was set on twelve and the minute hand was set on seven minutes to twelve. In other words, the clock was set at seven minutes until the midnight hour. The atomic scientists believe that when the hour hand and minute hand both reach midnight, humankind will have completely destroyed itself through atomic warfare.

Scientists still watch world conditions carefully. They particularly keep an eye on nuclear-arms developments and treaties that promise to eliminate such weapons. Whenever things look favorable to eliminating nuclear weaponry, the scientists move the minute hand farther from the twelve on the Doomsday Clock. Whenever things heat up in the arms race, they move it forward toward the twelve on the imaginary timepiece.

Since the Doomsday Clock was first created, its hands have seldom been out of the fourth quadrant (the last fifteen minutes on the clock's face.) The minute hand has come very near the midnight hour. For example, the hand moved to three minutes until midnight in 1949, when the Soviet Union exploded its first atomic bomb. The minute hand was moved to two minutes until midnight in 1953 following America's late-1952 explosion of the first hydrogen bomb, with the Soviets quickly matching the feat.

The clock's minute hand has also been moved back somewhat on occasion. For example, when the U.S. and the Soviet Union signed a partial test ban treaty in 1963, the hand was shifted back to twelve minutes until midnight.

The Doomsday Clock has continued to be manipulated throughout the decades since the atomic age was born with the first bomb's explosion in 1945. It is very apparent that those who should know believe this world sits upon a nuclear powder keg. All-out war could be right around the next corner.

Secondhand Smoke

The Doomsday Clock's minute hand has been warning of nuclear threats to the world for some time. But that imaginary clock's second hand, if it had one, would indeed be smoking from the heat of the many prophetic signals today. Movement of that symbolic indicator of the last time grows more frightening with each tick.

Previous chapters have covered these end-time, Tribulation-type issues and events. But, it is good to remind ourselves here of these things of major prophetic importance.

Again, these are:

- Many wars and rumors of wars around the world
- Israel at center stage and in a peace process
- Rome reviving in the form of the European Union and the international community
- Movement toward a one-world order
- Development of technology that can make it possible to control the masses
- The coming-together of all religions, and Christ being blasphemed
- Existence of a global economic structure and an overt effort to bring the current order crashing down so the new order can be instituted

- Occurrences of strange weather patterns and weird sightings
- People having the last-days characteristics outlined by the apostle Paul in 2 Timothy 3

Daniel the prophet said many end-time issues and events will come upon the world like "a flood" (Daniel 9:26) until all things prophesied are fulfilled. Jesus indicated that all of these things will be happening at the same time in the days just before His return to earth.

People have, for centuries, witnessed a few, scattered, similar issues or events during their lives. But ours is the only generation to see all of these major prophetic signals happening at the same time. And, the chief signal is this: Israel, God's timepiece, is again a nation in the land of promise!

Mideast Midnight

The midnight of world history is quickly approaching. Our generation has heard the hoof beats of the four horses of Apocalypse for some time. It was once a distant thunder, but, that rumbling now grows louder by the hour. Middle East war looms despite the talk of peace that seems impossible to achieve. More and more, the world community puts the blame on Israel for the lack of progress toward making earth a safer place.

IDF Says "Never Again"

Certain present-day political leaders in Israel seem bent toward making peace at any price, while the Israeli Defense Force (IDF) is willing to take all who would destroy it down with the nation rather than allow another Holocaust.

Israeli President Shimon Peres recently put forth the more dovish proponent's position in proposing to deal with those trying to force peace in the Middle East. His words were met with strong counterviews by Prime Minister Benjamin Netanyahu:

"The Middle East is replete with both new and old threats," [Peres] said. "One shouldn't underestimate these threats but not be alarmed by them either. Israel today is stronger than ever.

"Israel has its own means of defense—those created in the past, those being developed today and those that will be developed tomorrow. Our defense isn't static and isn't banal. The future offers a dimension of hope, not just of concern."

Last month, the president publically came out against an uncoordinated Israeli attack in Iran. In an interview…Peres said, "It is clear that we can cannot do it (attack) on our own. We can delay it (Iran's nuclear program), but we realize we have to proceed together with America. There are questions of cooperation and of timetables, but as severe as the danger is, at least this time we're not alone."

In response, one of the prime minister's aides said that "Shimon Peres has forgotten what his role is as president of the State of Israel."

[Ehud] Barak also addressed the Iranian threat…though he did not mention it by name. "Israel is surrounded by a stormy sea some of which is not ready to accept it as an equal member of the world's nations.

"The reality in which we live in sets before us grave challenges, the need for optimal exploitation of our resources and the need for preparation for any development, near or afar. The IDF will be the one to safeguard Israel's security and its future. The IDF will be the one to provide the solution when the time comes."

IDF chief [Benny] Gantz…added, "We have recently been hearing threats calling for Israel's destruction. The IDF is ready for any scenario. We will get to any place on time."

Earlier…Prime Minister Benjamin Netanyahu criticized the West, and mainly the US over their lack of efforts to delay Tehran's nuclear program.

"Until Iran doesn't see a red line, it will not stop the program. Iran must not be allowed to have nuclear weapons," he said at the opening of the weekly cabinet meeting.[96]

We must note with a degree of trepidation the November 2013 deal made by the Obama administration with Iran to delay sanctions against its nuclear ambitions for six months. The secretive agreement was made without Israel's input, and without serious efforts to curtail Iran's uranium enrichment program while that Israel-hating nation, in almost everyone's opinion, seeks to produce an atomic weapon.

One such opinion was registered in a forceful way that makes the warning worthy of serious consideration.

Among the many who decried the Obama Administration's catastrophic capitulation to the nuclear ambitions of the Islamic Republic of Iran, none spelled out its potential consequences as trenchantly as Israel's Economy Minister Naftali Bennett: "We awoke this morning to a new reality," he said Sunday. "A reality in which a bad deal was signed with Iran. A very bad deal. If a nuclear suitcase blows up five years from now in New York or Madrid, it will be because of the deal that was signed this morning." If that happens, it will also be because of the Shi'ite belief in the return of the Twelfth Imam. The two powers that the Iranian mullahs have long designated as the "Great Satan" and the "Little Satan"—America and Israel—would be the only targets of an Iranian attempt to hasten the Twelfth Imam's coming. A nuclear strike from Tehran into Israel could kill, estimates say, upwards of twenty million people, completely destroying the Jewish State. Barack Obama, by acceding to the Iranians' nuclear ambitions, has given a tremendous impetus to these revenge fantasies, probably not realizing or caring that Iran's mullahs take the prophesies of the Twelfth Imam very seriously indeed—seriously enough for them to bet the entire world upon them. Obama has just made the odds appear to them to be considerably more favorable than they were just a week ago.[97]

God Has the Last Word

Things look exceedingly bleak for Israel, as we've seen, because of the U.S. administration's allowing Iran to move ahead with its nuclear program, according to many observers inside of Israel and outside. On the other hand, those charged with the nation's security sound supremely confident in the Jewish state's military capability even in the ominous shadow of Iran's imminent threat.

We again consider the words of Ehud Barak, Israeli defense minister: "The IDF will be the one to safeguard Israel's security and its future. The IDF will be the one to provide the solution when the time comes."[98]

Those attuned to the prophetic Word of God sense with knowledge born of faith that the Lord has recorded, ahead of what will eventuate, that Israel will be the last nation standing when all is said and done.

Based upon that knowledge, we can say with certainty that those who desire to destroy Israel, the American administration that *foolishly* thinks it can diplomatically dissolve Iran's hatred for Israel, and the Israeli military hawks who believe the Israeli Defense Force can and will protect the nation no matter what are all wrong-headed in their declarations.

Behold, he that keepeth Israel shall neither slumber nor sleep. (Psalms 121:4)

Also I will bring again the captivity of my people of Israel, and they shall build the waste cities, and inhabit them; and they shall plant vineyards, and drink their wine; they shall also make gardens, and eat the fruit of them.

And I will plant them upon their land, and they shall no

more be pulled up out of their land which I have given them, saith the LORD, thy God. (Amos 9:14–15)

Be assured: It is God who will have the last word. As a matter of fact, He has already spoken that Word and it is recorded. We are seeing His promises beginning to come to pass during the day-to-day unfolding of history in these final months and years of the age.

A couple of factors with regard to God's promises shaping up include the following.

1. Iran's threats as of this writing/analysis are only that—threats. Iran doesn't yet have the nuclear force to obliterate the hated "little Satan." Bible prophecy foretells that Israel is not destroyed by nuclear firepower or any other. Ezekiel 38 and 39 make it clear that Persia and all the Gog-Magog coalition forces will be almost completely destroyed when they attack God's chosen nation. Therefore, we can say with a degree of certitude that Iran will not possess—at least will not be able to employ—nuclear weaponry against Israel that will come anywhere near destroying her.

2. God's being in complete control of things to come makes it fact—to those of us who believe in His promises to protect Israel—that *Persia* (present-day Iran) will not have to necessarily have its nuclear program destroyed or constantly delayed by an outside attack from Israel and/or the U.S. Iran's nuclear development facilities, intelligence reports say, lie deep in caverns of mountainous regions that are among the most earthquake-prone areas on the planet. These earthquake zones are capable of producing among the most severe tremblers possible. Perhaps this will be the fate of Iran's atomic weapons ambition.

The bottom line is that God's Word, rather than predicting nuclear-like devastation for Israel, foretells such catastrophic destruction upon those who try to destroy that people. And, it is the Lord God, not the Israeli Defense Force, who will unleash that destruction. When the God of heaven is finished with Israel's enemies, there will be no doubt whatsoever who defended that nation.

And it shall come to pass at the same time when Gog shall come against the land of Israel, saith the Lord GOD, that my fury shall come up in my face.

For in my jealousy and in the fire of my wrath have I spoken, Surely in that day there shall be a great shaking in the land of Israel;

So that the fishes of the sea, and the fowls of the heaven, and the beasts of the field, and all creeping things that creep upon the earth, and all the men that are upon the face of the earth, shall shake at my presence, and the mountains shall be thrown down, and the steep places shall fall, and every wall shall fall to the ground.

And I will call for a sword against him throughout all my mountains, saith the Lord GOD: every man's sword shall be against his brother.

And I will plead against him with pestilence and with blood; and I will rain upon him, and upon his bands, and upon the many people that are with him, an overflowing rain, and great hailstones, fire, and brimstone.

Thus will I magnify myself, and sanctify myself; and I will be known in the eyes of many nations, and they shall know that I am the LORD. (Ezekiel 38:18–23)

Middle East Magnet

Middle East oil remains the ever-growing factor that draws the world's attention to the region. Religious hatred is the fuse to the Mideast bomb that could be lit at any moment.

The Bible says there will come from that area a certain sort of peace—but, it will be a peace that destroys many people. What a strange peace that will be!

The one whom the Bible says will approve and guarantee the peace with "many" will appear to be the rider on the white horse. He will be the one for whom everyone has been looking. The "many" with whom he guarantees a seven-year treaty of peace will be the same "many" he will, three and a half years later, try his level best to completely destroy. He will, like Hitler, seek to murder every Jew in the world—with viciousness unmatched by any in history.

As covered earlier, all the armies of the world will gather at Armageddon. Those forces will turn from fighting each other to try to stop Christ from returning from heaven to earth. The sun will have gone dark, while at the same time heating up many times hotter than normal. Men will be "scorched" or "burned" by the heat. Antichrist will direct military fire at the returning King of Kings. This will indeed be mankind's midnight hour!

From Wartime to Peacetime

The Doomsday Clock agrees with true Bible prophecy watchers: Mideast midnight is approaching. But this fact shouldn't worry the Christian who truly seeks to understand God's truth that includes the whole Word, not just parts of the Bible.

Fully 28 percent of the Bible contains prophecy. About half of that prophetic Word has already come to pass and the other half remains to be fulfilled. In other words, 14 percent of prophecy in the Bible will yet come to pass.

Earthly war will soon fade into history. Peace will fill the whole world. Jesus Christ, the King of Kings and Lord of Lords, will break through the blackness of the Mideast midnight hour. He will speak, and the raging godless human forces will instantly be defeated. A new era will begin. The time of fallen human history will be vanquished, and King Jesus' millennial reign will begin.

So, Bible prophecy ultimately presents a picture, not of gloom and doom, but of glorious, joyous peace!

Call to Suppertime

These times in which we live are deceptive. That is, we are lulled into believing that everything is great. Christians in many places around the world are in great trials. They are murdered by the hundreds and tortured by the thousands, according to Voice of the Martyrs and other organizations who keep watch on Satan's war against the saints. However, Christians in America today are, for the most part, as caught up in this false feeling of security, as are those who do not know Jesus Christ as Savior and Lord.

Most who name Jesus as their Lord today hear little about the coming time of tremendous terrors for Jews and Christians (people saved during the Tribulation) during the last seven years of human history. Pastors and teachers, for one reason or another, often refuse to teach these all-important truths. Many times, this is because they aren't taught these things in the seminaries they attend.

God the Holy Spirit gave the apostle Paul something to say to our generation about that unfaithfulness to God's Word: "And they shall turn away their ears from the truth, and shall be turned unto fables" (2 Timothy 4:4). We've grown comfortable with the "feel-goodisms" and "do-goodisms" coming from our pulpits. We don't care to hear that horrors might be just around the corner. We want to hear about heaven, but not about hell, and about how to love each other, not about how to witness to those who are lost and bound for an eternity apart from God.

This is exactly how the Bible says it will be at the end of the age. It will be business as usual, with little thought for our true purpose as Christians. That purpose is to plant the seed of the gospel so that God will reap a harvest of souls.

Christ said: "Be ye therefore ready also: for the Son of man cometh at an hour when ye think not" (Luke 12:40). The Lord was talking to Christians. Certainly, His church as a whole is in a time when looking for His coming in the Rapture isn't popular!

We are told that He will return to the Mount of Olives after coming in the clouds with power and great glory. But the Bible also tells of an earlier return, not "to" the earth, but "above" it, in the air, in 1 Thessalonians 4:16–17:

> For the Lord himself shall descend from heaven with a shout, with the voice of the archangel, and with the trump of God: and the dead in Christ shall rise first: Then we which are alive and remain shall be caught up together with them in the clouds, to meet the Lord in the air: and so shall we ever be with the Lord.

That will be the "come up hither" of Revelation 4:1, Jesus Christ's call to all Christians, both dead and alive, to meet Him in the air. He will take them home to His Father's house (read John 14:2–4). It will be the Heavenly Father's call to suppertime. Christians will go back to the Father's house in heaven to enjoy the Marriage Supper of the Lamb.

Perfect Peace

Middle East war will explode not long after Christ's church is taken home. That isn't to say that there won't be military conflicts in the region, meanwhile. The explosive potential for armed conflict is constantly present. The wars of the recent past in that cauldron of hatred and the tremendous upheavals throughout the entire region surrounding Israel we've covered numerous times give just an inkling of what is to come.

But no matter when war becomes full blown on earth, all Christians who have lived or died during the Church Age will, immediately following the Rapture, enjoy peace, joy, and fulfillment beyond any that can be imagined this side of heaven. That peace will be true and everlasting.

Believers of the Church Age will, of course, stand before the Lord to be judged at the bema judgment seat of Christ. But, it will be a judgment of rewards, not one of sins committed in the earthly life. The Lord Jesus took all of those sins to the cross when He died. His sacrifice on that awful tree of crucifixion paid the sin debt in full for all who believe in Him.

The Bible says that the bema judgment is for the works we do in our earthly lives. Anything done with the pure motive of honoring Christ will be richly rewarded in ways we can't begin to fully understand right now. These rewards will be given in the form of crowns.

The Bible says also that unconfessed sin can result in loss of rewards at this judgment. Works done just to look good in the eyes of other people will not be accepted by the Lord as works done for Him. These works will be destroyed and only the works done with pure motive will remain.

But the bema judgment has nothing to do with salvation. Believers are forever secure in God's family at the moment they accept Jesus Christ as Savior. They will be forever with Christ in heaven!

Sadly and tragically, those who have rejected the Holy Spirit's call to salvation through Jesus Christ will face another, most terrible judgment. It is called the Great White Throne judgment (see Revelation 20:11–15), which will take place at the end of the Millennium. Everyone at that judgment will be lost. That is, they will have rejected God's offer of salvation and will be forever separated from God and heaven. This judgment is for eternal punishment. Those judged will be given punishment in accordance with the evil things they have done in their lives. This isn't my idea or some preacher's idea. It is a warning straight from God's holy, absolutely true Word.

The great, loving God doesn't want this for anyone. He has moved heaven and hell to bring all men, women, and children to Himself. He gave His only Son, Jesus Christ. What greater thing could He give? But God created us with a free will. That is, we can choose to love and obey Him…or not. It's up to us.

God's Holy Spirit, the third member of the Trinity, calls all people to salvation through the shed blood of Jesus, who died for us on the cross. God desires with all His heart that you come to Him. But, the cross is the only way you can come to Him. There is no other.

Accept Jesus Christ as your Savior right this moment. He will change your life forever. He will give you peace that surpasses understanding, even while the world rages around you.

Choose heavenly peace, not earthly war. Troubling issues and events about Mideast war and peace, as well as worry over all other prophetic signals of these last days, will then encourage you rather than frighten you.

When you see all these things begin to come to pass, you can then "look up, and lift up your heads; for your redemption draweth nigh" (Luke 21:28).

ABOUT THE AUTHOR

TERRY JAMES is author, general editor, and coauthor of more than twenty books on Bible prophecy and geopolitics, hundreds of thousands of which have been sold worldwide. He has also written fiction and nonfiction books on a number of other topics. His most recent releases are *Heaven Vision: Glimpses into Glory,* a collaboration with author Angie Peters in which the authors examine near-death experiences through the lens of what the Bible says about life after death and amazing promises about heaven, and *Do Our Pets Go to Heaven?*—a collaboration with Thomas Horn and others that explores the comforting and exciting scriptural answers to that compelling, ages-old question.

James is a frequent lecturer on the study of end-time phenomena, and interviews often with national and international media on topics involving world issues and events as they might relate to Bible prophecy. He is partner with Todd Strandberg and general editor in the www.raptureready.com website, which was recently rated as the number-one Bible prophecy website on the Internet.

NOTES

1. "Milestones: 1945–1952," *US Department of State; Office of the Historian*, http://history.state.gov/milestones/1945-1952/creation-israel.
2. "Palestinian Preacher: Put the Jews to the Sword," *Israel Today*, 11/27/13, http://www.israeltoday.co.il/NewsItem/tabid/178/nid/24273/Default.aspx?hp=readmore.
3. William Booth, "Israel's Netanyahu Calls Iran Deal 'Historic Mistake,'" *The Washington Post*, http://www.washingtonpost.com/world/israel-says-iran-deal-makes-world-more-dangerous/2013/11/24/e0e347de-54f9-11e3-bdbf-097ab2a3dc2b_story.html, 11/24/13.
4. "PM Netanyahu Addresses UN General Assembly," *IsraeliConsulateLA. org*, http://www.israeliconsulatela.org/index.php/he/featured-stories/item/pm-netanyahu-addresses-un-general-assembly-2. See also: "PM Netanyahu's Speech at the UN General Assembly," YouTube video, http://www.youtube.com/watch?v=RsG88a6IPl0, posted by IsraeliPM, 10/1/13.
5. Randall Price, *Jerusalem in Prophecy* (Eugene, Oregon: Harvest House 1990), 11.
6. "Israeli Rockets Slam into Gaza Police Complex," Associated Press, *Deseret News*, http://www.deseretnews.com/article/841922/Israeli-rockets-slam-into-Gaza-police-complex.html?pg=all, 5/10/01.
7. Maamoun Youssef, "Al Qaida Chief: Egypt Coup Shows Democracy Corrupt," Associated Press/Yahoo News, http://news.yahoo.com/al-qaida-chief-egypt-coup-shows-democracy-corrupt-142016067.html, 8/20/13.
8. Billy Graham, *Angels: God's Secret Agents* (Waco: Word, 1986), 47–48.
9. Bob Glaze, *Angels: A Historical & Prophetic Study* (Oklahoma City: Hearthstone, 1998), 65.
10. Matthew Henry, *Concise Commentary on the Whole Bible*, ChristiansUnite.com.
11. Reza Kahlili, "Revealed! Evidence Iran Crossed Nuclear 'Red Line,'" WND.com, http://www.wnd.com/2013/03/revealed-evidence-iran-crossed-nuclear-red-line/, 3/20/13.
12. Hal Lindsey, *Final Battle* (Los Angeles: Western Front, 1995), 22.
13. Readers Digest, *Everyday Life Through the Ages* (London: Reader's Digest, 1992), 53.

14. John Walvoord, *Armageddon, Oil, and the Middle East Crisis: What the Bible Says about the Future of the Middle East and the End of Western Civilization* (Grand Rapids, MI: Zondervan, 1991), 69.

15. Lindsey, 25.

16. Genesis 21:19, King James Version of the Bible, note 3, p. 31.

17. Ibid.

18. David Alexander, Pat Alexander, eds., *Eerdman's Handbook to the Bible* (Grand Rapids, MI: Eerdman's, 1973), 141.

19. Anthony C. Garland, *A Testimony of Jesus Christ: A Commentary on the Book of Revelation* (Camano Island, WA: SpiritAndTruth.org, 2004). http://www.spiritandtruth.org/teaching/Book_of_Revelation/commentary/htm/images/line_of_promise.jpg.

20. *Biblical Hermeneutics*, http://hermeneutics.stackexchange.com/questions/1593/isaacs-blessing-of-his-sons.

21. Maayana Miskin, "Feiglin Declares 'Time to Flood the Temple Mount,'" *Inside Israel,* http://www.israelnationalnews.com/News/News.aspx/170486#.UknrpNL6Vrc, 8/1/13.

22. Maayana Miskin, "Muslim Anger over Virtual 'Third Temple,'" *Inside Israel,* http://www.israelnationalnews.com/News/News.aspx/170220#.UknsLdL6Vrc, 7/24/13.

23. Henry H. Halley, *Halley's Bible Handbook* (Grand Rapids, MI: Zondervan), 411–412.

24. Beth Moore, *Jesus the One and Only* (Nashville: Lifeway, 2000), 195.

25. Walvoord, 91.

26. Tim LaHaye, commentary note on Matthew 24:1–25:46, *Prophecy Study Bible* (Chattanooga, TN: AMG, 2000), 1037.

27. "Archaeologists are still finding new evidence of this destruction," notes biblical scholar and author John Walvoord. For example, one report indicates that a " stone found during an excavation begun in 1968 by Benjamin Mazar on the southwest corner of the temple mount retaining wall was inscribed with the Hebrew words translated: 'The place of the trumpeting,'" which would have indicated the place "where the priest stood to announce the arrival and departure of the Sabbath."

28. Arthur W. Kac, *The Rebirth of the State of Israel: Is it of God or of Men?* (Whitefish, MT: Kessinger, 2007), 300–301.

29. "Archaeology in Israel: Masada Desert Fortress," *Jewish Virtual Library,* http://www.jewishvirtuallibrary.org/jsource/Archaeology/Masada1.html.

30. "Masada," *United Nations Educational, Scientific, and Cultural Organization,* http://whc.unesco.org/en/list/1040.

31. Kac, 58–59.

32. Paul Joseph Nzeribe and Lee Jay Walker, " Nigerian Armed Forces Attack Boko Haram: Christians Ordered Off a Bus and Killed," *Modern Tokyo Times,* http://moderntokyotimes.com/2013/09/07/nigerian-armed-forces-attack-boko-haram-christians-ordered-of-a-bus-and-killed/, 9/7/13.

33. "Five Christians Killed in Roadside Ambush near Jos, Nigeria," *Morning Star News*: Light Before Dawn, http://morningstarnews.org/2013/09/five-christians-killed-in-roadside-ambush-near-jos-nigeria/, 9/1/13.

34. Ibid.

35. Gillian Parker, "Is Barbaric Boko Haram Winning in Nigeria's North Country?" *Christian Science Monitor,* http://www.csmonitor.com/World/Security-Watch/2013/1001/Is-barbaric-Boko-Haram-winning-in-Nigeria-s-north-country-video, 10/1/13.

36. "Kenya Mall Shooting: Timeline of Events," *ABC News,* http://abcnews.go.com/International/kenya-mall-shooting-timeline-events/story?id=20334295, 9/22/13; also, "Nicholas Kulish, Jeffrey Gettleman, and Alan Cowell, "Attention Switches to Investigation of Kenyan Mall Siege," *New York Times,* http://www.nytimes.com/2013/09/26/world/africa/kenya-mall-shooting.html?pagewanted=all, 9/25/13.

37. Source: Colbert I. King, "Christians in the Crosshairs," *Washington Post/WP Opinions,* http://articles.washingtonpost.com/2013-09-27/opinions/42457301_1_christians-boko-haram-human-rights-watch, 9/27/13.

38. Kulish, et al.

39. Raymond Ibrahim, "Bloody Weekend: Trend of Muslim Rage Against 'Infidels' Continues," *Islam Translated,* http://www.raymondibrahim.com/islam/bloody-weekend-trend-of-muslim-rage-against-infidels-continues/, 9/25/13.

40. Fayaz Aziz, "Suicide Bombers Kill 78 Outside Pakistani Church," *Reuters,* http://www.reuters.com/article/2013/09/22/us-pakistan-blast-idUSBRE98L02K20130922, 9/22/13.

41. "Persecution," *Ethics & Religious Liberty Commission of the Southern Baptist Convention,* http://erlc.com/issues/quick-facts/persecution/.

42. "Black Death," *History Channel,* http://www.history.com/topics/black-death.

43. "Zionism," *Encyclopaedia Britannica,* http://www.britannica.com/EBchecked/topic/657475/Zionism.

44. Kac, 77.

45. David Allen Lewis, *Can Israel Survive in a Hostile World?* (Green Forest, AR: New Leaf Press, 2001), 151.

46. Ibid.

47. Chuck Missler, "A Prophet For Our Time: Ezekiel," *Koinonia House,* http://www.khouse.org/articles/biblestudy/19990101-226.html.

48. Thomas Ice, "Modern Israel's Right to the Land," http://ldolphin.org/landrights. html. Note: In his article, Ice cites the following Old Testament passages that predict this development: Ezekiel 20:33–38; 22:17–22; 36:22–24; 37:1–14; Isaiah 11:11–12; Zephaniah 2:1–2 and Ezekiel 38–39.

49. J. Vernon McGee, *Thru the Bible with J. Vernon McGee,* vol. 5 (Pasadena, CA: Thru the Bible Radio, 1983).

50. Walvoord.

51. "The World's Top Consumers and Producers of Oil," CNN.com, citing 2006 figures from the U.S. Energy Information Administration, http://www.cnn. com/2008/US/06/02/oil.map/.

52. Tim Chen, "American Household Credit Card Debt Statistics 2013," http://www. nerdwallet.com/blog/credit-card-data/average-credit-card-debt-household/.

53. Paul Feinberg, "The Mideast March to Megiddo," *Foreshocks of Antichrist,* ed. William T. James (Eugene, OR: Harvest House, 1997), 269.

54. Grant R, Jeffrey, "Russia's Day of Destruction in Israel," *Prophecy Online,* http:// www.grantjeffrey.com/article/rusisrl.htm.

55. Ibid.

56. Dave Breese, "The Soviet Phoenix Arises," *Foreshocks of Antichrist,* ed. William T. James (Eugene, OR: Harvest House, 1997), 247.

57. Ari Soffer, "Arab States to Single Out Israel at Nuclear Weapons Convention," *Israel National News,* http://www.israelnationalnews.com/News/News.aspx/172086#. UkxLBtL6Vrc, 9/20/13.

58. Jack Van Impe, "Jerusalem: War or Peace?," http://www.jvim.com/pt/2001/01003. html.

59. David Allen Lewis, "Israel—The Heart of Prophecy," *Storming Toward Armageddon: Essays in Apocalypse,* ed. William T. James (Green Forest, AR: New Leaf Press, 1992), 235– 236.

60. Zola Levitt, "Israel on the Spot," *Foreshadows of Wrath and Redemption,* ed., William T. James (Eugene, OR: Harvest House, 1999), 138–139.

61. Kac.

62. "The White Paper of 1939," *Jewish Agency for Israel,* http://jafi.org/ JewishAgency/English/Jewish+Education/Compelling+Content/Eye+on+Israel/ Activities+and+Programming/Israel-Ben+Gurion/Chapter+1++The+White+Paper +of+1939.htm.

63. Michael Benson, *Harry S. Truman and the Founding of Israel* (Westport, CT: Greenwood, 1997), 96–97.

64. Ibid.

65. Ibid.

66. Drew Desilver, "World's Muslim Population More Widespread than You Think," Pew Research Center, http://www.pewresearch.org/fact-tank/2013/06/07/worlds-muslim-population-more-widespread-than-you-might-think/m 6/7/13.

67. "The Making of a Martyr: When Death Means More than Life: The Making of a Suicide Bomber," ABCNews.com, 12/6/01.

68. Kac, 353–354.

69. "Ancient Jewish History: The Ark of the Covenant," Jewish Virtual Library, http://www.jewishvirtuallibrary.org/jsource/Judaism/ark.html.

70. "Historical Evidence for Jesus' Prophecy—The Temple, Bible History, http://www.biblehistory.net/newsletter/jesus_temple.htm.

71. Dan Perry, "Israel," Associated Press, http://www.nandotimes.com, 6/2/01.

72. Uri Dan, "Duel on the Temple Mount," Freeman Center for Strategic Studies, 1/01.

73. David Allen Lewis, "Israel in Tribulation," Prophecy Study Bible, ed. Tim LaHaye (Chattanooga, TN:AMG, 2000) 936.

74. John Loeffler, "Mid-East Update 2000: The Struggle for Jerusalem," Koinonia House, http://www.khouse.org/articles/2000/290/, 9/00.

75. "Portrait of IHH," Meir Amit Intelligence and Terrorism Information Center, http://www.terrorism-info.org.il/en/article/18108, 5/27/10.

76. "Timeline of Gaza Flotilla Raid," Telegraph, http://www.telegraph.co.uk/news/worldnews/middleeast/israel/8737182/Timeline-of-the-Gaza-flotilla-raid.html, 9/2/11.

77. Source: Elliott Abrams, "UN Report on Flotilla Incident Exonerates Israel, *Weekly Standard,* http://www.weeklystandard.com/blogs/un-report-flotilla-incident-exonerates-israel_592127.html, 9/3/11.

78. "Anwar Sadat, Architect of a New Mid-East," *Time,* www.time.com, 1/2/78.

79. Ibid.

80. *Jack Van Impe Presents,* week of June 10, 2001.

81. David Breese, "Europe and the Prince that Shall Come," Rapture Ready, http://www.raptureme.com/terry/james4.html.

82. "About the Temple Institute," Temple Institute, http://www.templeinstitute.org/about.htm.

83. Abby Stevens, "Jewish Organization Opens Holy Temple Visitors' Center in Jerusalem," *Deseret News,* http://www.deseretnews.com/article/865583894/Jewish-organization-opens-Holy-Temple-Visitors-Center-in-Jerusalem.html 7/31/13.

84. "The Ark," Temple Institute, http://www.templeinstitute.org/ark_of_the_covenant.htm.

85. Jake Wallis Simons, "The Rabbi, the Lost Ark and the Future of the Temple

Mount," Telegraph, http://www.telegraph.co.uk/news/worldnews/10287615/The-rabbi-the-lost-ark-and-the-future-of-Temple-Mount.html, 9/12/13.

86. Kevin Bermeister, "Temple Mount Is the Key to Peace," Algemeiner, http://www.algemeiner.com/2013/08/07/the-temple-mount-is-the-key-to-peace/, 8/7/13.

87. Sinem Tezyapar, "A New Muslim Vision: Rebuilding Solomon's Temple Together," Jewish Press, http://www.jewishpress.com/indepth/opinions/a-new-muslim-vision-rebuilding-solomons-temple-together/, 3/12/13.

88. "The Antichrist: What We Know about Him," http://www.arewelivinginthelastdays.com/article/antichrist/antichrist.htm.

89. Aaron Klein, "Hagel Pushes Wealth Redistribution to Third World," World Net Daily, http://www.wnd.com/2013/01/hagel-pushes-wealth-redistribution-to-third-world/#cDgV86hDYOgoT1Qz.99, 1/19/13.

90. Claudio Lavanga, "Could Putin-Pope Francis Visit Mark Beginning of Centuries-Old Rift?" NBCnews.com, http://worldnews.nbcnews.com/_news/2013/11/25/21611511-could-putin-pope-francis-visit-mark-beginning-of-end-of-centuries-old-rift, 11/25/13.

91. Dave Breese.

92. Some consider the 200 million prophesied to come across the Euphrates in this Scripture to be demonic forces, not human forces. I don't agree. I think they will be human beings, possessed by demonic forces.

93. "The Growing Chinese Threat," Volume 1, Issue 7, 8/99, Discerning the Times Digest and NewsBytes.

94. John Milner, "Israel Slams Bad Nuclear Deal," European Jewish Press, http://www.ejpress.org/article/news/eastern_europe/69055, 11/24/13.

95. Ibid.

96. Noam (Dabul) Dvir, "Peres: Don't Be Alarmed by Threats," YNETnews.com, http://www.ynetnews.com/articles/0,7340,L-4276177,00.html, 9/12/12.

97. Robert Spencer, "Now the Twelfth Imam…and Nuclear Armageddon…Can Come," Front Page Magazine, http://www.frontpagemag.com/2013/robert-spencer/now-the-twelfth-imam-can-come/?utm_source=FrontPage+Magazine&utm_medium=email&utm_campaign=1e8b693867-Mailchimp_FrontPageMag&utm_term=0_57e32c1dad-1e8b693867-156519425, 11/26/13.

98. Dvir.